→→ TELL IT WITH PRIDE ←←

"The black soldiers marched
side by side
with their white comrades
in arms to the assault.
Tell it with pride to the world."

JULY 31, 1863

TELL IT WITH PRIDE

THE 54TH MASSACHUSETTS REGIMENT AND AUGUSTUS SAINT-GAUDENS' SHAW MEMORIAL

Sarah Greenough and Nancy K. Anderson with Lindsay Harris and Renée Ater

Foreword by Richard J. Powell

NATIONAL GALLERY OF ART, WASHINGTON

THE EXHIBITION IS MADE POSSIBLE THROUGH THE GENEROUS SUPPORT OF GROW,
AN INITIATIVE OF THE ANNENBERG FOUNDATION

ADDITIONAL SUPPORT IS PROVIDED BY THE TRELLIS FUND

The exhibition was organized by the National Gallery of Art, Washington.

Exhibition dates:

National Gallery of Art, Washington
September 15, 2013 – January 20, 2014

Massachusetts Historical Society, Boston
February 23 – May 26, 2014

Copyright © 2013 Board of Trustees, National Gallery of Art, Washington. All rights reserved. This book may not be reproduced, in whole or in part (beyond that copying permitted by Sections 107 and 108 of the U.S. Copyright Law, and except by reviewers from the public press), without written permission from the publishers.

10 9 8 7 6 5 4 3 2 1

Produced by the Publishing Office,
National Gallery of Art, Washington
www.nga.gov
Judy Metro, *editor in chief*
Chris Vogel, *deputy publisher*
Wendy Schleicher, *design manager*

Designed by Wendy Schleicher
Edited by Tam Curry Bryfogle

Sara Sanders-Buell, *permissions coordinator*
Mariah Shay, *production assistant*
John Long, *assistant production manager*

Separations by Robert J. Hennessey
Map on page 114 by Tom Willcockson, Mapcraft, Woodstock, Illinois

Typeset in Requiem, The Sans, and P22 Declaration Pro. Printed on Satimatte Naturelle by NINO Druck GmbH, Germany

Library of Congress Cataloging-in-Publication Data

Tell it with pride : the 54th Massachusetts Regiment and Augustus Saint-Gaudens' Shaw Memorial / Sarah Greenough and Nancy Anderson ; with Lindsay Harris and Renée Ater. — 1st edition.
    pages   cm
"The exhibition was organized by the National Gallery of Art, Washington. Exhibition dates, National Gallery of Art, Washington, September 15, 2013 – January 20, 2014, Massachusetts Historical Society, Boston, February 23 – May 26, 2014."
    Includes bibliographical references and index.
    ISBN 978-0-300-19773-0 (hardback)
    ISBN 978-0-89468-384-8 (paperback)
1. United States. Army. Massachusetts Infantry Regiment, 54th (1863 – 1865) — Exhibitions. 2. African American soldiers — Portraits — Exhibitions. 3. African American soldiers — Monuments — Exhibitions. 4. Robert Gould Shaw Memorial (Boston, Mass.) — Exhibitions. 5. United States — History — Civil War, 1861 – 1865 — Art and the war — Exhibitions. I. Greenough, Sarah, Seeing what ought to be. II. Anderson, Nancy K. For all time to come. III. Harris, Lindsay R. Before the eyes of thousands. IV. Ater, Renée. Commemorating black soldiers. V. National Gallery of Art (U.S.) VI. Massachusetts Historical Society.
E513.554th T45 2013
973.7'415 — dc23   2013018395

Hard cover edition published by the National Gallery of Art, Washington, in association with Yale University Press, New Haven and London

Yale University Press
302 Temple Street
P.O. Box 209040
New Haven, CT 06520-9040
www.yalebooks.com/art

Endpapers / inside cover
Adapted from anonymous letter to the Shaw family announcing the death of Robert Gould Shaw, July 31, 1863 (pl. 43)

Images at section openings

p. ii: Robert Knox Sneden, *Charleston Harbor, S.C., Bombardment of Fort Sumter*, 1862 – 1865. Virginia Historical Society, Richmond

pp. iv – v: George N. Barnard, *Ruins in Charleston, South Carolina* (detail), 1865 – 1866, albumen print (pl. 54)

p. vi: Richard Benson, *Robert Gould Shaw Memorial* (detail), 1973, pigmented ink jet print (pl. 75)

p. x: Ambrotype of Sergeant Henry F. Steward, 1863 (pl. 22)

p. 154: Albumen print of Colonel Robert Gould Shaw, 1863 (pl. 16)

Notes to the Reader

Dimensions are given height before width before depth, in inches followed by centimeters.

Transcripts of letters retain the original spelling and punctuation.

Director's Foreword | **EARL A. POWELL III** | xi

Lenders to the Exhibition | xiii

Foreword | **RICHARD J. POWELL** | xv

THE 54TH MASSACHUSETTS REGIMENT
AND THE BATTLE OF FORT WAGNER | 1

Seeing What Ought to Be: Photography and
the 54th Massachusetts Regiment | **SARAH GREENOUGH** | 2

PLATES 1 – 56 | 21

THE LEGACY OF THE 54TH MASSACHUSETTS REGIMENT
AND THE BATTLE OF FORT WAGNER | 79

For All Time to Come: Memorializing Robert Gould Shaw and
the 54th Massachusetts Regiment | **NANCY K. ANDERSON** | 80

Before the Eyes of Thousands: The 54th Massachusetts Regiment and
the Shaw Memorial in Twentieth-Century Art | **LINDSAY HARRIS** | 94

Commemorating Black Soldiers: The African American Civil War
Memorial in Washington, DC | **RENÉE ATER** | 112

PLATES 57 – 80 | 127

Roster of the 54th Massachusetts Regiment
COMPILED BY LINDSAY HARRIS, ZOË SAMELS, NICOLE STRIBLING, AND MEGAN SWEENEY | 155

Transcripts of Letters in the Exhibition | 182

Notes | 185

Selected Bibliography | 196

Acknowledgments | 200

Index | 204

Photography Credits | 209

DIRECTOR'S FOREWORD

This exhibition and publication celebrate the magisterial Shaw Memorial, 1900, by Augustus Saint-Gaudens (1848 – 1907), on long-term loan to the National Gallery of Art from the United States Department of the Interior, the National Park Service, and the Saint-Gaudens National Historic Site. Widely considered one of the finest examples of nineteenth-century American sculpture, the monument commemorates the July 18, 1863, storming of Fort Wagner by Colonel Robert Gould Shaw and the 54th Massachusetts Volunteer Infantry, among the first regiments of African Americans formed during the Civil War. Although one-third of the troops who participated in the battle were killed or wounded, including Shaw himself, many viewed it as a turning point in the war, for the African Americans proved themselves exemplary soldiers, displaying bravery and dedication to country that equaled the nation's most revered heroes. Then, as today, these soldiers captured the imagination: they were common men propelled by deep moral principles, willing to sacrifice everything for a nation that had taken much from them but now promised liberty.

Commemorating the 150th anniversary of the Battle of Fort Wagner, *Tell It with Pride: The 54th Massachusetts Regiment and Augustus Saint-Gaudens' Shaw Memorial* honors the monument, the soldiers it acclaims, and the works of art it has inspired over the past century. The first part of the exhibition and catalogue focuses attention on the 54th Massachusetts. When Saint-Gaudens worked on the memorial (1883 – 1900), he did not model any of the heads on actual members of the 54th regiment besides Shaw, whose likeness was based on a photograph. Our project seeks to make real these anonymous African American soldiers, giving them both names and faces, where possible, by showing vintage photographs of the 54th as well as the men and women who recruited them and who nursed, taught, and guided them. It also presents critical documents related to the 54th, such as the Emancipation Proclamation, a letter to President Abraham Lincoln on the question of equal pay, and the Medal of Honor awarded to the African American whose actions first warranted this distinction, Sergeant William H. Carney. The second half of the presentation looks at the legacy of the 54th and the Battle of Fort Wagner, examining nineteenth-century efforts to memorialize those who fought, including Saint-Gaudens' work on the Shaw Memorial itself. *Tell It with Pride* also illustrates the continuing inspiration the 54th, its defining battle, and the Shaw Memorial have given to twentieth- and twenty-first-century artists as diverse as Lewis Hine, Richard Benson, Carrie Mae Weems, William Earle Williams, and Ed Hamilton. It succinctly demonstrates how perceptions of these people and events have changed, becoming more complex, inclusive, and incisive over time as society has grown more willing to tackle the difficult issues they raise.

As the Shaw Memorial is beloved throughout the National Gallery, it is fitting that *Tell It with Pride* is truly a team effort. Conceived by Sarah Greenough, senior curator and head of the department of photographs, the project was co-organized with Nancy K. Anderson, curator and head of the department of American and British paintings. They have been joined by a distinguished group of catalogue authors, including Lindsay Harris, research associate in the department of photographs, Richard J. Powell, John Spencer Bassett Professor of Art and Art History at Duke University, and Renée Ater, associate professor of American art and director of academic programs at the University of Maryland. We thank them for their dedicated participation.

We are especially grateful for the support of Dennis Fiori, president of the Massachusetts Historical Society, whose institution so graciously lent many of the objects in the exhibition and will present the show in Boston. All of the lenders are to be thanked for allowing us to display their prized material within this context. Their trust and generosity have given us the opportunity to gain new insight into the Shaw Memorial and the sacrifices it honors.

In addition, we would like to thank GRoW, an initiative of the Annenberg Foundation, and Gregory Annenberg Weingarten for their enthusiastic support of the exhibition in Washington. Betsy Karel and the Trellis Fund are also to be thanked for their steadfast commitment to our photography exhibitions and their support of this show. Without both foundations' sponsorship, *Tell It with Pride* would not have been possible.

EARL A. POWELL III
NATIONAL GALLERY OF ART

LENDERS TO THE EXHIBITION

American Antiquarian Society, Worcester, Massachusetts

The Art Institute of Chicago

The Boston Athenaeum

Boston Public Library

Anne P. and Ronald S. Coddington

Carl J. Cruz

Chris Foard

Greg French

George Eastman House, Rochester, New York

Gettysburg National Military Park

The Gilder Lehrman Collection, New York

Harvard University, Houghton Library

Jack Shainman Gallery, New York

Kansas State Historical Society, Topeka

Library Company of Philadelphia

The Library of Congress, Washington, DC

Massachusetts Historical Society, Boston

Moorland-Spingarn Research Center, Howard University, Washington, DC

National Archives, Washington, DC

National Gallery of Art

National Museum of African American History and Culture, Washington, DC

National Park Service, Washington, DC

National Portrait Gallery, Washington, DC

The New York Public Library, Schomburg Center for Research in Black Culture

Oberlin College Archives, Oberlin, Ohio

Ohio Historical Society, Columbus

Pamplin Historical Park and the National Museum of the Civil War Soldier, Petersburg, Virginia

David M. Rubenstein

Saint Gaudens National Historic Site, Cornish, New Hampshire

San Francisco Museum of Modern Art

Smithsonian American Art Museum, Washington, DC

West Virginia University Libraries, Morgantown

Williams College Museum of Art, Williamstown, Massachusetts

FOREWORD: AUGUSTUS SAINT-GAUDENS' DEVOTIONAL MEMORIAL

RICHARD J. POWELL

Augustus Saint-Gaudens' Memorial to Colonel Robert Gould Shaw and the 54th Massachusetts Regiment (fig. 1) is an anomaly. Is there more accurate or suitable terminology for such a singular, evocative creation, and this artist's astonishing, sculptural farewell to the nineteenth-century? Over one hundred years old, bigger than life itself, multi-dimensional, and abounding in competing histories and significations, the Shaw Memorial appears like a shimmering reverie from the faded past: a grand conception that, unlike so much bygone material culture, entreats — no, *demands* — our undivided attention and engages us today in a meditation about our own vocations, sense of duty, and mortality. The Shaw Memorial's genre and sculptural form recall other famous monuments (most notably François Rude's high relief tribute to the French Revolution on the façade of the Arc de Triomphe de l'Étoile in Paris), but such easy, visual analogies fail to differentiate the Shaw Memorial's intrinsic affect, a product of its design as much as its particular expository program. Above all, the Shaw Memorial's status in the parallel universes of art and visual culture is held aloft by its uncanny timelessness and daring figural expressivity that, remarkably, draw twenty-first-century audiences deep into its sinewy, arrested-in-motion ranks.

Part sculptural relief and part freestanding, the Shaw Memorial revels in liminality, like a stereoscopic, turn-of-the-century tableau vivant. Colonel Robert Gould Shaw and his horse stand tall and independent from their concave, theatrical niche and the surrounding regiment, which ironically makes this part of the sculptural group the most conventional component in this striking commission. Unitarian minister and former Civil War officer Thomas Wentworth Higginson, writing about the Shaw Memorial in *Century Illustrated Magazine,* concluded that Colonel Shaw and his horse (or what he referred to as "the head and the front" of the sculpture) "presented a difficult but not a complicated problem." On the standard public art worksheet, the equestrian unit ticks off all of the qualities one expects from this sculptural type — physical perfection, erect stature, nobility in attitude, and stoicism in expression — and therefore fulfills the basic requirements for a three-dimensional, monumental, dedicatory portrait. But in contrast to Colonel Shaw and his horse, the retinue of marching men hails from an entirely different visual realm and spatial dimension. "*How* the equestrian figure dominates the composition," exclaimed Higginson (with emphasis added), "and yet *how essentially* a part of one's impression is the presence of the troops!"[1]

Even the term "sculptural relief" doesn't sufficiently describe what Augustus Saint-Gaudens conjured and ultimately realized in these raised sections of the memorial. In spite of their limited visibility (which Higginson artfully described as "the moderation of what would be too prominent as details if they were not so well subordinated by giving each object a place where it will tell and not tell too much"), these sandwiched men nonetheless provide discerning viewers with the most appreciable surprises and emotional uplift throughout this work.[2] A complete figure here, a singular head there, a bearded elder in one place, and a teenage combatant someplace else: this cornucopia of African American manhood, of distinct physiognomies and different ages, is simply unlike anything else in the history of art (with perhaps the rather remote, though thematically related exception of the spectacular and enigmatic relief bronze plaques from the kingdom of Benin in Renaissance-era Nigeria).[3] Realizing the 54th Massachusetts in such a radical, compressed fashion psychologically pushed the Shaw Memorial beyond Saint-Gaudens' moment of fevered nationalism and encroaching industrialization and instead propelled it into the future, and into our own collapsed space and critical times.

Could Saint-Gaudens have imagined how his memorial would function in 2013, what it could communicate to postmodern spectators significantly transposed in time from his fin-de-siècle juncture, and even more alienated from the memories and traumas of America's Civil War? Or would he have even cared that, in an unimaginable future, the descendants of the peoples who shared comparable histories of war, service, and sacrifice with Colonel Shaw, the 54th Regiment, and other Americans might stand in awe before his memorial and marvel at its imaginative assembly of real-life figures and elegiac apparitions?

Sculpting a life-size frieze of twenty or more soldiers, each individually conceived, sartorially detailed, shown carrying their respective rifles, blanket rolls, and other war gear, and all marching in unison, strikes me as not only artistically ambitious, but extreme. Add to these representational feats the audacious task of representing the 54th Regiment as racially and historically accurately as possible, and one understands the enormous challenge that Saint-Gaudens faced with this commission, especially in that cultural era of blackface minstrelsy and rampant racism. "Now look at the drummer-boy," noted Higginson in 1897, "and the grizzled old man in the front ranks, at the one who is third from the nearest in the first row of soldiers, at him who comes first behind the horse, and the next one, with the Arab cast of features, the three together in the last file." "See what variety of types and what gradation of expressions are shown in these heads," Higginson continued, "and note the rhythm of the march, the individuality of the bodies, of the arms and legs and hands and feet."[4] With the coercing of the sculpture's narrative to such a descriptive (and performative) degree, one wonders just what inner demons (or spiritual catalysts) drove Saint-Gaudens to create this commemorative-to-end-all-commemoratives?

The answer might reside in the work's ability to traverse the lofty, fine art echelon it clearly occupies (and to leap ahead of its exclusive military history), to communicate something special, principled, and heartfelt for today's viewers. And arguably, that special "something" involves the memorial's quiet upending of its presumed themes of hero veneration and the art requiem, shrewdly replacing these with an elaborate, multifigured essay on loyalty and commitment beyond one's own self-interest. The Shaw Memorial's message of social cohesion, comrades-in-arms, and steadfastness while confronting perils — exemplified in Saint-Gaudens' literal shaping and layering of humanity — extends to Saint-Gaudens himself, a point the pioneering, black art and cultural critic Freeman Henry Morris Murray made in his 1916 examination of the Shaw Memorial. "[What] we see…in this immortal work," wrote Murray, "is not the result, on the sculptor's part, of a lucky hit, a fortuitous chance, or a sudden and unsought inspiration.… Masterpieces of this character are the result of much hard work and skillful technical manipulation; but they are still more the consummation of prolonged study based on discernment, artistic taste, sympathy, and sincerity. In short, inspiration—or certainly the essential element in it—is devotion."[5] Saint-Gaudens' devotion (or rather, his dedication) to both his craft and fellow man is, according to Murray, the key ingredient that flows through and out of the commemorative and its particular history, accounting for much of its transmissible, late nineteenth-century allure and contemporary relevance.

"Yes, and now we have brochures about the Shaw Memorial in that room, too," replied a National Gallery of Art security officer when I asked him (during a recent, impromptu visit) if the circa 1900 plaster version was still on display. Not only did the officer know exactly which artwork (among the thousands in the Gallery's permanent collection) I was inquiring

FOREWORD — Augustus Saint-Gaudens Devotional Memorial

Fig. 1 Augustus Saint-Gaudens' Shaw Memorial, 1900, patinated plaster, U.S. Department of the Interior, National Park Service, Saint-Gaudens National Historic Site, Cornish, New Hampshire (pl. 65)

1

about, but he seemed eager to volunteer as my informational guide and duly appointed docent. I'm guessing that the Shaw Memorial is one of the most beloved and captivating of the National Gallery of Art's many treasures for those (like the security guards and other staff members) who encounter it daily as well as the visiting public. As evidenced in the Shaw Memorial's devotional breadth, its representations of mutual support, self-sacrifice, and commitment — encrypted in Saint-Gaudens' "unusual language" of merged bodies and common destinies — prompt the most unlikely communions and shared experiences between strangers when entering its wide orbit of influence. "Take some extra brochures home and share them with your family and friends," my guide reminded me as I left him at his post and walked down the National Gallery of Art's long, Tennessee marble hallway toward Gallery 66 and its impressive, altarlike homage to fallen heroes and higher allegiances.

xvii

THE 54TH MASSACHUSETTS REGIMENT
AND THE BATTLE OF FORT WAGNER

Seeing What Ought to Be:
Photography and the
54th Massachusetts Regiment

"Poets, prophets, and reformers are all picture makers — and this ability is the secret of their power and of their achievements. They see what ought to be by the reflection of what is, and endeavor to remove the contradiction."

— FREDERICK DOUGLASS [1864 OR 1865]

SARAH GREENOUGH

SHORTLY AFTER NINE O'CLOCK on the morning of May 28, 1863, a little more than a thousand members of the 54th Massachusetts Volunteer Regiment arrived in Boston, where they were to set sail later that afternoon for combat in the South. Although many New Englanders had visited the 54th at Camp Meigs on the outskirts of Boston, there was keen interest to see this new troop, composed of African Americans soldiers and led by white officers.[1] Almost as soon as President Abraham Lincoln had signed the Emancipation Proclamation on January 1, 1863, Massachusetts governor John A. Andrew had begun to found the regiment (pls. 1–2). He solicited help from the abolitionist George Luther Stearns and formed "the Black Committee" of prominent citizens, both black and white, including Frederick Douglass, Amos A. Lawrence, William Lloyd Garrison, and Wendell Phillips (pls. 3–5). Assisted by African Americans working in Cleveland and New York City as well as Pennsylvania and Upstate New York, they secured enlistments for the 54th from fifteen Northern states, all four border states, five Confederate states, and even Canada and the West Indies (pls. 6–13).[2] Now both supporters and skeptics alike wondered if "they marched well, they wheeled well, they stood well, they handled their guns well," and if they had an "air of completeness, and order, and *morale*," as had been reported in the newspapers.[3] As the regiment marched to the foot of the State House, the 54th cut an unusual sight. The soldiers wore their new uniforms, adorned with appropriate military insignia identifying their rank, and brass buttons embossed with eagles. Some had caps that noted their regiment and others had brass belt buckles embossed with the letters "US." These were all objects and symbols that few African Americans before them had ever had the privilege to wear, and the honor was lost on no one. Yet what was perhaps even more startling at the time was the sight of line after line of African American soldiers carrying rifles on their shoulders, marching off to do battle for the Union.

The events of the day had been carefully calculated to heighten the symbolism inherent in this regiment and the sentiment of the crowd. Large numbers of spectators lined the sidewalks, balconies, and windows along the route, cheering and waving flags and handkerchiefs. As many newspapers and subsequent accounts noted, often in stirring language, the 54th marched past Wendell Phillips' home, where Garrison was seen resting his hand on a bust of John Brown.[4] After going by the State House and down Beacon Street, the regiment paused briefly at the home of its Harvard-educated, twenty-five-year-old colonel, Robert Gould Shaw, where he raised his sword in tribute to his abolitionist parents and his young bride. They then proceeded onto the Common, where Shaw led them past a reviewing stand filled with dignitaries, including the governor, the mayor of Boston, and officers from other regiments. Accompanied by the rousing music of John Brown's hymn, they walked over the ground that, as was noted at the time, was "moistened by the blood of Crispus Attucks," an African American and the first person shot to death by the British during the 1770 Boston Massacre. Continuing past the sites hallowed by earlier martyrs, they marched by the infamous spot where two escaped slaves, John Sims and Anthony Burns, had been captured by bounty hunters in 1851 and 1854 and returned to slavery in Georgia and Virginia.[5] When the 54th arrived at Battery Wharf and began to board the steamer that would take them to South

Fig. 1 Robert Knox Sneden, *Genl. Q. A. Gillmore's Line of Earthworks in Front of Fort Wagner, Morris Island, SC, July 1863*, 1863–1865. Virginia Historical Society, Richmond

Carolina, the men bid farewell to friends and supporters. Douglass, whose sons Charles and Lewis were soldiers in the regiment, was among those who gathered for a parting glimpse of this historic troop. Many, although by no means all, believed that the 54th comported itself well: "No white regiment from Massachusetts surpassed the Fifty-fourth in excellence of drill," a reporter for the *New York Daily Tribune* wrote two days later, "while in general discipline, dignity, and military bearing the regiment is acknowledged by every candid mind to be all that can be desired."[6]

That same day, perhaps during a break in the ceremonies, the surgeon for the 54th, thirty-year-old Major Lincoln Ripley Stone, from nearby Salem, Massachusetts, stopped at a photographer's studio and had his portrait made (pl. 38). Seated, with his cap resting on his leg, Stone did not look directly at the camera but off to the side. Either the camera operator or more likely Dr. Stone himself selected a plain backdrop — no elaborate painted background, grand columns, or drapery denoting power and prestige for this son of a Unitarian pastor, transcendentalist, and abolitionist. He presented a quiet, thoughtful, even distant expression to the camera, befitting a medical doctor who had previously served for almost two years with the 2nd Massachusetts Regiment and, as a veteran of the Battle of Antietam, knew only too well the horrors that awaited him. We do not know if he had the picture taken as a keepsake to send to family or friends — he was not married, so no wife anxiously awaited the photograph to study his visage or gaze into his eyes — or merely as a reminder of this momentous day, for the only inscription on the back is the date, "May 28, 1863." We do know, however, that the sitting probably did not take long, for Dr. Stone was able to rejoin the rest of the regiment in time to sail with them, first for Port Royal and then on to Beaufort, South Carolina.[7]

The next fifty-one days would forever ensure a place in history for the 54th. Soon after they arrived in Beaufort, the regiment was ordered to participate in the June 11 plunder and destruction of the undefended coastal town of Darien, Georgia, under the command of Colonel James Montgomery. Although Shaw was eager to distance the 54th from this event, which he deplored as "barbarous," he was even more determined that his men should prove that they were fit soldiers.[8] The opportunity came a little over a month later, when they were ordered to assist Major General Quincy A. Gillmore in his attack on Fort Wagner on Morris Island. Fort Wagner, along with Fort Sumter and several other forts, guarded Charleston, South Carolina, bastion of the Southern cause and birthplace of the rebellion (fig. 1 and p. ii). Their first battle, on July 16 on James Island, south of Fort Wagner, was a dramatic test for the 54th. One survivor recalled the sight of wounded comrades as a "trial" and "the screaming shot and shells flying overhead" as "a deadly sound," then noted proudly: "the dark line stood staunch, holding the line at the most vital point. Not a man was out of place."[9] Their valor won them acclaim, but it brought them no rest. Indeed, they spent most of the next two days on a grueling march, with almost no food or shelter, as they moved into position to attack Fort Wagner. Although Gillmore had bombarded Fort Wagner from the sea throughout most of the daylight hours of July 18, it was all but impregnable. Rising thirty feet above the beach, it had fourteen cannons, the largest of which fired a 128-pound shot, and on the side from which an assault had to be mounted, the fort had a water-filled ditch, ten feet wide and five feet deep; buried land mines and razor-sharp stakes provided additional defense.

As the sun began to set and sand mixed with smoke rising from the fort and fog from the sea, distant thunder combined with the booming, flashing cannons to create a hellish scene. Shaw determined that he would not direct the fighting from afar but would go in advance with the national flag to "give the men something to rally round." Urging his soldiers to "prove yourselves men," he led the charge. As the 54th approached, Confederate soldiers, most of whom had spent the day inside the fort's "bombproof," rushed to their battle stations and sent a "sheet of flame" in

2

the form of hot lead pouring down onto the 54th.[10] Many lost their lives in this initial barrage, but Shaw somehow survived, passed through the ditch, and began to climb the parapet. Beside him was a twenty-three-year-old African American sergeant, William H. Carney, who had seen the regiment's color sergeant drop the national flag. "As quick as a thought," he recalled many years later, "I threw away my gun, seized the colors and made my way to the head of the column."[11] As Shaw and Carney reached the top of the parapet, one with his sword and the other with the flag, Shaw waved his weapon, shouted "Forward 54th!" and fell dead.[12] Carney briefly planted the flag on the parapet, where he guarded it despite being wounded and coming under heavy assault. Even with several other regiments backing up the 54th, all eventually had to retreat. When they did, Carney "wrapped the precious colors about the staff," he later remembered, "cautiously picked my way among the dead and dying," and limped back to safety.[13] When he was reunited with other survivors from the 54th, he proudly handed over the flag and proclaimed: "Boys, I but did my duty; the dear old flag never touched the ground."[14] Of the 600 men who participated in the assault on Fort Wagner, more than 280 were killed, missing and presumed dead, or wounded, with the exact fate of many never to be determined.[15] On viewing the wreckage the following day, even a Confederate general said the carnage before the fort was "indescribable."[16]

Although defeated in battle, the 54th was hailed for its exemplary "bravery." The liberal press praised the men's "nobility," "honor," "courage," and "discipline" and lauded their actions on the field as "manly, heroic, and sublime."[17] They were immortalized in eulogies, songs, and poems. Monuments to them were proposed as early as the fall of 1863, long before the final outcome of the war was settled.[18] Lavish laments focused on Shaw, while Carney's actions, although acknowledged, were far less widely celebrated. Perhaps in an effort to correct this imbalance, Carney had his photograph taken, probably in the spring or early summer of 1864 (fig. 2).[19] Artfully arranged, the picture is replete with symbolism. Carney stands in front of a painted backdrop of soldiers' tents. A common background for Civil War portraits, suggesting the soldiers' communal life, it was especially appropriate given Carney's illustrious return of the flag to the 54th after the battle (fig. 3). His sergeant stripes, confirmation of the respect he had won within his company, are plainly visible on his right arm, and in his right hand he holds a cane, evidence of the wounds he received in battle. Yet it is the use of the American flag that is the most telling. As the symbol of the sovereignty of the nation and the union of the states, the flag assumed profound importance during the war, prompting many Northern soldiers to be depicted with one (pl. 25). As Wendell Phillips noted in 1861, African Americans also embraced the emblem of the country: "To-day the slave asks God for a sight of this

Fig. 2 Unknown photographer, *Sergeant William H. Carney*, 1864, albumen print. West Virginia University Libraries, West Virginia and Regional History Collection

Fig. 3 Flag of the 54th Massachusetts Volunteer Regiment, 1863. Bureau of State Office Buildings, State House, Boston, Massachusetts, State House Flag Collection,

banner, and counts it the pledge of his redemption."[20] In Carney's photograph, the flag was carefully placed in his arm so that both one star in the upper right and the tears and damage inflicted on it are clearly evident. It was draped so that its folds mimicked the folds of his trousers, and, of course, it does not touch the floor. His right arm is outstretched in an almost unnaturally straight line so that it runs precisely parallel to the staff of the flag, as if to suggest that he and the flag are inextricably bound together, that he has become, in a sense, one with this emblem of freedom.

Interest in the 54th Massachusetts has continued unabated since the end of the Civil War. The first regimental history was published by one of the survivors, Captain Luis Emilio, in time for the thirtieth anniversary of the war in 1891, with a revised and expanded edition released in 1894.[21] In 1904 Robert T. Teamoh published a biography of Shaw, *Sketch of the Life and Death of Col. Robert Gould Shaw*, while in 1965, at the close of the centennial celebrations of the Civil War, Peter Burchard published *One Gallant Rush: Robert Gould Shaw and His Brave Black Regiment*, a more popular study focusing on Shaw.[22] This became the basis for Edward Zwick's 1989 Oscar-winning film *Glory*,

3

starring Matthew Broderick and Denzel Washington. Historians have also probed deeply into the broad military, social, and political history of the 54th in such significant publications as *Where Death and Glory Meet: Colonel Robert Gould Shaw and the 54th Massachusetts Infantry* by Russell Duncan (1999) and *Hope and Glory: Essays on the Legacy of the Fifty-Fourth Massachusetts Regiment*, edited by Martin H. Blatt, Thomas J. Brown, and Donald Yacovone (2001).[23] Building on pioneering works such as Dudley Taylor Cornish's *The Sable Arm: Negro Troops in the Union Army, 1861–1865* (1956), James M. McPherson's *The Negro's Civil War: How American Negroes Felt and Acted during the War for the Union* (1965), and Benjamin Quarles' *The Negro in the Civil War* (1953), more recent scholars have focused attention specifically on the African American contributions to the war effort, including those of the 54th.[24] In addition, numerous primary materials by members of the 54th, including letters and other documents by Shaw, Corporal James Henry Gooding, and others, have been published both in print and online.[25]

But in the midst of all this attention, the works of art related to the 54th—with the exception of Edmonia Lewis' sculptures of Carney and Shaw and Augustus Saint-Gaudens' Shaw Memorial—have not been either collected or systematically analyzed. And what has been neglected perhaps most of all is the important role that photography played in the lives of members of the 54th. In recent years scholars have addressed the ways in which nineteenth-century African Americans were represented in photography and how they used the medium to present an image of themselves to the world, but the photographs of the 54th have remained largely unexplored.[26] Almost every account of the 54th reproduces at least one photograph of a soldier from the regiment, yet the pictures themselves have not been dissected for the clues they provide about the individuals, as evidence of social and economic status, or as reflections of changing relations between the races immediately after the Emancipation Proclamation.[27] Differences between how white and black soldiers of the 54th were depicted—or had themselves

7

depicted — have never been considered. Nor have any of these pictures been discussed as conscious emblems of the soldiers' self-identity or as indicative of how they used photography to chart or take pleasure from the new social and political opportunities available to them.

Since the mid-eighteenth century, portraiture had been a distinguishing characteristic of middle-class identity. During the Civil War, as many African Americans began to take what they hoped would be the first steps toward achieving that status, they exploited the cheapest, most readily available, and most malleable process of making portraits: photography. Indeed, while photography served unprecedented military and civilian uses in the Civil War itself, it was also intimately woven into the fabric of the 54th. It was used as a means of self-promotion by those who recruited men to enlist in the 54th, including Frederick Douglass, Lewis Hayden, Robert Purvis, Charles Lenox Remond, John S. Rock, and Sojourner Truth. It was cherished for its talismanic properties by the soldiers themselves, who not only longed to possess likenesses of their loved ones but also had pictures made of themselves in their new circumstances. And it was employed by the soldiers to make visible their deepest hopes about the implications of the Emancipation Proclamation as they explored and establish new identities for the lives they hoped to lead. In their seminal compilation of Civil War letters and documents, Ira Berlin, Joseph P. Reidy, and Leslie S. Rowland note that during this tumultuous time "ordinary men and women…under the tutelage of unprecedented events" seized "the moment to challenge the assumptions of the old regime and proclaim a new social order."[28] So too did several people associated with the 54th use photography to propose new visions for themselves and their country.

"POETS, PROPHETS, AND REFORMERS":
PHOTOGRAPHY AND THE RECRUITERS, NURSES,
TEACHERS, AND SUPPORTERS OF THE 54TH

In early December 1861, almost eight months after the Civil War erupted with the Battle of Fort Sumter and on the second anniversary of John Brown's death, Frederick Douglass delivered a long lecture at the Tremont Temple in Boston.[29] Throughout the 1840s and 1850s Douglass had used the power of his words, both written and spoken, to embed himself into the American consciousness, becoming the most celebrated African American of his time and an ardent champion of the abolitionist cause. He focused a significant portion of his talk that day, however, not on pressing social or political matters, but on photography. He praised the inventor of the daguerreotype process, Louis-Jacques-Mandé Daguerre, as the "great father of modern pictures [who] by the simple but all abounding sunshine has converted the planet into a picture gallery."[30] Like so many others in the nineteenth century, Douglass believed that this process would be distinguished not only by the "multitude, variety, perfection, and cheapness" of its pictures but also by its democratic nature: "The humbled servant girl whose income is but a few shillings per week may now possess a more perfect likeness of herself than noble ladies and court royalty, with all its precious treasures could purchase fifty years ago."[31] Douglass also passionately believed that the "picture making facility" was an essential characteristic of being human: "The process by which man is able to invert his own subjective consciousness into the objective form, considered in all its range, is in truth the highest attribute of man's nature.… It is the picture of life contrasted with the fact of life, the ideal contrasted with the real, which makes criticism possible. Where there is no criticism there is no progress — for the want of progress is not felt where such want is not made visible by criticism."[32] Photography made this human faculty both far easier to exercise and far more accessible than ever before. "The farmer boy gets an iron shoe for his horse, and metallic picture for him-

Fig. 4 Unknown photographer, *Frederick Douglass*, 1850–1860, albumen print. Library of Congress, Prints and Photographs Division

self at the same time," Douglass asserted, "and at the same price."[33]

More specifically, Douglass celebrated the power of portrait photography. From an early point in his career, he realized that images, and especially photographs, could be valuable tools to promote his reputation and his cause. He reproduced portraits of himself as frontispieces to his 1845 and 1855 autobiographies, and throughout the 1850s and 1860s he had numerous photographic portraits made of himself that circulated widely (fig. 4). "A man who now o'days publishes a book, or peddles a patent medicine," he asserted, "and does not publish his face to the world with it may almost claim and get credit for simple modesty."[34] As a skillful orator who knew how to captivate his audience, Douglass understood that having one's photographic portrait taken was a performance, demanding as much from the sitter as from the photographer.[35] Projecting what one of his admirers called a "majestic wrath," he learned to translate the charisma he exuded in person through his physical presence, words, and gestures into the poses and expressions he assumed for the camera (pl. 5).[36] By the 1860s, he also began to explore the gap between the performer and the performance, the inside and the outside, for he recognized that one of the great powers of photography lay in the ability it gave people to step outside themselves. Portraits allow us "to see our interior selves as distinct personalities as though through a looking glass," he observed, and thus make "ourselves objective to ourselves."[37] As Maurice O. Wallace and Shawn Michelle Smith have observed, Douglass saw pictures as a means to "see ourselves as if from the outside and, from this more distanced view, to contemplate and assess ourselves, drawing up plans for improvement."[38]

Thus when he issued his call, "Men of Color, to Arms!" in March 1863, urging African Americans to enlist in the 54th, he drew upon his reputation, established in part through photography, and also upon a sophisticated understanding of the ways in which the medium could be a catalyst for personal and social change. But Douglass was not the only recruiter for the 54th seeking to use photography to advance the abolitionist cause. In the tempestuous decade leading up to the Civil War and throughout the war itself, those within the tight-knit antislavery community supported one another intellectually, financially, morally, and physically, and they also followed each other's example. The abolitionists Lewis Hayden, Charles Lenox Remond, and Robert Purvis; the journalist, physician, and proponent of black nationalism Martin Robison Delany; and the physician and attorney John S. Rock all had strong, forceful, determined photographic portraits made of themselves to insert their ideas, actions, and images into the national dialogue (pls. 6–13).[39] So too did many of the women who aided the 54th, including the nurses Clara Barton and Helen Louise Gilson who tended the soldiers' wounds and the teacher Charlotte L. Forten who taught some of them to read and write at her school in Port Royal and formed a close friend-

4

5

ship with Shaw (pls. 47, 50, 49).[40] Their photographs portray them as tender, thoughtful, but also resolute. The escaped slave, abolitionist, and Union spy Harriet Tubman, who led armed assaults in the Beaufort area during the war and rescued many enslaved people — and who was with the 54th shortly before the Battle of Fort Wagner — as well as the nurse and teacher Susie King Taylor also used photographs and reproductions to create strikingly original images of themselves as staunch, powerful figures (fig. 5; pls. 52, 51). And the fearless Martha Gray, who traveled from New Bedford, Massachusetts, to South Carolina to care for her ill husband and other members of the 54th, commemorated her reunion with him in a photograph (fig. 6).[41]

Yet none of the recruiters for the 54th used photography more creatively than the former slave, abolitionist, and women's rights activist Sojourner Truth. Unlike Douglass, who was intrigued with the daguerreotype process (even though it was outmoded by the time he gave his talk in Boston), Truth embraced the most up-to-date technology of her time, the carte de visite. Patented in 1854 in Paris by André-Adolphe-Eugène Disdéri, the carte de visite was a small albumen photograph mounted on a card that could be sent through the mail. Four, eight, or a dozen exposures could be made at once, significantly reducing costs: by the early 1860s, a dozen cartes de visite could be purchased for as little as $1.50.[42] The process became wildly popular in 1859 when Emperor Napoleon III stopped at Disdéri's studio to have his portrait taken while leading a column of troops out of Paris on his way to Italy. Soon "cardomania" swept the world, as royalty and people of middle-class means alike collected portraits of friends, family, and celebrities — actors, writers, statesmen, politicians, military leaders — which they stored in specially made albums. As Oliver Wendell Holmes wrote in 1859, cartes de visite were "the social currency, the sentimental 'green-backs' of civilization."[43]

Sojourner Truth astutely recognized that photographers reaped large profits from the sale of celebrity cartes de visite. Unwilling to let others benefit from her labor or reputation, she transformed herself into a "commodity" and had several different cartes de visite made of herself between 1863 and 1875, which she purchased in large quantities and sold at rallies and lectures (pl. 14).[44] She had allowed others to write her biography, with conflicting results, but she took much more control over the construction of her visual image, carefully selecting details relating to her dress, pose, and even the setting and props. She could have chosen columns, drapery, or painted backdrops, but in almost all of her cartes de visite she was depicted in front of a plain background that focused attention on her appearance. In most of the photographs, she is seated next to a table on which rests a book and flowers (possibly stock items supplied by the photographers), and she holds her knitting, a sign of domesticity. Combining echoes of African American slavery with Northern temperance, she wore clothes that newspapers at the time described as a "'mixture' of what 'used to be worn by female slaves of the South' with the dress of the Quakers."[45] Yet within this

Fig. 5 H.B. Lindsley, *Harriet Tubman*, 1860–1875, albumen print. Library of Congress, Prints and Photographs Division

Fig. 6 H.C. Foster, *Sergeant and Mrs. William H.W. Gray*, 1864, albumen print. Collection of John D. Hayden

carefully scripted performance, the caption below many of her cartes de visite is even more unusual. Playing with both the nineteenth-century idea that photographs secure the "shadow" of nature and the daguerreotypists' admonition to "Secure the Shadow 'ere the Substance Fade," Truth had printed: "I Sell the Shadow to Secure the Substance." Further subverting traditional photographic practice of the time, she — not the photographer — had the copyright registered in her own name, thus claiming ownership over her image and how she was presented to the world.

Drawing on the public fascination with cartes de visite and the widespread desire to collect images of notable figures, Truth was able to reach a significant audience and earn money from her "shadow" as she traveled around the country lecturing on women's rights and abolition and seeking recruits for the Union army and the 54th. Other portraits of her, probably made between 1863 and early 1865, further confirmed both her support for the 54th and her skill in using photography to define herself. Wearing an elegant silk dress and shawl, Truth seated herself so that she looked directly at the photographer and thus also the viewer (pl. 53), not slightly off to the side or past the camera, as she had done in most of her cartes de visite. Yet it is not just her gaze that is remarkable. It is also the cased photograph, open and prominently displayed on her lap, most likely a portrait of her grandson, James Caldwell, a nineteen-year-old private in Company H of the 54th Massachusetts.[46] With her right hand (injured during her last year of slavery) tucked under her shawl, she points directly at her grandson's portrait with her powerful left index finger, lest we overlook the diminutive object. Her direct engagement with the viewer may be a way of showing the very personal connection she and her family had with this famous regiment and a means of highlighting the sacrifice they were making to eradicate slavery. But the determination of her gaze and gesture may also have been an appeal for Caldwell's safe return, for he was captured in the battle on James Island on July 16, 1863, and not exchanged until March 1865.[47]

"THE HISTORY FROM WHICH THERE WOULD BE NO APPEAL": THE PHOTOGRAPHS OF THE 54TH SOLDIERS

In 1882 when Walt Whitman bid "good-bye to the war" in his autobiographical rumination, *Specimen Days*, he noted the great interest he found in the "rank and file" soldiers: they "were of more significance," he asserted, "even than the political interests involved." But he lamented that the war's "interior history will not only never be written — its practicality, minutiae of deeds and passions, will never be even suggested."[48] However, despite Whitman's fear that highly personal experiences of the war would "never get in the books," we can, perhaps, begin to construct an alternative history of the 54th by examining a few of the letters and photographs of the soldiers themselves:

Dear sister i take my pen in hand to inform you that I am well and all the rest of them are well we are very well pleas with soildieren but we wont have it so easy when we leave Boston we spect to leave about the first of June and it may be sooner for what we know for the rigiment is nearly fill out David and george got there on Wenday David saide for to tell you that we didant no when we would get any money but i dont think it will be very long.... we also gut our arms this day they are springfield rifles wich we have they are aloud to kill a great [unclear: disants?]....

— JACOB E. CHRISTY TO MARY JANE DEMUS, MAY [?], 1863, CAMP MEIGS, READVILLE, MASSACHUSETTS[49]

My Dear Sister i have took my pen in han to let you no that i am well and i hope that thes fu lines may find you injoyen the same state of health and the rest of the days that ar in Camp ar well give my love to all the rest of the frens you can tell them that we ar all well and ar giten along verry well and we expect to move soon to north carlina and you may look for a nother letter sune and i will send you my litnes as soon as i can git it taken the rigment ar ful now and we [unclear: ar] gut ar unform and arms tel father that i will send sum monney home to pay Clark for my boots as soon as we git ar buntey that will be soon we ar ten mils byont boston

— SAMUEL A. CHRISTY TO MARY JANE DEMUS, MAY 9, 1863, CAMP MEIGS, READVILLE, MASSACHUSETTS

... i Wish you Wod right as son as you can i am in the hosply i Was in the battle Was sot in the head But i am Able to go a boat a gane....

— DAVID DEMUS TO AN UNKNOWN RECIPIENT, JULY 26, 1863, BEAUFORT, SOUTH CAROLINA

Dear sister.... On the 18 of July we landed on mres island and We made a charge of Port Wagner We lost agrate meny men the revls Was tow harde for us Jacob Christey was wonded and [unclear: tomed] [unclear: Curtches] [unclear: hes watches sirers cruelten] was kild and all the rest of them was wonded Daved Deames was wonded tomes stoner robert lines is ammonks the missin....i have saw more than i ever expected to see be for i left home i have gut thrue this tim i was struck on the best plate with a ball and that was all that save me it was throw gods will that the ball struck the plate....

— WILLIAM CHRISTY TO MARY JANE DEMUS, AUGUST 2, 1863

Mi Dear Wife i tak mi pen in hand to inform you that i am Well as can be fer a Woned man i hav not now pane.... i am [unclear: versor] to tell you that cant get mi liteenes taking hear but i Want you tow sent yor likens to me you can sende yor likens to me you can send me your likens like Talop Walkson Wife did and i Wich that you Wod send you likess in the nex letter and peas to rite as son as you Can and let me now how you ar all geting a long nothing more at present but still remac yor Dear hus bean David A. Demes

— DAVID A. DEMUS TO MARY JANE DEMUS, AUGUST 18, 1863, HILTON HEAD, SOUTH CAROLINA

These poignant letters exchanged among members of the Demus and Christy families from Mercersburg in Franklin County, Pennsylvania, speak with the authentic voice that Whitman craved. They reveal "the actual soldier of 1862 – '65," as he wrote, "with all his ways, his incredible dauntlessness, habits, practices, tastes, language, his fierce friendship, his appetite, rankness, his superb strength and animality lawless gait, and a hundred unnamed lights and shades of camp."[50] In simple, untutored but legible prose, the letters also offer insight into the profound events the soldiers experienced within a very short time, while simultaneously indicating the issues of concern to their daily lives, especially the question of pay, as well as the importance they placed on their uniforms and guns. The young men who wrote these letters were between the ages of sixteen and twenty-three; most worked as laborers or farmers, although Joseph Christy was a woodcutter. The Christy brothers lived with their father, a widower, who owned a small farm worth about $200, and their sister Mary Jane, who was a domestic worker. In 1860 Mary Jane married David Andrew Demus, who worked as a farmhand.[51] David Demus and his brother George, along with his brothers-in-law, Jacob, Joseph, Samuel, and William Christy, were among the forty-five recruits from Franklin County who joined the 54th in late April 1863. Although the local newspaper tried to discourage recruits, quoting one of the "sable brethren" as saying that the war was nothing more than "two dogs fighting over one bone," Franklin County contributed more soldiers to the 54th than almost any other area in the country.[52] As with all the newly enlisted soldiers, the recruiting officer assured the Demus and Christy brothers that they would get the same pay as white soldiers: $13 a month, plus $8 a month for their families, and an enlistment bonus of $50. The soldiers' pay soon became the subject of a bitter dispute between the 54th and the federal government, prompting Corporal James Henry Gooding of the 54th to write to President Lincoln in September 1863 and demand, as so many others would do in the years to come, equal pay for equal work (pl. 45).[53]

Yet Whitman, who had a deep appreciation for photography's lucid and loving descriptions of the ordinary world and its democratic nature, would also have immediately noted that the frequent references to "likenesses" in the letters demonstrated the soldiers' fascination with photography, as well as their easy access to it. And, as someone who once referred to a photograph of himself as "this heart's geography's map … / This condensation of the universe," he would have recognized and celebrated the profound talismanic properties the soldiers ascribed to the medium, and the solace, joy, and inspiration it gave them.[54]

No photographs of the Demus or Christy brothers are known to have survived, although they had many opportunities to have their portraits taken — in studios near Camp Meigs in Readville, Massachusetts, or in Beaufort, Port Royal, and Hilton Head, or Morris Island in 1863; in Olustee, Florida, where they arrived in early 1864; or again on Morris Island later in 1864. Many other recruits to the 54th did take advantage of these opportunities. Some had their portraits made at a photography studio near Camp Meigs before they left Boston in May 1863 (pl. 19). Eager to explore and preserve his new identity and pose with the attributes of his profession, Private James Matthew Townsend from Company I, who was born free in Gallipolis, Ohio, had his portrait taken in the four weeks between the time the 54th soldiers received their uniforms and guns and when they left for South Carolina.[55] He was so proud of his rifle that he took it with him to the photography studio, resting one hand on its barrel, both to steady himself and to claim further ownership of it. The gun, which was taller than he was, fills the entire frame of the picture. Showing photography's ability to freeze a fleeting expression, transforming the moment into the eternal, Townsend's fully frontal pose, with one leg slightly forward from the other, and his barely parted lips combine to give the portrait an air of immediacy and anticipation. With his strong moral "conviction that the war would result in

7

the emancipation of his race," Townsend may have wished to send copies of this carte de visite to family and friends in Ohio to show them, as he would later say, that he was ready to be "well up in the line of battle, where the fight is up and where the smoke is ascending and the hurry and clash of arms are heard."[56]

Townsend may have brought a friend with him the day he had his portrait made, for a photograph of an unidentified 54th soldier from Company I (pl. 20) was also made at the same studio near Camp Meigs.[57] This man, like Townsend, looked directly into the camera, but he did not pose with his rifle. Instead, he steadied himself for the long exposure time by resting his hand on a table. The unknown soldier also conveys anticipation, but not so much through facial expression as through his outstretched fingers, which evoke the gesture of a pianist waiting to play a chord. Yet, unlike Townsend's photograph, his is an ambrotype. More expensive than a carte de visite and with richer tones that were often augmented with hand-coloring, an ambrotype is a direct positive image made on glass, thus each one is unique. In addition, in order to protect their fragile surfaces, many ambrotypes were placed in frames with brass mats, as this one was, and also in cases. This makes viewing an ambrotype an intimate experience, as one opens the case in one's hands and slowly moves it back and forth to examine the image on its somewhat reflective surface. By having his portrait made as an ambrotype, this soldier chose to preserve this historic occasion with a record of himself that was both precious and personal.[58]

Other soldiers of the 54th had their portraits made in Boston. Drawing on the example of his father, Frederick Douglass, twenty-two-year-old Sergeant Major Lewis Douglass, one of the highest-ranking African Americans in the regiment, had a commanding full-length carte de visite made of himself by the Boston firm of Case & Getchell (pl. 21). Assertively folding his arms across his chest, Lewis Douglass directly confronted the camera, wore a determined expression, and proudly displayed his stripes. The strength of character he displays in this photograph won him the respect of his fellow soldiers as a calm and courageous leader and served him well when, as he wrote, "the grape and canister, shell and minnies swept down on us like chaff" at Fort Wagner.[59] Another portrait of Sergeant Major Douglass, made after he was discharged from the army for medical reasons in 1864, demonstrates how he was able to modulate his expression for the camera to a remarkable degree (pl. 46). With his wife, Amelia, who was fully aware of all that he had endured, standing protectively at his side, Douglass looks pensively down, as if reflecting on the profound cost of the war. "How I got out of that fight alive I cannot tell, but I am here," he wrote to his then fiancée, Amelia, two days after the Battle of Fort Wagner: "My Dear girl I hope

Fig. 7 Abraham Fisher, *Private Theodore J. Becker*, 1863, albumen print. Museum of African American History, Boston and Nantucket, Massachusetts

again to see you. I must bid you farewell should I be killed. Remember if I die I die in a good cause. I wish we had a hundred thousand colored troops we would put an end to this war."[60]

At least two other 54th soldiers had their portraits made in Boston. Thirty-two-year-old Theodore J. Becker, who was older than most of the enlisted men, a physician from nearby Fitchburg, Massachusetts, and the hospital steward for the 54th, had his carte de visite made in the studio of Abraham Fisher on Washington Street in early May (fig. 7). Henry Steward, who had risen quickly from a private to a sergeant after enlisting in April 1863, probably had his picture taken soon thereafter (pl. 22). As in so many of the photographs of the soldiers of the 54th regiment, much of the unpretentious yet powerful veracity of this image resides in its simple details. Steward, who was born free in Lenawee County in Michigan, had worked hard to get others to join the 54th.[61] His palpable pride in the regiment and his own accomplishments, as well as, one suspects, in the promise he saw for his people, is patently evident in his erect posture and his precisely vertical sword and sheath; even the column he chose to stand next to conveys a sense of strength, clarity of purpose, and democratic ideals. Like the unknown soldier from Company I, Steward opted for a more expensive ambrotype. Proud of his profession, uniform, and rank, and no doubt honored and humbled by this auspicious moment in history, he paid an additional fee to have his buttons, belt buckle, and other elements in his cap, sword, and eagle breastplate tinted with gold paint to highlight their significance. To a great extent, Steward embodies all that Frederick Douglass spoke of when he addressed an audience in National Hall in Philadelphia on July 6, 1863, seeking additional recruits for the colored troops: "Once let the black man get upon his person the brass letters, U.S.; let him get an eagle on his button and a musket on his shoulder and bullets in his pocket, and there is no power on the earth or under the earth which can deny that he has earned the right of citizenship in the United States."[62]

Several enlisted men of the 54th appear to have had their photographs taken in South Carolina. By the time the 54th reached there in the summer of 1863, the Union had been in control of the Beaufort, Port Royal, Hilton Head area for over a year and a half. Former slaves had flocked to the area, but so too had civilians such as shopowners, barbers, teachers, ministers, and photographers, all of whom were eager to provide goods and services to the many soldiers and sailors who now inhabited the region. Some of the photographers were itinerant, traveling with sutlers behind advancing regiments; others opened more permanent studios, often in abandoned buildings. Samuel A. Cooley, for example, set up a studio in Beaufort on June 1, 1863, and opened additional ones on Folly Island, Hilton Head, and Morris Island. H. C. Foster, who had photographed in the region throughout 1864, opened a "Photographic Gallery" in September of that year on Morris Island near Bluff Battery, newly renamed "Fort Shaw."[63] These were the kinds of establishments where the members of the 54th — both African American and white — had their portraits made. Money, not aesthetics, was the objective of these photographers: as their advertisements made clear, they employed "skillful operators" who made "likenesses," not artists with lofty ambitions.[64] Their ventures were profitable if they attracted enough clients, moved them through the process quickly, and standardized their practice. Thus the power of the portraits lay far less in the ability of the photographer to draw forth the character of his sitter than in the intention, charisma, and performance of the subject himself. For the African American members of the 54th, the transaction was complicated by the fact that this was the first time in American history that armed people of color in uniforms were presenting themselves to a civilian population as liberators. Some soldiers displayed great confidence, as Sergeant Steward had done; others, especially younger ones, appeared to be intimidated or uncertain; while still others, like many of their white counterparts, remained reserved.

8

Private Abraham F. Brown, who probably had his portrait made shortly after the 54th arrived in South Carolina in June 1863, seemed to warm to the process of being photographed. In one portrait he is seated in front of a painted backdrop of a camp scene with tents, lines of soldiers, and a wagon wheel in the foreground (pl. 24). He faces forward with his large hands calmly folded in his lap, but his eyes look off to the left and do not engage the photographer directly. The other portrait is not technically resolved, but Brown is far more animated, which gives the image the feeling of a casual snapshot (pl. 23). Standing in a shallow space with a painting of a flag above his shoulder, Brown has one hand on a chair and one on his lapel, as if he has just risen and is about to address an audience. Both portraits are tintypes, a resilient, direct positive process that flourished during the Civil War. Tintypes were cheaper and dried faster than ambrotypes, so the results could be quickly inspected. Thus, like twentieth-century photo booth portraits, they encouraged playful experimentation. Like ambrotypes, they also could be hand-tinted, as was the larger of Brown's tintypes, with the addition of gold paint to his buttons and red to his cheeks. A sailor born in Toronto, Canada, Brown appears to have been a man of some means, as he wears a pocket watch that was also tinted with gold.[65]

Several other 54th soldiers, including John Wilson, had their photographs taken in 1864 when the regiment returned to Morris Island after serving in Florida. A painter from Cincinnati, Ohio, Wilson had distinguished himself as a leader in Company G as soon as he arrived at Camp Meigs on April 14, 1863, and was promoted to sergeant by May 10.[66] When Lewis Douglass was discharged from the army in April 1864, Wilson was promoted to sergeant major, one of only five African American noncommissioned officers in the regiment at that time. A little over a month later, on June 3, 1864, he had his portrait made (pl. 26).[67] With his jacket elegantly draped below his leg, he prominently displays both his sergeant major stripes and his cap with its bugle and the numerals "54." Photographed in front of a painted backdrop of a camp scene, as if to indicate his rise from the ranks, the twenty-three-year-old Wilson projects a strong presence. Although many cartes de visite depict full-length figures set within a contrived architectural surrounding, Wilson's body fills the picture frame. Seated sideways on the chair, he faces the camera, his erect posture and direct engagement with the viewer anchoring this dynamic composition.

Among the most poignant — and troubling — of the photographs made on Morris Island at this time are three of drummer boys and one of a fifer: John Gooseberry, Alexander Howard Johnson, Henry Augustus Monroe, and David Miles Moore (pls. 29–31; fig. 8). Their small stature and bewildered expressions, coupled with clothes several sizes too large, make

Fig. 8　Unknown photographer, *Private David Miles Moore, Company C, 54th Massachusetts Regiment*, 1864, albumen print. West Virginia University Libraries, West Virginia and Regional History Collection

Fig. 9　H. C. Foster (?), *Private Isaiah Spriggs, Company A, 54th Massachusetts Regiment*, 1864, albumen print. Museum of African American History, Boston and Nantucket, Massachusetts

Fig. 10　H. C. Foster, *Sergeant Joseph A. Palmer, Company K, 54th Massachusetts Regiment*, 1864, albumen print. Museum of African American History, Boston and Nantucket, Massachusetts

them appear vulnerable and lost. In truth, they ranged in age from thirteen to twenty-five and were not significantly younger than many of the other soldiers when they enlisted. And evidence indicates they were resilient. For example, Johnson, sixteen, whom Shaw referred to as the "original drummer boy," was with the colonel when he died at Fort Wagner and carried important messages to other officers during the battle. Monroe, who enlisted at age thirteen almost as soon as the call for recruits was issued in February 1863, was an exceptional student in his hometown of New Bedford, Massachusetts, distinguishing himself in an all-white class.[68] H. C. Foster probably made the portraits of Gooseberry and Johnson as well as those of James W. Bush, Isaiah Spriggs, and Joseph A. Palmer (pl. 28; figs. 9, 10).[69] The fact that all of these men, two of whom were sergeants, appear just as wary as the youngest drummer boy, raises the possibility that Foster's studio may have not have been welcoming to African American members of 54th.

The portrait of Sergeant William H. Carney mentioned earlier in this essay (see fig. 2) may have been made at the same studio where the photographs of Monroe, Moore, and Wilson were taken, for the backdrop and floor appear similar. Because of the contrived, careful construction of that photograph, which would have been hard for Carney himself to orchestrate, and because of the hesitancy Carney seems to express — the stiffness of his pose, his slightly downcast eyes and tilted head — it raises several ques-

9

10

tions: not only who helped him execute it, but who conceived it — Carney or someone else? And if someone else, was it the photographer, a fellow soldier, or possibly even an officer? The answer may lie in the reproduction history of the portrait. Although Carney's image, deeds, and words were used as early as November 1864 to recruit other African Americans to enlist in the Union army (pl. 66), this iconic photograph was not circulated widely or reproduced until it appeared as the frontispiece in Captain Luis Emilio's regimental history of 1894. Carney had given the flag to Emilio immediately after the battle, and in 1894 when Emilio captioned the photograph, he noted that Carney was posed "With the Flag He Saved At Wagner," suggesting that he might have had a hand in its creation.[70] As a first-generation Spanish-American born in Salem, Massachusetts, Emilio was sensitive to discrimination and took offense when the 54th was not given proper military respect.[71] Just as important, he fully understood the power of photography and had himself photographed numerous times during his army career. Like many of the other white officers from the 54th, such as Major Lincoln Ripley Stone, Second Lieutenant Charles Hallett, and even Shaw himself, Emilio was at ease having his photograph taken and was comfortable expressing different emotions in front of the camera, from compassion, to reflection, to stern, impenetrable resolve (pls. 16, 35–40). And as the cost of a photograph was minimal for Emilio and the other officers, they experimented freely with their poses. In 1861, for example, a seventeen-year-old Emilio had himself depicted in the gray, blue, and red Zouave uniform of the 23rd Massachusetts Volunteer Infantry, even though other officers disparaged them as the "Jewels" for such outlandish attire.[72] And on October 12, 1863, an older Emilio struck more casual poses, first with fellow officers from the 54th and then by himself, displaying an easy assurance that bespoke not only the camaraderie of a group of friends who had endured ordeals together but also his own confidence in himself, his position, and the process of being photographed (pls. 35, 36).

11

Despite his heroic actions, Carney exudes no such relaxed self-possession in the portrait that was made of him in 1864. Overwhelmed by the flag, he is, in fact, a cipher and difficult to read. He was a "shy man … a very quiet and very unassuming man," a descendant said of him: "not a person who wanted" all the attention that was showered on him. "He just happened to be in a place, [and] did what he thought was his duty."[73] Carney *did* fare better than many of his comrades, who knew only too well the fragility and fickleness of life: Abraham Brown accidentally shot himself while cleaning his gun and died on July 11, 1863; Henry Steward died on September 27, 1863, most likely of chronic diarrhea; John Gooseberry survived the war but died "poor and needy" at the age of thirty-eight; and Private Samuel Benton, who was said to be "moon struck," was court-martialed for murder (pl. 32).[74]

Fig. 11 Henry F. Hatch, *William H. Carney*, c. 1887, gelatin silver print. Carl J. Cruz Collection

But many others, capitalizing on their military service, enjoyed far more prominent public careers. Lewis Douglass was a newspaper editor and a District of Columbia assemblyman; James Townsend attended Oberlin, was an ordained deacon, a member of the Indiana General Assembly, and appointed by President Benjamin Harrison to be recorder of the General Land Office in Washington, DC; and Henry Augustus Monroe, who received his doctorate of divinity, was a preacher, teacher, customs inspector for the port of Baltimore, and publisher of the *Standard Bearer*, a newspaper dedicated to African American issues.[75]

Carney's rewards for his distinguished service came more slowly. After his discharge from the army in 1864, he returned to his adopted home of New Bedford, Massachusetts, where he was made superintendent of streetlights. Although the appointment was significant, as he supervised whites, the position did not suit him, and he soon left for California. He returned to New Bedford by the late 1860s and worked for thirty-two years in the postal service, his limp noticeable as he delivered mail throughout the city, often wearing his Civil War greatcoat for warmth (pl. 67). Sometime around 1887 he had another portrait made of himself (fig. 11). Although he wears several medals, including the Gillmore Medal of Honor and one from the Grand Army of the Republic, he looks off to the side and does not engage the photographer or the viewer.[76]

We see a far different, much more relaxed person in one of the last photographs made of him by a New Bedford photographer between 1900 and 1908 (pl. 69). Filling almost the entire frame of the picture, Carney looks directly at the camera and wears only one medal: the nation's highest award for bravery, the Congressional Medal of Honor. Thanks to the efforts of both W.E.B. Du Bois, one of a new generation of African American activists who was the driving force behind the Exhibit of the American Negro at the 1900 Paris Exhibition, and Christian Fleetwood, a former sergeant major in the 4th Regiment of the U.S. Colored Volunteer Infantry, Carney finally received the Medal of Honor in May 1900 (pl. 68). Although the medal was ignominiously sent through the mail, depriving Carney of the honor and pleasure of receiving it in front of his comrades-in-arms, he nevertheless accepted it graciously, writing the assistant secretary of war, G. D. Meiklejohn, "I prize it most highly."[77] Denied his public ceremony, Carney turned to photography to commemorate his award and document himself as the first African American Medal of Honor recipient.[78] Smiling and looking directly at the photographer, James E. Reed, one of the few African American photographers at the time to own and operate his own photography studio in Massachusetts, Carney expresses deep pride in his accomplishments and his medal.[79] Yet he also shows that he had learned how to present himself for public view. Like Douglass, Truth, and many others associated with the 54th, Carney had come to understand how he could use photography to create an image of himself that he wanted the world and history to see — a proud, confident, distinguished hero. Just as the photographs of the soldiers of the 54th offer mute testimony of their participation in the war, their service and their sacrifice, refuting stereotypes with diversity and generalizations with the lucidity of facts, and just as they remind Americans of what they can be and should aspired to become, so too does the photograph of Carney allow him to reach through time and touch the future. Photographic portraits provide us with "the best history," Whitman wrote, "the history from which there would be no appeal."[80]

These burin'd eyes, flashing to you, to pass to future time,

To launch and spin through space revolving, sideling — from these to emanate,

To You, whoe-er you are — a Look....

A Traveler of thoughts and years — of peace and war,

Of youth long sped, and middle age declining,...

To draw and clench your Soul, of once, inseparably with mine,

Then travel, travel on.[81]

PLATES 1 – 56

RECRUITERS OF THE
54TH MASSACHUSETTS REGIMENT

⊱⊰

"Massachusetts now welcomes you to arms
as her soldiers. She has but a small colored
population from which to recruit. She has full
leave of the General Government to send one
regiment to the war, and she has undertaken
to do it. Go quickly and help fill up this first
colored regiment from the North."

— FREDERICK DOUGLASS, MARCH 2, 1863

EMANCIPATION PROCLAMATION

January 1, 1863, ink on paper, 21 ⅛ × 13 ½ (53.7 × 34.2)

David M. Rubenstein

Washington only

2

Mathew Brady

GOVERNOR JOHN A. ANDREW

1861 – 1866, albumen print, 3 ½ × 2 ¼ (8.8 × 5.5)
Harvard University, Houghton Library, MS Am 1084 (59),
Gift, Military Order of the Loyal Legion of the United States,
Commandery of the State of Massachusetts, 1974

RECRUITERS

3

Pach Brothers

GEORGE LUTHER STEARNS

1866–1867, albumen print, 5¾ × 4 (14.6 × 10.3)

Kansas State Historical Society

4

Southworth & Hawes

WENDELL PHILLIPS

c. 1850, daguerreotype, 8 1/8 × 6 1/8 (20.6 × 15.6)
Courtesy of the Boston Public Library, Print Department
Washington only

5

Samuel J. Miller

FREDERICK DOUGLASS

1847 – 1852, daguerreotype, 4¾ × 3½ (12.1 × 8.8)
Art Institute of Chicago, Major Acquisitions Centennial Endowment
Washington only

6

Samuel Broadbent

CHARLES LENOX REMOND

c. 1858, daguerreotype, 3⅝ × 2⅝ (9.2 × 6.6)
Courtesy of the Boston Public Library, Print Department
Washington only

7

Unknown photographer

ROBERT PURVIS

c. 1840 – 1849, daguerreotype, 3½ × 2⅝ (9 × 6.5)
Courtesy of the Boston Public Library, Print Department
Washington only

8

James U. Stead

HENRY HIGHLAND GARNET

c. 1881, albumen print, 4½ × 3⅝ (11.5 × 9.1)

National Portrait Gallery, Smithsonian Institution

9

David C. Burnite

THOMAS MORRIS CHESTER

c. 1870, albumen print, 3⅝ × 2½ (9.2 × 6.4)

The New York Public Library,

Schomburg Center for Research in Black Culture,

Photographs and Prints Division

Washington only

10

Frederick DeBourg Richards

DR. JOHN S. ROCK

1863–1864, albumen print, 3⅝ × 2⅜ (9 × 5.9)

Collection of Greg French

11

Harry Shepherd

JOHN MERCER LANGSTON

c. 1870–1880, albumen print, 5½ × 3⅞ (14 × 9.8)

Courtesy of Oberlin College Archives

12

Edward L. Allen

LEWIS HAYDEN

c. 1860–1869, albumen print, 3⅝ × 2¼ (9 × 5.5)
Ohio Historical Society, Wilbur H. Siebert Collection

RECRUITERS

13

Abraham Bogardus

MAJOR MARTIN ROBISON DELANY

1865, albumen print, 3 ⅜ × 2 ⅛ (8.6 × 5.3)
Courtesy of the National Park Service,
Gettysburg National Military Park Museum

14

Unknown photographer

SOJOURNER TRUTH

1864, albumen print, 3¼ × 2¼ (8.1 × 5.7)
National Portrait Gallery, Smithsonian Institution

> Commonwealth of Massachusetts.
>
> Executive Department.
>
> Boston, Jan. 30th 1863
>
> Francis G. Shaw, Esq. Staten Island. N.Y.
>
> Dear Sir:
>
> As you may have seen by the newspapers, I am about to raise a Colored Regiment in Massachusetts. This I cannot but regard as perhaps the most important corps to be organized during the whole war, in view of what must be the composition of our new levies; and therefore I am very anxious to organize it judiciously in order that it may be a model for all future Colored Regiments. I am desirous to have for its officers, particularly

15

LETTER FROM GOVERNOR JOHN A. ANDREW TO FRANCIS G. SHAW

January 30, 1863, ink on paper, 9 7/8 × 7 1/2 (25.1 × 19.1)
Courtesy of the Massachusetts Historical Society

THE 54TH MASSACHUSETTS REGIMENT

※

"The regiment has established its reputation as a fighting regiment.... I wish we had a hundred thousand colored troops — we would put an end to this war."

— LEWIS DOUGLASS TO AMELIA LOUGEN, JULY 20, 1863

16

John Adams Whipple

COLONEL ROBERT GOULD SHAW

1863, albumen print, 3 3/8 × 2 3/8 (8.4 × 6)

Boston Athenaeum

ENLISTMENT ROLL OF COMPANY A,
54TH MASSACHUSETTS INFANTRY REGIMENT

May 4–8, 1863, ink on paper, 21 × 13¾ (53.3 × 34.9)
Courtesy of the Massachusetts Historical Society

18

J. E. Farwell and Co.

TO COLORED MEN. 54TH REGIMENT!
MASSACHUSETTS VOLUNTEERS, OF AFRICAN DESCENT!

1863, ink on paper, 43 ¼ × 29 ⅝ (109.9 × 75.2)
Courtesy of the Massachusetts Historical Society

19

Unknown photographer

PRIVATE JAMES MATTHEW TOWNSEND

1863, albumen print, 3 3/8 × 2 3/8 (8.6 × 5.8)

Collection of Greg French

20

Unknown photographer

UNIDENTIFIED PRIVATE, COMPANY I,
54TH MASSACHUSETTS REGIMENT

1863, ambrotype, 3 ½ × 2 ½ (8.7 × 6.4)
The Gilder Lehrman Institute of American History

21

Case & Getchell

SERGEANT MAJOR LEWIS H. DOUGLASS

1863, albumen print, 3 3/8 × 2 1/4 (8.6 × 5.5)

Moorland-Spingarn Research Center, Howard University

22

Unknown photographer

SERGEANT HENRY F. STEWARD

1863, ambrotype, 4⅛ × 3⅛ (10.5 × 8)
Courtesy of the Massachusetts Historical Society

23

Unknown photographer

PRIVATE ABRAHAM F. BROWN

1863, tintype, 3 1/8 × 2 5/8 (8 × 6.5)
Courtesy of the Massachusetts Historical Society

24

Unknown photographer

PRIVATE ABRAHAM F. BROWN

1863, tintype, 3 1/8 × 2 3/4 (8 × 7)

Courtesy of the Massachusetts Historical Society

25

Unknown photographer

PRIVATE CHARLES H. ARNUM

1864, tintype, 4 × 2⅝ (10 × 6.5)

Courtesy of the Massachusetts Historical Society

26

Unknown photographer

SERGEANT MAJOR JOHN H. WILSON

June 3, 1864, albumen print, 3 5/8 × 2 3/8 (9.1 × 5.8)
West Virginia University Libraries,
West Virginia and Regional History Collection

27

Unknown photographer

PRIVATE WILLIAM J. NETSON, MUSICIAN

c. 1863 – 1864, tintype, 3 3/8 × 2 5/8 (8.5 × 6.5)

Courtesy of the Massachusetts Historical Society

28

H. C. Foster

SERGEANT JAMES W. BUSH

1864, albumen print, 3 ⅜ × 2 (8.5 × 5)
Courtesy of the Massachusetts Historical Society

29

Unknown photographer

PRIVATE HENRY A. MONROE, MUSICIAN

c. 1863, albumen print, image: 3 ⅜ × 2 (8.5 × 5)
Courtesy of the Massachusetts Historical Society

30

H. C. Foster (?)

PRIVATE JOHN GOOSEBERRY, MUSICIAN

1864, tintype, 4 × 2 2/3 (10 × 6.8)
Courtesy of the Massachusetts Historical Society

31

H. C. Foster (?)

PRIVATE ALEXANDER H. JOHNSON, MUSICIAN

1864, tintype, 3 ⅛ × 2 ⅝ (8 × 6.5)

Courtesy of the Massachusetts Historical Society

32

Unknown photographer

PRIVATE SAMUEL J. BENTON

1863 – 1865, tintype, 2 ⅝ × 2 (6.5 × 5.2)
West Virginia University Libraries,
West Virginia and Regional History Collection

54TH MASSACHUSETTS REGIMENT

33

Unknown photographer

PRIVATE CHARLES A. SMITH

c. 1880, tintype, 3½ × 2⅜ (8.7 × 6)

Courtesy of the Massachusetts Historical Society

34

Unknown photographer

PRIVATE RICHARD GOMAR

c. 1880, tintype, 3⅜ × 2⅜ (8.5 × 6)

Courtesy of the Massachusetts Historical Society

35

Unknown photographer

SECOND LIEUTENANT EZEKIEL G. TOMLINSON,
CAPTAIN LUIS F. EMILIO,
AND SECOND LIEUTENANT DANIEL SPEAR

October 12, 1863, tintype, 3¼ × 2½ (8.3 × 6.2)
Library of Congress, Prints and Photographs Division

36

Unknown photographer

CAPTAIN LUIS F. EMILIO

1863–1865, tintype, 2 5/8 × 2 1/8 (6.6 × 5.33)

Pamplin Historical Park and
The National Museum of the Civil War Soldier

37

Unknown photographer

SECOND LIEUTENANT CHARLES O. HALLETT

c. 1865, albumen print, 3¾ × 2¼ (9.3 × 5.6)

Pamplin Historical Park and
The National Museum of the Civil War Soldier

38

Unknown photographer

MAJOR LINCOLN R. STONE, SURGEON

May 28, 1863, 3 ⅝ × 2 ¼ (9.2 × 5.5)

Pamplin Historical Park and
The National Museum of the Civil War Soldier

39

Unknown photographer

CAPTAIN NORWOOD P. HALLOWELL

1862 – 1863, albumen print, 3 ½ × 2 ⅜ (8.8 × 5.9)
Pamplin Historical Park and
The National Museum of the Civil War Soldier

40

John Adams Whipple

CAPTAIN CABOT J. RUSSELL

c. 1863, albumen print, 3 ½ × 2 ⅜ (8.9 × 5.9)

American Antiquarian Society

Washington only

41

Currier & Ives

THE GALLANT CHARGE OF THE
54TH MASSACHUSETTS (COLORED)
REGIMENT: ON THE REBEL WORKS
AT FORT WAGNER, MORRIS ISLAND,
NEAR CHARLESTON, JULY 18TH, 1863,
AND DEATH OF COLONEL ROBT. G. SHAW

1863, hand-colored lithograph,
8¼ × 12½ (20.7 × 31.6)
Boston Athenaeum,
Gift of Raymond Wilkins, 1944

CASUALTY LIST OF THE 54TH MASSACHUSETTS INFANTRY
REGIMENT FROM THE ASSAULT ON FORT WAGNER, SC

July 16–18, 1863, ink on paper, 12¼ × 7¾ (31.1 × 19.7)
National Archives, Washington, DC

Beaufort S.C.
July 31st 1863

I regret to inform you that Col Shaw is killed. The 54th mass., of which he was Col, fought so bravely that Gen. Gilmore put them in a white Brigade. When the attack was to be made on Fort Wagner, the Gen selected his best troops, and among the rest, the 54th. The black soldiers marched side by side with their white comrades in arms to the assault. (Tell it with pride to the world.) The parapet is 30. feet high. Col. Shaw was the first man to mount that high parapet. He waved his sword and shouted "come on boys", and then he fell dead. He died well. Neither Greece nor Rome can excell his heroism.

43

ANONYMOUS LETTER TO SHAW FAMILY ANNOUNCING SHAW'S DEATH

July 31, 1863, ink on paper, 7¼ × 7⅝ (18.2 × 19.2), Harvard University,
Houghton Library, MS Am 1910 (14), Robert Gould Shaw letters to his family,
Gift, Mrs. Lloyd K. Garrison, Mrs. Alexander D. Harvey, Frances Jay,
and Mrs. Lawrence Fox, 1975

44

Frank Vizetelly

ASSAULT ON BATTERY WAGNER, MORRIS ISLAND,
NEAR CHARLESTON, ON THE NIGHT OF THE 18TH JULY —
THE RUSH OF THE GARRISON TO THE PARAPET

July 18, 1863, pencil, gray wash, Chinese white on paper, 9 × 11 (22.9 × 28)
Harvard University, Houghton Library, MS Am 1585 (22),
Frank Vizetelly drawings, Gift, Colonel John Glas Sandeman, 1902

Camp of 54th Mass Colored Regt

1863

Morris Island, Dept of the South, Sept 28th

Your Excelency Abraham Lincoln;

Your Excelency will pardon the presumtion of an humble individual like myself, in addressing you, but the earnest Solicitation of my Comrades in Arms, besides the genuine interest felt by myself in the matter is my excuse, for placing before the Executive head of the Nation our Common Grievance: On the 6th of the last Month, the Paymaster of the department informed us, that if we would decide to recieve the sum of $10 (ten dollars) per month, he would come and pay us that sum, but, that, on the sitting of Congress, the Regt would, in his opinion, be allowed the other 3 (three.) He did not give us any guarantee that this would be, as he hoped, certainly he had no authority for making any such guarantee, and we can not supose him acting in any way interested. Now the main question is, Are we Soldiers, or are we Labourers. We are fully armed, and equipped, have done all the various Duties, pertaining to a Soldiers life, have conducted ourselves, to the complete satisfaction of General Officers, who were if any, prejudiced against us, but who now accord us all the encouragement, and honour due us: have shared the perils, and Labour, of Reducing the first stronghold, that flaunted a Traitor Flag: and more, Mr President. Today, the Anglo Saxon Mother, Wife, or Sister, are not alone, in tears for

45

LETTER FROM CORPORAL JAMES HENRY GOODING
TO PRESIDENT ABRAHAM LINCOLN

September 25, 1863, ink on paper, 9 ⅝ × 7 ½ (24.5 × 190.1)
National Archives, Washington, DC

AFTER THE BATTLE

✈

"My dear Amelia:
I have been in two fights, and am unhurt....
Our men fought well on both occasions.
The last was desperate — we charged that
terrible battery on Morris Island known as
Fort Wagner, and were repulsed with a loss of
300 killed and wounded. I escaped unhurt
from amidst that perfect hail of shot and shell."

— LEWIS DOUGLASS TO AMELIA LOUGEN, JULY 20, 1863

46

Unknown photographer

LEWIS AND AMELIA DOUGLASS

c. 1866, albumen print, 2 5/8 × 2 1/8 (6.6 × 5.33)
U.S. Department of the Interior, National Park Service,
Frederick Douglass National Historic Site,
Washington, DC

47

Charles R. B. Claflin

CLARA BARTON, NURSE

c. 1864, albumen print, 4 × 2 ¼ (10 × 5.5)

Chris Foard

48

Unknown photographer

DR. M. M. MARSH

c. 1863, albumen print, 3 ¾ × 2 ¼ (9.5 × 5.7)

Chris Foard

49

Charles Milton Bell

CHARLOTTE L. FORTEN, TEACHER

c. 1870, albumen print, 3½ × 2½ (8.9 × 6.4)
The New York Public Library,
Schomburg Center for Research in Black Culture,
Photographs and Prints Division
Washington only

50

Black & Case

HELEN LOUISE GILSON, NURSE

c. 1865, albumen print, 3⅝ × 2¼ (9 × 5.7)
Chris Foard

51

Unknown photographer

SUSIE KING TAYLOR, NURSE

1902, halftone frontispiece from *Reminiscences of My Life in Camp*, 5 ½ × 3 ⅛ (13.8 × 8)

Chris Foard

52

John G. Darby

HARRIET ARMINTA TUBMAN, SPY

1868, wood engraving frontispiece from *Scenes in the Life of Harriet Tubman*, 7 × 4 ⅜ (17.8 × 11)

Library Company of Philadelphia

53

Unknown photographer

SOJOURNER TRUTH, ADVOCATE

c. 1863 – 1870, albumen print, 3⅝ × 2¼ (9.1 × 5.6)
National Museum of African American History and Culture,
Smithsonian Institution
Washington only

54

George N. Barnard

RUINS IN CHARLESTON, SOUTH CAROLINA

1865–1866, from the album "Photographic Views of Sherman's Campaign," albumen print,
10 ⅛ × 14 ⅛ (25.7 × 35.9)
Collection of the San Francisco Museum of Modern Art, fractional gift of Paul Sack, and collection of the Sack Photographic Trust

55

George N. Barnard
RUINS OF THE PINCKNEY MANSION,
CHARLESTON, SOUTH CAROLINA
1865, from the album "Photographic Views
of Sherman's Campaign," albumen print,
10 × 14 (25.4 × 35.6)
Collection of the Sack Photographic Trust

56

George N. Barnard

RUINS OF THE RAILROAD DEPOT,
CHARLESTON, SOUTH CAROLINA

1865, from the album "Photographic Views
of Sherman's Campaign," albumen print,
10 ⅛ × 14 ⅛ (25.7 × 36.2)
Collection of the Sack Photographic Trust

AFTER THE BATTLE

THE LEGACY OF THE
54TH MASSACHUSETTS REGIMENT AND
THE BATTLE OF FORT WAGNER

For All Time to Come:
Memorializing Robert Gould Shaw and
the 54th Massachusetts Regiment

*"It is not merely for today,
but for all time to come...."*

—ABRAHAM LINCOLN, AUGUST 22, 1864

NANCY K. ANDERSON

*I*N JANUARY 2011, MAUREEN FALLON, mother of a young Marine lieutenant wounded in Afghanistan and hospitalized at Walter Reed Army Medical Center, called the National Gallery of Art to ask a favor. Her son, who had lost his sight following the explosion of a roadside bomb in Helmand Province, was about to be transferred to a rehabilitation facility near Chicago. Before leaving Washington, she asked, could he come to the museum to touch the Shaw Memorial? Anxious and apologetic, she continued without pause, "I know you don't allow visitors to touch the works of art...."[1]

A short time later, Lieutenant Timothy Fallon, accompanied by his parents, brother, and fiancée, arrived at the National Gallery early one morning before the museum opened to the public. Met by a staff security officer, who had also served in the Marine Corps, the Fallon family was soon joined by the conservator and curator responsible for the care of the sculpture, who accompanied them to the gallery where the Shaw Memorial is on permanent exhibition. There, in silence, Lieutenant Fallon moved his hand, slowly, across the faces of the soldiers Augustus Saint-Gaudens had sculpted more than one hundred years earlier in honor of those who had served with the 54th Massachusetts Volunteer Regiment during the Civil War (see pl. 65). It was a private experience for the wounded soldier, and few questions were posed by others present.

Months later, however, when asked how he had first come to know the Shaw Memorial, Lieutenant Fallon recalled seeing the 1989 film *Glory*.[2] A young boy at the time, he had been struck by the still images of Saint-Gaudens' sculpture at the conclusion of what he described as an "action" film. Later, on a family visit to Washington, Timothy and his brother were surprised when they suddenly came upon the plaster version of the memorial at the National Gallery. Maureen Fallon remembers the boys racing back to find their parents — several galleries away — bursting with the news of their discovery.

When Timothy Fallon arrived at the National Gallery in January 2011 to touch the sculpture he had first seen as a boy, he returned as a platoon commander and a combat veteran. Lieutenant Fallon had lost his sight when shrapnel from an improvised explosive device penetrated his eyes. During the difficult days following his injury, he feared that he would no longer be able to enjoy paintings, photographs, or films, and he confessed that on the morning of the planned visit to the National Gallery he nearly "begged off," believing that he could not "possibly appreciate the work by feeling over it like some fool lost in the dark." Yet touch and memory served, and in his recollection of his experience at the National Gallery written more than a year after his visit, Lieutenant Fallon brought the insights of a soldier to Saint-Gaudens' masterpiece:

This piece should kindle pride in any officer who has led men into battle. Shaw is erect, weapon drawn, at the fore of his men, atop a horse where he can best direct his unit's actions. He is sharing their danger and leading from the front.... An officer's first duty is to mission, and his second is to his troops.... The Shaw Memorial depicts only one officer, and the rest of the figures are the men who must do the majority of the fighting, bleeding, and dying.

Lieutenant Fallon, fully aware that the members of the 54th Massachusetts Regiment fought not only against the institution of slavery but also against the widely held belief that they were unworthy both as soldiers and citizens, recalled the emotion he felt as his hand traced "the faces of the dead warriors tramping into a hailstorm of fire and war":

1

All the self-pity and silence of the morning dissipated in a few seconds as I was able to explore the fine and even hidden aspects of this extraordinary work. Yes, I had lost the ability to see it in its entirety, but I could feel the contours, the angles, the shapes as they had lain in the sculptor's mind. I could almost sense his extreme care even as I had tensed while feeling the most fragile part of the piece, Shaw's sword. And even as the sculptor had reflected on the grim minds behind determined, set faces marching into battle, I could feel the tight set of jaws, open eyes, and unbowed, level heads.... It has been 150 years since the Civil War, but this memorial to freedom fighters and the man who led them is as relevant today as it might have been the morning after the failed, but determined assault on Fort Wagner.

The Shaw Memorial was formally dedicated in Boston on May 31, 1897 — Memorial Day (fig. 1). Praise for Saint-Gaudens' extraordinary sculpture appeared even before the official unveiling. Two days prior to the dedication, a writer for *Harper's Weekly* described the memorial as "unsurpassed."[3] The following month *Century Magazine* declared the monument "the greatest work of plastic art yet produced in America."[4] Appreciation for Saint-Gaudens' achievement has only grown with the passage of time. Lieutenant Fallon's personal response to the memorial, informed by the experience of war, is a poignant reminder of the continuing power of the monument. Strikingly innovative and deeply moving, Saint-Gaudens' Shaw

Fig. 1 Augustus Saint-Gaudens' Shaw Memorial, 1897, bronze, Boston, Massachusetts. From the Carol M. Highsmith "This is America!" Collection at the Library of Congress

Fig. 2 Brigadier General Rufus Saxton, c. 1860–1870. Library of Congress, Prints and Photographs Division, Civil War Glass Negative Collection

Memorial is rightfully judged one of the most extraordinary sculptural works ever produced, but it was not the first work of art created to honor Shaw and the 54th Regiment. The earliest "memorials" may have been those completed by two African American artists working in Boston in 1864.

"THE SPLENDID 54TH IS CUT TO PIECES"

Of all the letters sent home by members of the 54th Massachusetts Regiment following the assault on Fort Wagner, perhaps none is more wrenching than that sent by Lewis Douglass to his mother and father, Anna and Frederick Douglass. Dated July 20, the letter was composed two days after the defeat on Morris Island. Frederick Douglass published his son's letter in the August 1863 issue of his journal *Douglass' Monthly*. In his letter, Lewis Douglass wrote of the heroism displayed by the regiment earlier in July when they were severely outnumbered by the enemy during an encounter on James Island. The young soldier noted, "This performance on our part, earned for us the reputation of a fighting regiment."[5] With little food or rest, the regiment continued on to Morris Island, where they soon faced the heavily fortified battery Wagner near Charleston Harbor. Again the men of the 54th displayed astonishing bravery, but, as Douglass lamented, "The splendid 54th is cut to pieces."

Below the letter from his son, in that August issue of his journal, Frederick Douglass printed a second letter. Dated July 27 and addressed to "the colored soldiers and freedmen in this Department," this letter had been issued by Brigadier General Rufus Saxton (fig. 2), Union commander and military governor of the Department of the South.[6] In his letter, Saxton proposed a monument to Robert Gould Shaw, whom he called a "martyr" to the cause of freedom. Writing within days of the defeat at Fort Wagner, Saxton appealed for contributions: "I trust that you will honor yourselves and his glorious memory by appropriating the first proceeds of your labor as freemen towards erecting an enduring monument to the hero, soldier, martyr, Robert Gould Shaw."

By the end of the war, contributions for the proposed monument from multiple sources exceeded $3,000.[7] Yet lingering prejudice, unstable ground on Morris Island (the proposed site of the monument), and disagreements among proponents doomed the project. Later, the funds were used to establish the first free school for black children in Charleston — appropriately named for Shaw.[8]

A similar effort to erect a monument honoring Shaw and the 54th Massachusetts Regiment was discussed in Boston shortly after word of the battle arrived in that capital of antislavery activism.[9] Joshua B. Smith (fig. 3), an African American businessman

2

3

4

acquainted with the Shaw family, initiated the plan but curtailed his efforts when counseled by Senator Charles Sumner (fig. 4) to wait until the conclusion of the war.[10] Within months of the surrender at Appomattox, Smith revived his plan with a personal contribution of $500. A committee was formed, and American sculptor William Wetmore Story was consulted.[11] Implementation of the plan, however, was delayed by multiple factors, including the deaths of Massachusetts governor John Andrew and Senator Sumner, both ardent supporters of the project.

Although early plans for public monuments in South Carolina and Massachusetts were thwarted or delayed, commemorative works honoring Shaw and the 54th Regiment were created by African American artists within months of the battle of Fort Wagner. Three notable works by two artists, none of which appear to have survived, were exhibited in Boston in the fall of 1864.[12]

COLORED LADIES' SANITARY FAIR

In June 1861, President Abraham Lincoln authorized establishment of the United States Sanitary Commission, an agency intended to coordinate volunteer relief efforts on behalf of Union troops.[13] During the course of the war, the commission organized a number of large and successful fairs intended to raise money for the benefit of sick and wounded soldiers.[14] In 1864, a plan for a fair modeled on those sponsored by the United States Sanitary Commission, but more modest scope, was announced in Boston. Christiana Carteaux Bannister (fig. 5), an African American woman who had built a successful hair salon business, announced that "the Colored Ladies of Massachusetts" were organizing a benefit fair for the colored soldiers and their families.[15] As published in *The Liberator*, under the heading "An Appeal to the Public," the announcement began:

Fig. 3   Joshua B. Smith, from "Portraits of American Abolitionists," The Massachusetts Historical Society, Boston

Fig. 4   Senator Charles Sumner of Massachusetts. Library of Congress, Prints and Photographs Division

Fig. 5   *Christiana Carteaux Bannister*, c. 1880, oil on canvas. Collection of the Newport Art Museum by extended loan of the Rhode Island Black Heritage Society in trust of Bannister House, Providence

Fig. 6   Edward Mitchell Bannister, c. 1880, albumen print by Gustine L. Hurd. The National Portrait Gallery, Smithsonian Institution, Gift of Andra and Jacob Terner

Fig. 7   Edmonia Lewis, c. 1870, albumen print by H. Rocher. Boston Athenaeum

5

6

7

It being a well-known fact that the brave men composing the 54th and 55th Regiments Mass. Vols. have, since they have been in their country's service, received no pay, and also that hundreds of them have fallen in defense of the American flag, leaving here in our midst their poor, suffering and destitute wives and children, the Colored Ladies of Massachusetts, knowing the urgent necessity there is, just at this time, of doing something for these suffering ones, are preparing to hold a Fair in this city.... Donations, either of goods or money, will be most thankfully received....[16]

The proposed fair opened on October 18, 1864, in Boston's Mercantile Hall. From the outset, solicitations for goods and services that could be sold at the fair were described as exclusively for the benefit of "the colored Massachusetts regiments."[17] It was at this fair that two African American artists working in Boston, Edward Bannister and Edmonia Lewis (figs. 6, 7), contributed what may have been the first works of art commemorating the courageous charge by Colonel Shaw and the 54th at Fort Wagner.

Edward Bannister, husband of Christiana Carteaux Bannister (president of the Colored Ladies' Sanitary Commission of Boston and chief organizer of the fair), had arrived in Boston as a young man, perhaps as early as 1848.[18] Initially employed as a photographer and a barber, Bannister became an active member of Boston's abolitionist community. In 1857 he married Christiana Carteaux, who was deeply involved in antislavery activities and closely connected (through family) with Charles Lenox Remond (pl. 6), a prominent African American abolitionist and recruiter for the 54th Regiment. Bannister and his wife were members of the Twelfth Baptist Church, known as the "Fugitive's Church," whose congregation included a number of escaped slaves, and whose leader, Reverend Leonard Andrew Grimes, had served as a "conductor" on the Underground Railroad. Bannister was also a member of the "Colored Citizens of Boston" and the "Union Progressive Association," two organizations at the forefront of black abolitionist activities. In December 1862, the artist was listed as a member of the "Committee of Arrangements" for the grand celebration of "President Lincoln's Emancipation Proclamation" held at Tremont Temple in Boston on January 1, 1863.[19] It was the issuance of the Emancipation Proclamation that allowed Massachusetts governor John Andrew to call for the formation of the 54th Volunteer Regiment the following month.

Given the antislavery activities of both Edward and Christiana Bannister, it is not surprising that Edward would contribute one of the most important objects — a portrait of Robert Gould Shaw — to the fair organized to benefit the wounded soldiers who had served under Shaw's leadership. Bannister's portrait of Shaw (described in newspaper accounts as three-quarter length) hung in a place of honor directly behind the speaker's platform. A banner embroidered with the words "Our Martyr" hung above the portrait.[20] On October 19, 1864, the *Boston Transcript* announced that the portrait of Shaw "by the young colored artist Edward M. Bannister" was valued at two hundred dollars and would be raffled.[21] The painting was not, in fact, raffled at the conclusion of the fair. Subsequent reports indicate that a large number of raffle tickets remained unsold on the final day of the fair, and the artist (or his wife) decided to place the painting on exhibition at a local gallery to extend the period during which tickets could be purchased. A later article noted, "the drawing will take place as soon as the list is full" — that is, as soon as all the raffle tickets had been sold. Bannister's portrait of Colonel Shaw, undoubtedly one of the earliest works of art created to memorialize the fallen hero, has not been seen since the nineteenth century.[22]

A second work of art by an African American artist donated to the Colored Ladies' Sanitary Fair also seems to have disappeared. Unlike Bannister, who chose the martyred white leader of the 54th Massachusetts Regiment as the subject of his painting, Edmonia Lewis executed what was described as a "small sculpture" honoring one of the black heroes of the battle, Sergeant William Harvey Carney.[23] Later awarded the Medal of Honor for his bravery during the assault on Fort Wagner, Sergeant Carney had "caught the colors" and carried them forward when the regimental color-bearer fell wounded. Though severely injured himself, the young soldier "brought the colors off, creeping on his knees, pressing his wound with one hand and with the other holding up the emblem of freedom." Upon reaching safety, he was said to have declared, "Boys, I but did my duty; the dear old flag never touched the ground."[24]

In an article on the Colored Ladies' Sanitary Fair, the *Anglo-African* described Edmonia Lewis' work as "a small statue representing Sergt. Carney of the 54th regiment, in a kneeling attitude holding up the colors lest they touch the ground."[25] On the final evening of the fair, Sergeant Carney brought the flag he had rescued at Fort Wagner to Mercantile Hall, where he spoke to those in attendance. Whether the sculpture was purchased or raffled is not clear, and no image of

Fig. 8 Edmonia Lewis' *Colonel Robert Shaw*, photographed by Augustus Marshall, 1864. The Massachusetts Historical Society, Boston, Dall-Healey Family Photographs

the work appears to have survived. At the present time, the location of this sculpture remains unknown.

Edmonia Lewis had only recently arrived in Boston when she donated the sculpture.[26] Of African American and Native American heritage, she had traveled from Oberlin College with letters of introduction to prominent abolitionists. Like Bannister, she became involved in antislavery activities and may have been encouraged to contribute to the fair by the artist and his wife.[27]

The work for which Lewis became most widely known, a bust of Robert Gould Shaw, also dates from 1864. Lydia Marie Child, an antislavery activist who had befriended the artist shortly after her arrival in Boston, described seeing a clay model of the bust in Lewis' studio in the fall of 1864.[28] Early in November, shortly after the Colored Ladies' Sanitary Fair closed (October 26), the *Boston Evening Transcript* encouraged readers to pay special attention to "a bust of the hero Col. Robert G. Shaw by Miss Edmonia Lewis" at the National Sailors' Fair, which had opened in Boston two days earlier.[29] The *Transcript* reported that Lewis had been "modeling for about a year in this city and undertook to make this likeness of one whom she had never seen, out of grateful feeling 'for what he had done for her race.'"[30] The paper also noted, "Col. Shaw's family consider it an excellent likeness and have had it photographed by Mr. Marshall, allowing the artist to sell copies for her own benefit" (fig. 8).[31] Two days later, however, the *Transcript* published a correction: "The bust of Col. Shaw, modeled by Edmonia Lewis, is not exhibited at the National Fair.... The molds not being finished, from which the casts are to be taken, ordered by Col. Shaw's family and others."[32] Instead, the newspaper announced, the bust would be placed on view at a local gallery later in the month. Like Bannister's portrait of Shaw and Lewis' sculpture of Sergeant Carney, the original bust of Shaw modeled by Lewis in 1864 has disappeared.

Shortly after the Civil War, Lewis left Boston and traveled to Europe, where she joined a group of American sculptors working in Rome. She reportedly took with her a commission from a member of the Shaw family for a marble version of her bust of Shaw. The only known version of the bust, in the collection of the Museum of African American History in Boston, is marble and is inscribed "Rome 1867."[33]

Thus three works of art created by two African American artists to commemorate Shaw and the 54th Massachusetts Regiment are known to have been exhibited in Boston in the fall of 1864. Unfortunately, no photographs or drawings of Bannister's oil portrait of Shaw or Lewis' sculpture of Carney have come to light, and the works themselves appear to be lost. Although one hundred plaster copies of Lewis' bust of Shaw are reported to have been produced and sold for $15 each (she is said to have financed her trip abroad through the sale of these copies), no example appears to have entered a public collection.

Since its unveiling in 1897, Saint-Gaudens' Shaw Memorial (see fig. 1) has been justly celebrated for its departure from the traditional "hero on a horse" monument that placed the honored commander/martyr atop a pedestal in splendid isolation. Saint-Gaudens' decision to place Shaw beside his marching regiment was revolutionary. Equally revolutionary was Edmonia Lewis' decision to concentrate solely on Sergeant Carney—perhaps the most celebrated African American hero of the battle—as the subject of her small sculpture. It is, therefore, especially regrettable that no image of this work of any kind is known to have survived.

Lewis' need for funds to continue her studies abroad as well as the dictates of the market would have been factors in the production of one hundred copies (possibly apocryphal) of her bust of Shaw.[34] Boston's abolitionist community, Lewis' most secure patron base, could well afford copies of her bust of Shaw, the hero drawn from their own ranks, but no reference has come to light suggesting that any copies were made of her sculpture of Carney. Those for whom the Colored Ladies' Sanitary Fair served as a "benefit" were probably not in a position to purchase even plaster copies of sculpture. A patronage base for works of art celebrating African American heroism would emerge only later (see pl. 71).

Edward Bannister and Edmonia Lewis created their works commemorating Shaw and his regiment of African American soldiers at what appeared to be one of the most hopeful and celebratory moments in the long struggle against slavery. Although a more nuanced document than many perceived, the Emancipation Proclamation issued by President Lincoln in January 1863 enabled antislavery advocates to begin recruiting African Americans to serve in regiments that would engage not only the Confederate enemy but also systemic racism.

Nowhere was the difficulty of the struggle more passionately chronicled than in the pages of *The Liberator*, William Lloyd Garrison's abolitionist newspaper.[35] In August 1863, shortly after the battle at Fort Wagner, Garrison published an article praising the gallantry of the volunteer regiment and the stoic resolve of the wounded. In the same issue, he reprinted an article from the *Boston Transcript* that angrily drew attention to the appalling social chasm between the heroism displayed by the soldiers of the 54th and the recent barbarity of rioters in New York who had turned their anger at draft inequities into a race riot. During the same week that Shaw and his men led the charge on Fort Wagner, African American men were lynched in New York. In a single paragraph, the *Transcript* reported on the "heroic conduct" of the soldiers of the 54th Regiment and "the unfathomable baseness of the miscreants in New York City, who wreaked every outrage on the defenseless brethren of such soldiers, and who, recreants themselves to their country's call, were furious at the idea that men whose skins were black should presume to be patriots and heroes."[36] The earliest works of art honoring Shaw and his regiment were created at a time when extraordinary displays of courage justified hope for social change, but concurrent demonstrations of explosive racial hatred foretold the powerful forces of resistance that would continue with Reconstruction and beyond.

"THROUGH MY EXTREME INTEREST IN IT"

Less than six months after the Colored Ladies' Sanitary Fair closed in Boston, Robert E. Lee had surrendered at Appomattox and President Lincoln had been assassinated. Postwar "reconstruction" began, and despite initial gains, the legislative dismantling of civil rights for African Americans—purportedly achieved through civil war—began in earnest.

It was against this background that efforts to erect a public monument in Boston honoring Robert Gould Shaw and the men of the 54th Regiment were revived. Joshua B. Smith (see fig. 2)—the African American entrepreneur who had previously proposed a monument honoring Shaw in 1863 — rallied earlier supporters, Senator Charles Sumner and Governor John Andrew, and with $500 of his own money set in motion the new initiative.[37] In the fall of 1865, twenty-one prominent Bostonians formed a committee to raise funds for an equestrian statue honoring Shaw.[38] Although the original concept was clearly focused on a traditional monument of the type created to celebrate generations of military heroes, the stated purpose of the fundraising campaign spoke to the broader implications of the battle at Fort Wagner: "The Monument is intended not only to mark the public gratitude to the fallen hero who at a critical moment assumed a perilous responsibility, but also to commemorate that great event wherein he was a leader by which the title of colored men as citizen soldiers was fixed beyond recall."[39]

By spring of the following year slightly more than $3,000 had been raised.[40] The initiative floundered at first, perhaps because of the deaths of Governor Andrew and Senator Sumner, who had spearheaded the renewed effort.[41] Yet Edward Atkinson, who served as treasurer for the committee, continued to invest the funds, and by the early 1880s more than $16,000 had accrued. Atkinson credited architect Henry Hobson Richardson, his Boston friend and neighbor, with reviving the project.[42] After learning that plans for the memorial had stalled, Richardson, who had known Shaw, volunteered his own services and recommended that Augustus Saint-Gaudens be hired as the sculptor of the proposed monument. In his *Reminiscences,* Saint-Gaudens later wrote: "like most sculptors at the beginning of their careers, [I] felt that by hook or crook I must do an equestrian statue," and with the Shaw Memorial, he confessed, "I had found my opportunity."[43] Saint-Gaudens signed a contract to undertake the commission in February 1884. At the time, it was understood by all that the project would be completed in two years, but the project grew upon Saint-Gaudens, as Atkinson wrote, "in its importance, in its significance, and also in the size of the panel."[44]

Twenty years earlier, Senator Sumner had envisioned an equestrian statue: "no common stone or shaft will be sufficient.... It must be an equestrian statue." Noting that in Europe "only members of the royal family are allowed the honor of an equestrian statue," Sumner had declared, "this is no reason why a grateful republic should not decree an equestrian statue to a youthful hero, whose duty was on horseback, and who was last seen in our streets on horseback."[45] Years later, however, when Saint-Gaudens began working on his initial sketches for the monument, Sumner and Richardson were both gone, and early calls for an equestrian statue had been tempered by members of the Shaw family, who — as Saint-Gaudens recorded in his *Reminiscences* — "objected on the ground that, although Shaw was of a noble type, as noble as any, still he had not been a great commander, and only men of the highest rank should be so honored."[46] The Shaw family was also undoubtedly aware that the funds raised by surviving members of the 54th Massachusetts Regiment soon after the battle at Fort Wagner were given "for the purpose of erecting a monument in memory of Col. Robert G. Shaw and those who died with him."[47] In the eyes of many, the monument was not intended to honor Shaw alone.

Responding to this more complex mandate, Saint-Gaudens began "casting about for some manner of reconciling my desire with their ideas." Recalling the process years later, he wrote, "I fell upon a plan of associating him directly with his troops in a bas-relief, and thereby reducing his importance."[48] By reducing Shaw's importance, of course, Saint-Gaudens heightened the importance of the soldiers.

The commission that Saint-Gaudens had agreed to complete in two years became an object of such importance to the sculptor that he ignored the contract, turned a deaf ear to protests, took on additional work to pay bills, and continued refining his sculptural concept for more than a decade. As he later explained:

9

In justice to myself I must say here that from the low-relief I proposed making when I undertook the Shaw commission, a relief that reasonably could be finished for the limited sum at the command of the committee, I, through my extreme interest in it and its opportunity, increased the conception until the rider grew almost to a statue in the round and the negroes assumed far more importance than I had originally intended. Hence the monument, developing in this way infinitely beyond what could be paid for, became a labor of love.[49]

The evolution of the Shaw Memorial has been carefully chronicled, first by William A. Coffin and Edward Atkinson in a multipart article published in *Century Magazine* in June 1897 and more recently by Gregory C. Schwarz in a publication for the National Park Service and by Lois Goldreich Marcus in an article published in *Winterthur Portfolio*.[50] Coffin, Schwarz, and Marcus all discuss Saint-Gaudens' extraordinary attention to detail, including his concern that the soldiers' uniforms be accurate to the last button. Perhaps most notable in his quest for accuracy was the artist's search for African American men willing to serve as models. Shaw, whose appearance was based on a photograph, was the only figure included in the monument not drawn from life studies. By his own count, Saint-Gaudens modeled "about forty heads," from which he selected twenty-three for the final sculpture (pls. 59–64).[51] In his *Reminiscences*, the sculptor described at length the difficulties he encountered in persuading men, suspicious of his motives, to pose.[52] He persisted nevertheless, and the individuality he achieved in the faces of the soldiers is one of the most compelling features of the memorial.

For all the energy Saint-Gaudens invested in the realistic depiction of the soldiers, the compositional element he continued to rework — even after the bronze version of the memorial had been installed on Boston Common — was the symbolic figure above the marching soldiers (fig. 9). The sculptor's son Homer, in a comment added to his father's *Reminiscences*, described Saint-Gaudens as driven "nearly frantic in his efforts to combine the ideal with the real."[53] Most often described as an angel, the allegorical figure was criticized by Paul Bion, a French sculptor whom Saint-Gaudens had met when studying abroad and whose opinion he valued.[54] Saint-Gaudens had sent Bion a photograph of the still-unfinished monument and was disheartened when Bion responded that the sculpture would be better without the allegorical figure.[55] By this time, the figure had already been through multiple revisions. The size, profile, placement, and even the flowers in the figure's hand had been altered several times. Stung by Bion's criticism, Saint-Gaudens set to work again. He did not, however, remove the angel. Homer Saint-Gaudens' comment that his father struggled to reconcile the real and ideal in his design — struggled to unite a symbolic figure whose art historical lineage was centuries old with scrupulously realistic African American soldiers entirely new to American sculpture — mirrors in its tension and complexity the cultural environment in which Saint-Gaudens created his masterpiece.

Fig. 9 Detail of allegorical figure from Shaw Memorial as installed at the National Gallery of Art

Fig. 10 Veterans of the 54th Regiment at the unveiling ceremony for the Shaw Memorial in Boston, May 31, 1897. Photograph by Augusta Saint-Gaudens. U.S. Department of the Interior, National Park Service, Saint-Gaudens National Historic Site, Cornish, New Hampshire

"NOT VICTORY COMPLETE"

As noted earlier, the draft protest that became a race riot in the summer of 1863 took place within days of the assault on Fort Wagner. African American men were lynched in New York City, an African American orphanage was burned, African American homes were looted — all during the same week that members of the 54th Massachusetts Regiment, in a deliberate attempt to win acceptance as worthy citizen soldiers, placed themselves at the front of the charge on Fort Wagner.

Among the most moving images associated with the Shaw Memorial are the photographs taken by Saint-Gaudens' wife, Augusta, of the surviving members of the 54th marching in front of the monument on May 31, 1897, the day the memorial was dedicated (fig. 10). The heroism displayed thirty-four years earlier by the uniformed veterans marching before the sculpture received widespread publicity and renewed praise. John Appleton, a survivor of the battle, declared: "It was soon to be the proudest boast of the survivors that they 'charged with Shaw at Wagner.'"[56]

Having struck a blow for freedom and demonstrated exceptional bravery, the surviving members of the 54th Massachusetts Regiment must have felt — in the year of Emancipation — that change was imminent. However, as Deborah Willis and Barbara Krauthamer recently wrote in *Envisioning Emancipation*, "only the formal institution of slavery died in 1865."[57] Despite passage of the "Reconstruction Amendments" to the Constitution (Thirteenth: abolition of slavery, 1865; Fourteenth: rights of citizenship, 1868; Fifteenth: right to vote, 1870), full participation by African Americans in American society was both actively challenged and subtly undermined following the war. Andrew Johnson, who had assumed the U.S. presidency following Lincoln's assassination, opposed equal rights for African Americans and worked against Republican attempts to establish a new social order in the South. Soon restrictive legal provisions adopted by Southern states to exert control over former slaves —"Black Codes"— were instituted. As early as 1866, racial hatred spawned violent vigilante groups, including the Ku Klux Klan. Bitter white supremacists, intent on denying African Americans the civil rights they had helped win through civil war, created legal barriers, including poll taxes and literacy tests, to maintain a racial hierarchy supposedly dismantled at the end of the war. Violence, intimidation, and fraud significantly suppressed the emerging African American vote. By the mid-1870s laws permitting racial segregation were gradually modified to *require* segregation. In 1892, just a few years before Saint-Gaudens' memorial was unveiled, Ida B. Wells, outraged by the lynching of three African American men whom she knew to be innocent of any offense, began her anti-lynching crusade, publishing a series of editorials and a widely circulated pamphlet, "Southern Horrors." Multiple lynchings had taken place in New York in July 1863 as the 54th Massachusetts Regiment fought on Morris Island. By 1897, when the monument to Shaw and the 54th was dedicated, the number of lynchings of African American men had grown exponentially.

It was against this backdrop that Booker T. Washington addressed the assembled crowd at the dedication of the Shaw Memorial. Pointedly observing that the sacrifices of Shaw and the members of the 54th had not been fully rewarded, he declared

10

that the monument stood "for effort, not victory complete."[58] As many in the audience undoubtedly knew, slavery in America had been abolished, but equal rights had not been achieved.

Celebrated philosopher and Harvard professor William James also spoke at the dedication ceremony. James' brother, Garth Wilkinson James, had been severely wounded at Fort Wagner. In his address, James spoke of the horrible "falsehood" that disfigured the American republic — a land of freedom "with human slavery enthroned at the heart of it." He noted that "law and reason" had failed to rid the nation of this "self-contradiction." Only war had settled the matter.[59] James spoke of the "earnestness with which both the officers and men of the Fifty-fourth embraced their mission of showing that a black regiment could excel in every virtue known to man." Turning his attention to Saint-Gaudens' monument, James pointed to the radical nature of the design, calling it "the first soldiers' monument to be raised to a particular set of comparatively undistinguished men." Shaw's soldiers were "undistinguished" only in the narrow racial divide of the time, for as James declared, the 54th fought with such valor that they "became a model in all possible respects" and "champions of a better day for man." James' praise for Saint-Gaudens' monument was unqualified. It was his hope that the memorial would stand "for all time" to inspire future unselfish public deeds.

Generous in his praise of Robert Gould Shaw, the 54th Massachusetts Regiment, and Saint-Gaudens, James concluded his remarks with a statement that must have struck some in the audience as widely off the mark: "The warfare is accomplished; the iniquity pardoned. No future problem can be like that problem. No task laid on our children can compare in difficulty with the task with which their fathers had to deal."[60] Certainly slavery, the "horrible falsehood" at the heart of the nation since its birth, had been legally abolished, but racial oppression, insidious in its workings, was pervasive in American society. The idealism and sacrifices celebrated in the Shaw Memorial may have been inspirational, as they clearly were for James, but the "iniquity" he described as "pardoned" remained a grim reality.

WINNING EVERY AWARD

William Coffin, in the article he wrote on Saint-Gaudens for *Century Magazine* in 1897, recalled visiting the artist in his studio in the fall of 1896. After more than a decade of work, the sculptor had finished the Shaw Memorial and was preparing the piece for casting. Coffin took the opportunity to ask Saint-Gaudens why the project had taken so long. The artist replied that it was not the actual execution of the memorial that took the time, it was "the thinking about it."[61]

Even after the monument had been cast in bronze and installed on Boston Common, Saint-Gaudens continued "thinking about it." In the fall of 1897, he closed his New York studio where the memorial-in-progress had been a fixture for many years and moved to Paris. Saint-Gaudens had prepared a full-scale plaster model of the monument, which he shipped to Paris and, during the early months of 1898, altered yet again. In April he placed the latest version on view at the Paris Salon. Still unsatisfied, he continued to modify the design for the next two years before contributing the fourth and final version to the Exposition Universelle in Paris in 1900 (see p. 97, fig. 1). He was awarded the Grand Prix, a gold medal, and later the Legion of Honor. Auguste Rodin, whose studio Saint-Gaudens had visited, was said to have doffed his hat before the Shaw Memorial.[62] Saint-Gaudens had won every prize.

FOR ALL TIME

Kirk Savage has written with insight and eloquence about Saint-Gaudens' public monuments, including the Shaw Memorial. In *Standing Soldiers, Kneeling Slaves: Race, War, and Monument in Nineteenth-Century America*, his pioneering study of public sculpture following the

Civil War, Savage wrote, "A monument fixes a permanent image meant to define a historical event for all time."[63] The historic event commemorated in the Shaw Memorial, the disastrous assault on Fort Wagner, was understood at the time to mark a turning point in American history. In their display of uncommon courage, African American men had fought for freedom and a new social order. It was Saint-Gaudens' achievement that he succeeded in creating a work of art that gave the event permanent form.

At the same time that Saint-Gaudens was "thinking about" the Shaw Memorial, he was completing a statue of Abraham Lincoln for a public park in Chicago. In discussing the process by which the sculptor arrived at the figure of Lincoln, Savage wrote: "For all Saint-Gaudens's fidelity to contemporary details, the figure stands apart from history and its messy irresolutions and becomes a pure embodiment of moral perfection."[64] The same can be said of the Shaw Memorial.

Robert Gould Shaw's family intended that the memorial "should typify patriotic devotion, and embody a modern spirit with heroic attributes."[65] Their son and brother was representative of a type. It was their wish that Shaw and his troops be "bound together" in common cause, both in history and in art. The monument was to be a distillation. From an historic event, an ideal was to be celebrated. In the Shaw Memorial, Saint-Gaudens again gave form to moral perfection.

Unresolved social issues still haunt American society. Booker T. Washington's 1897 observation that the victory was not complete is still decidedly true. In the Shaw Memorial, however, Saint-Gaudens created an object that stands apart from history — an object that more than one hundred years after its dedication a wounded American soldier simply wanted to touch.

Before the Eyes of Thousands:
The 54th Massachusetts Regiment
and the Shaw Memorial
in Twentieth-Century Art

"The artist must be the medium through which humanity expresses itself."

—ROMARE BEARDEN, 1934

LINDSAY HARRIS

On the evening of July 18, 1863, Colonel Robert Gould Shaw readied his 54th Massachusetts Volunteer Infantry to lead the assault on Fort Wagner off the coast of South Carolina. Barely two months had passed since the troop had marched out of Boston, where some twenty thousand spectators had lined Beacon Street to send off the first northern regiment composed of African American soldiers. After weeks at sea and days spent tramping across beaches and swamps from Beaufort, where they landed, to Morris Island, the 54th was on the brink of attacking one of the strongest fortifications in the South.[1] Fort Wagner, a formidable parapet rising out of the sand, was the gateway to Charleston, a Confederate stronghold and prime target of the Union army. In what would be his final remarks to his men, Shaw presaged the potential of the 54th to emerge as a powerful visual symbol of the Civil War in American art: "I want you to prove yourselves," he encouraged them. "The eyes of thousands will look on what you do tonight."[2]

In the century and a half since the assault on Fort Wagner, in which Shaw and many of his men were killed, the capacity of the 54th Massachusetts and their fair-haired colonel to open the nation's eyes to issues of race and citizenship in the United States has permeated American culture. Poets like Paul Laurence Dunbar, Ralph Waldo Emerson, and James Russell Lowell have praised the bravery of the troops, the drama of their actions at Fort Wagner, and the tragedy of their burial without ceremony in a common grave. Their valor inspired marching songs by other Union soldiers and melodies by American songwriters like Charles Ives.[3] Schools, housing complexes, parks, and neighborhoods across the country bear the name Shaw in honor of the "blue-eyed child of fortune."[4] Hollywood portrayed the regiment's story in the award-winning film *Glory* (1989). Yet it is within the realm of the fine arts that a single, extraordinary work gave concrete public form to the 54th as an icon of the Civil War in the American consciousness and, for artists, established a focus for efforts to wrest meaning from that decisive moment in the nation's history.

Since its dedication on Boston Common on May 31, 1897, Augustus Saint-Gaudens' memorial to Robert Gould Shaw and the 54th Massachusetts has been hailed time and again as a "masterpiece," "the finest piece of American sculpture," and the "noblest work of public art" in the country.[5] The bronze relief depicts Shaw in the foreground, on horseback, alongside the regiment's African American soldiers, who march with bayonets over their shoulders behind a drummer boy (p. 82, fig. 1). Shaw is portrayed with an accurate likeness, and while Saint-Gaudens did not represent the African American soldiers as stereotypes, neither did he convey the identities of the actual men who served in the 54th. Instead, he created a regiment of individual but anonymous African American soldiers of varying ages, heights, gaits, and expressions.

The so-called Shaw Memorial has long been acknowledged as a singular example of American public art.[6] It honors both a famous hero and the unknown common soldiers he commanded, integrating two seemingly opposite subjects in a single monument. Its depiction of numerous unnamed soldiers, rather than the single, anonymous standing figure that had become standard for memorials to the Civil War dead, was also novel.[7] So too was its representation of clearly African American soldiers at a time when the majority of soldier monuments depicted men with Anglo-Saxon features.[8] Its interracial subject, while not unique, was uncommon for the period, as were its sponsors, who ranged from Joshua B. Smith, a former slave living in Boston who initiated the campaign, to Massachusetts senator Charles Sumner.[9]

Innovative in its style and scope, the Shaw Memorial also broke new ground in representing the 54th Massachusetts. The monument was raised to honor the regiment's brave assault — and tragic defeat — at Fort Wagner. Yet the relief does not depict the troop in battle, a scene that popular prints of the period had made readily familiar (pl. 41). Rather, the memorial evokes the day in May 1863 when the regiment marched out of Boston with great fanfare. By representing the regiment's send-off near the very location where it occurred, Saint-Gaudens imagines viewers of the monument as new generations of spectators who gather to see the pioneering troop depart. This shift in focus extended the visual narrative of the 54th and has opened up new ways for artists to illuminate its importance in American history. Some have turned to photography to interpret the shifting significance of the Shaw Memorial at different moments in time. Others have recreated the story of the 54th in new works of public art. Still others have adapted the series format in painting and photography to recount new narratives of the regiment's history from viewpoints that earlier versions overlooked.

As we commemorate the sesquicentennial of the Civil War, it seems fitting to look beyond the virtues of the Shaw Memorial itself to consider the legacy of this singular work, the battle it honors, and the men it venerates in American art and culture over the decades that followed. How has Saint-Gaudens' "masterpiece" kept alive and relevant the memory of the 54th Massachusetts in American consciousness? What symbols and strategies have artists developed to represent the 54th, and how has this visual vocabulary changed in the twentieth century? How has the 54th served as a focus for artists to advance various social and political agendas? How has their art shaped our understanding of the promises and betrayals of the Civil War? To understand the continuing resonance of the 54th and the Shaw Memorial in the twentieth century, we must look at how the art they inspired both interprets the memory and meaning of the Civil War and expresses the evolving ideals and inequities of American culture during this period.

THE 54TH MASSACHUSETTS AND THE "NEW NEGRO" IN THE NEW CENTURY

The power of the Shaw Memorial to serve as a barometer for perceptions of race in the United States became apparent the moment it was unveiled to the public. In a speech at the dedication, Tuskegee Institute president Booker T. Washington articulated the meaning of Saint-Gaudens' sculpture, and the regiment it embodied, at the dawn of the twentieth century. The sacrifice at Fort Wagner would be redeemed "not in malice, nor in narrowness; nor artificial progress, nor in efforts at mere temporary political gain, nor in abuse of another section or race," he insisted, but in "patience and natural effort."[10] Change would be gradual. Reiterating the message of his famous "Atlanta Compromise" speech that had inaugurated the Atlanta Fair in 1895, Washington encouraged his fellow African Americans "to withstand temptation, to economize, to exercise thrift, to disregard the superficial for the real.... This is the key that unlocks every door of opportunity, and all others fail." Only advancements "in industry, property, intelligence and moral responsibility" would enable African Americans to combat racial discrimination.[11]

Behind the podium, Saint-Gaudens' forward-marching depiction of the 54th served as a potent symbol of Washington's faith in progress as an antidote to prejudice in the new century, a belief many African Americans shared. While the Civil War had brought an end to slavery, it had not brought an end to racism or inequality in the postbellum United

Fig. 1 Corridor leading to the U.S. Paintings Galleries, Grand Palais, Paris Exposition, 1900, with Augustus Saint-Gaudens' *Amor Caritas* and *Shaw Memorial*. Archives Nationales, Paris

States. In 1896, only one year before the dedication of the Shaw Memorial, the Supreme Court officially denied African Americans an equal place in society when it validated racial segregation in *Plessy v. Ferguson*. Derogatory stereotypes of African Americans cropped up at every turn — in plantation fictions, newspaper cartoons, and minstrel shows, on song sheets, board games, postcards, and elsewhere. To counter the prejudice that lay beneath these racist displays, African Americans took pains to construct public self-images that mirrored the mores of white culture and demonstrated their social advancement. So prevalent was this tendency by 1895 that the *Cleveland Gazette*, announcing the passage of the New York Civil Rights Law, wrote of "a class of colored people, the 'New Negro,'...who have arisen since the war, with education, refinement, and money."[12] The emergence of the New Negro in the American consciousness thus dovetailed with the presentation of the Shaw Memorial to the American public.

The Paris Universal Exposition of 1900 made evident for international audiences the significance of Saint-Gaudens' monument as a symbol of the New Negro, who had risen from slave to soldier during the Civil War and now faced the challenge of defining himself as an American citizen. On one bank of the Seine, the U.S. national pavilion, organized by Commissioner Ferdinand W. Peck, presented four works by Saint-Gaudens. Among them was a revised plaster cast of the Shaw Memorial painted in gold leaf (fig. 1). After completing the bronze in Boston, Saint-Gaudens had continued to modify his memorial to the 54th regiment, reworking the faces of the soldiers and, more radically, the appearance of the angel soaring above the troop. The success of the monument's updated composition, praised by none other than Auguste Rodin, earned Saint-Gaudens the exposition's Grand Prize for sculpture.[13]

In addition to confirming his achievement in the realm of art, Saint-Gaudens' award also reflected a greater purpose of the U.S. Commission at the Paris fair: to demonstrate how conditions in the United States had enabled African Americans to advance in society and how the "race problem" had been solved through political compromise.[14] Across the river from the American pavilion, the judges also awarded a Grand Prize that year to Thomas Junius Calloway, who had been invited by Peck, at Booker T. Washington's behest, to organize an exhibition on the contemporary life of the "American Negro."[15] Calloway greatly admired Washington as "the wisest servant of his race," and he supported the educator's embrace of African American progress as a way to improve race relations within American society.[16] Taking to heart Washington's message at the dedication of Saint-Gaudens' bronze in Boston three years earlier, Calloway's American Negro Exhibit "put before the public statistics and other evidences of our progress" to encourage "our young men and women…to get an education, property and a basic character." Only by showing "what the Negro under difficulties has accomplished," he maintained, will it be possible "to overcome that sordid pessimism which sees no hope for racial assimilation or adjustment."[17] Saint-Gaudens' memorial thus offered an artistic counterpart to Calloway's "evidence" of African American progress at the Paris Exposition.

The American Negro Exhibit featured several smaller displays devoted to African American achievement that provide a critical framework for understanding the meaning of the Shaw Memorial and the 54th Massachusetts at the time. The first of these, the Medal of Honor Men exhibit, presented the photographs and official records of African American soldiers and sailors who had distinguished themselves in combat since the Civil War (fig. 2). Of the fifteen men honored in the display, ten had fought in the Civil War, including William H. Carney, who had served as a sergeant in Company C of the 54th Massachusetts (pl. 69). During the assault on Fort Wagner on July 18, 1863, Carney, with "most distinguished gallantry," as the assistant secretary of war later wrote, "seized the colors of the regiment and advanced with them" after the flag bearer was killed.[18] Almost immediately, Carney's declaration to his comrades that "The old flag never touched the ground, boys!" became the stuff of legend and a rallying cry for other African Americans to enlist in the Union army (pl. 66). Yet it was not until the Medal of Honor Men display in Paris, more than thirty years after the battle, that Carney earned public recognition for his bravery at Fort Wagner, across the Seine from Saint-Gaudens' gilded memorial to the valor of his entire regiment.

While both the Shaw Memorial and the Medal of Honor Men display celebrated the heroism and accomplishment of African American soldiers, the greater message of the American Negro Exhibit suggested that the battle for civic equality within American society was far from over. Other photography shows in the exhibition also provided visual "evidence,"

2

Fig. 2 Medal of Honor Men, recognizing those who had received medals of honor in United States Army and Navy, compiled by W.E.B. Du Bois, c. 1900. Library of Congress, Washington, DC, Prints and Photographs Division, Daniel Murray Collection

Fig. 3 Frances Benjamin Johnston, "The Old Folks at Home," 1899–1900, platinum print. The Museum of Modern Art, New York, Gift of Lincoln Kirstein

Fig. 4 Frances Benjamin Johnston, "A Hampton Graduate at Home," 1899–1900, platinum print. The Museum of Modern Art, New York, Gift of Lincoln Kirstein

in Calloway's words, to show that the "road to salvation" for the New Negro was through achievement.[19]

A display of photographs of the Hampton Normal and Agricultural Institute, taken by Frances Benjamin Johnston expressly for the Paris Exposition, aimed to support the claim that, as Frederick Douglass noted as early as 1853, "the most telling, the most killing refutation" of racism and discrimination "is the presentation of an industrious, enterprising, thrifty and intelligent free black population."[20] The photographs, which in 1966 were exhibited at the Museum of Modern Art and published as a catalogue called *The Hampton Album*, show students attending lessons, building houses, and tilling fields to illustrate the school's guiding principle: Work leads the way to integrity and economic self-reliance.[21]

Such was the philosophy of Hampton's founder Samuel Chapman Armstrong, the son of American missionaries to the Sandwich Islands. After graduating from Williams College in 1862, Armstrong volunteered to lead the 9th U.S. Colored Troops during the Civil War. As he later wrote, the war showed him the "excellent qualities and capacities" of African American soldiers and their obvious "ambition to improve."[22] After the war Armstrong established the Hampton Institute to ensure the welfare of "the large masses" of newly emancipated African Americans who, as he saw it, "need to be educated and elevated; and who especially need earnest and active friends to see that they receive justice, to counsel and direct them, to gather up the rising generation in schools, and to encourage the[m]…to industry."[23]

In a series of before-and-after comparisons, Johnston's photographs at the Paris Exposition demonstrated for an international audience the impact of a Hampton education on African American progress. Rather than living in the rudimentary log cabin of the "old folks," shown in one photograph, the Hampton graduate, in a second image, sat with "unstrained ease" and "dignity" at the linen-clad dining table of his modern home (figs. 3, 4).[24] The radiant faces of his wife and children, their respectable clothes, silver

3

4

cutlery, and shiny piano illustrated just how far the American Negro had advanced since slavery, and just how well they had assimilated into mainstream American life.

In another display at the American Negro Exhibit, W.E.B. Du Bois compiled three albums of photographs to illustrate the upward mobility that education helped African Americans achieve.[25] Produced in collaboration with students from Atlanta University, *Types of American Negroes, Georgia, U.S.A.*, and *Negro Life in Georgia, U.S.A.* each featured photographs and studio portraits of well-to-do African Americans surrounded by the trappings of middle-class urban life. Rural settings and signs of hard labor or poverty were nowhere to be seen. In the pages of Du Bois' albums, the American Negro appeared as a child posed with an open book; a woman seated upright in a fashionable dress and hat; a poised man in a waistcoat and tie; a family gathered on the porch of their stately home (figs. 5 – 8).

Both Du Bois' albums and Johnston's photographs were part of a larger attempt to counter the ubiquitous stereotypes of African Americans in popular culture with representations of seriousness and dignity.[26] Yet the racial affinity between sitter and photographer in Du Bois' albums took this effort one step further. While unattributed in the American Negro Exhibit, the majority of the photographs Du Bois compiled for his project were taken by Thomas E. Askew, the first professional African American photographer in Atlanta.[27] Askew and Du Bois both lived in Atlanta at the turn of the century, as did many of the African Americans represented in the photographs. Unlike the Hampton Institute photographs, which were taken by an elite, white woman at the vanguard of socially progressive issues, Du Bois' albums presented photographs of African Americans taken by a photographer from the same community. The photographs thus furnished the American Negro Exhibit with a respectable *self-portrait* of African American identity, a form of representation African American leaders deemed essential to help erode the inequities of prejudice.

By the 1920s, efforts to disseminate images of the richness of African American life had not brought about the significant change in social status that African Americans had hoped to gain. The poet Langston Hughes described "the desire to pour racial individuality into the mold of American standardization" as "the mountain standing in the way of any true Negro art [or progress] in America."[28] Sharing Hughes' doubt in the effectiveness of cultural assimilation, African American leaders and intellectuals, such as Du Bois, Alain Locke, Fannie Barrier Williams, and Jessie Redmon Fauset, stressed the need to embrace African and African American heritage as well as the cultural norms of mainstream American life.

Images of African American soldiers emerged as potent illustrations of strength and determination, as Jim Crow laws and the growth of the Ku Klux Klan undermined African Americans' self-image and opportunities for social advancement. The end of the First World War kindled new interest in images of recent African American military heroes, such as the four "colored troops" whose charge up San Juan Hill on July 1, 1898, turned the tide in the Spanish-American war.[29] Earlier martyrs also resurfaced as popular subjects, including the 54th Massachusetts, whose bravery at Fort Wagner had transformed the regiment into a symbol of African American patriotism.

An image taken by social documentary photographer Lewis Hine around 1920 shows the relevance of historic figures like the 54th Massachusetts to New Negro ideology during this period. That year Hine traveled to Atlanta, Georgia, to record the positive impact of education and employment on local African American communities. The series he produced, titled "Southern Negroes," possibly after Du Bois' earlier photographic albums of the same region, comprised a dozen or so portraits of men, women, farmers, clergymen, and workers in one of Atlanta's burgeoning factories. One photograph depicts a mother and father, seated in their living room, reading to their two daughters (pl. 71). Above the mantelpiece behind them, in the center both of the wall and of Hine's composition, hangs a photographic reproduction of the Shaw Memorial.

The family portrait reveals several strategies middle-class African Americans developed during this period to demonstrate their education and

Fig. 5 Photograph by Thomas E. Askew, in W.E.B. Du Bois, *Types of American Negroes, Georgia, U.S.A.*, vol. 1, no. 53 (1900). Library of Congress, Washington, DC, Daniel Murray Collection

Fig. 6 Photograph by Thomas E. Askew, in W.E.B. Du Bois, *Types of American Negroes, Georgia, U.S.A.*, vol. 1, no. 66 (1900). Library of Congress, Washington, DC, Daniel Murray Collection

Fig. 7 Unknown photographer, in W.E.B. Du Bois, *Types of American Negroes, Georgia, U.S.A.*, vol. 1, no. 91 (1900). Library of Congress, Washington, DC, Daniel Murray Collection

Fig. 8 Photograph by Thomas E. Askew, in W.E.B. Du Bois, *Negro Life in Georgia, U.S.A.*, no. 352 (1900). Library of Congress, Washington, DC, Daniel Murray Collection

5

7

6

8

refinement to the public eye. It also illustrates a new perception of the Shaw Memorial and the 54th Massachusetts. Rather than sit idly in front of the 5-by-7-inch box camera Hine set up in their living room, the family pictured has chosen a more industrious pretense for their portrait: reading. The woman, seated on the left with the younger daughter, points to a section in a massive illustrated book that the girl is likely still too young to comprehend, while on the right, the man places his arm around the elder daughter and directs her attention to the book on his knee. Actively engaged in educating the next generation about the past, the parents demonstrate to the photographer, and to the viewer, their high esteem for history, literacy, and education. They also show how far they — as representatives of the New Negro — have advanced in the generation since slavery, when it was illegal for African Americans to learn to read.

The family's dress, demeanor, and setting in this photograph also serve as signs of racial advancement. The woman wears a long, conservative dress, and her husband has put on his three-piece suit for the picture. The girls wear clean, crisp dresses and bows in their hair, and everyone's shoes are well polished. Clearly visible on the man's left hand is a wedding ring, a symbol of domestic stability within the African American family, which slavery had made all but impossible. A patterned rug protects the floor, a fireplace screen keeps the hearth tidy, and a handful of pictures adorn the otherwise bare wooden walls. Behind the woman, an open door leads to an adjacent room, suggesting that the family has progressed from the one-room cabin of their forebears.[30] Refined but not ostentatious in their tastes, and industrious rather than indolent in their leisure, the family in Hine's photograph exemplifies the cardinal values of "thrift, economy, and push" that, according to Booker T. Washington, "awakened Negro[es]" should espouse "to lift themselves up."[31]

The reproduction of the Shaw Memorial above the mantelpiece in Hine's image also illustrates the affinity of the New Negro for protagonists of African American history. This was particularly true for historical figures whose determination to forge a new role for themselves within society reinforced contemporary African Americans' aspiration for a "self-willed beginning."[32] The 54th Massachusetts — a pioneering regiment of African American soldiers who *volunteered* to fight for emancipation, and who inspired thousands of African American men to do the same — epitomized the bravery of African American Civil War soldiers writ large. Further, Saint-Gaudens' memorial to the troop provided a widely hailed masterwork of *public* art that celebrated a distinctive aspect of African American heritage in no less central a location than opposite the Massachusetts State House in Boston.

Saint-Gaudens himself had ensured the visibility of his bronze relief well beyond its fixed location on Boston Common. To commemorate the inauguration of the memorial in 1897, the artist commissioned publishers Curtis and Cameron to issue a photograph of the monument as part of the Copley Prints series of reproductions "of all the good art that might be found in the country." Such images were "especially suitable for the decoration of school-room walls" to educate children about the nation's past, the publishers noted in their catalogue.[33] As Hine's photograph shows, some also appeared on the living room walls of African American homes.

The resonance of such images was particularly strong in the early 1920s, when Hine took this family portrait, as both the violence of the First World War and subsequent riots in several American cities were a vivid recent memory. The gallant action of African American soldiers during the Civil War had led many African Americans to perceive military service as a "golden opportunity" and to hope that their loyalty to the nation would help improve race relations.[34] Yet not all Americans shared their idealism. In the second decade of the twentieth century, many African Americans had begun to move to northern cities, drawn by labor shortages and the chance to leave behind the markers of slavery in the South. Despite the optimism that came with this Great Migration, problems in housing, unemployment, and crime began to surface, causing racial tensions to mount across the country. The influx of returning veterans — black and white — and ongoing job scarcity exacerbated these hostilities, which erupted in race riots across the country in the summer of 1919.[35] By the time Hine set out for Atlanta to produce the "Southern Negroes" series the following year, it was clear that a new generation of Americans was on the verge of a "second Emancipation," primed to extend the fight for freedom on the Civil War battlefield and claim the privileges of full citizenship.[36]

The significance of a middle-class African American family decorating their home at this time with an image of the Shaw Memorial was not lost on Hine, who had made a career of taking photographs to rouse public interest in the condition of people for whom, as he put it, "the odds are all against them."[37] By 1920 Hine had begun to turn away from his earlier documentary use of the camera to expose the negative impact of industry on its most exploited victims — immigrants, women, and children — to take "interpretive" photographs that conveyed the "human virtue" of work and self-improvement.[38]

The principal outlet for Hine's photographs during this period was *Survey* magazine, then the premier journal of social work in the United States, and its special monthly publication *Survey Graphic*.[39] While Hine never published the portrait of the African American family, it is possible he produced it, and the rest of his "Southern Negroes" series, with this magazine in mind. He may even have intended the series for a special issue of *Survey Graphic* devoted to African American culture, which the journal's editor-in-chief Paul Kellogg produced in collaboration with author and activist Alain Locke in March 1925. That issue, which featured articles and drawings on African American themes by an interracial coterie of writers and artists, became the basis for Locke's landmark book on the cultural renaissance of African Americans in the 1920s, *The New Negro*. The book omitted several pieces from the magazine version, however, including an article by African American physician and writer Rudolph Fisher on life in the South during the Great Migration. The piece includes a portrait of an African American farmer taken by Hine, who may well have hoped to publish other "Southern Negroes" portraits in this context.[40]

MARCHING THROUGH THE LONG CIVIL RIGHTS MOVEMENT

When Locke's book, *The New Negro*, appeared in 1925, it announced the arrival of the Harlem Renaissance, a spectacular outpouring of creativity in literature, music, and art within black America that celebrated African American history and traditions.[41] With the onset of the Great Depression following the stock market crash of 1929, this "flowering of Negro literature" faded.[42] Yet many of its ideas continued to inspire African American artists and writers during what scholars have called "the long civil rights movement."[43] This period of racial change took root in the New Deal era of the 1930s and grew in subtle increments to become more radical by its "halcyon decade" of the 1960s. A variety of tactics to combat racial marginalization emerged during these years, and artists responded with an equally wide range of techniques to advance their various social and political agendas. Yet an appeal to African American history unified much of their work. Some artists commemorated African American leaders; others evoked their actions to encourage participants in the ongoing struggle for democracy at hand; still others sought to highlight the significance of African Americans that all too often remained in the shadows, or even invisible, in representations of the nation's history. Within this imagery, African American military service, and the 54th Massachusetts in particular, symbolized the courage and determination of past heroes for a younger generation that was striving to overcome the inequalities of the day.

Several artists in the 1930s and 1940s mined the participation of African Americans in the Civil War in their work. Aaron Douglas, Jacob Lawrence, William Henry Johnson, Horace Pippin, and James Van Der Zee, to name a few, recalled the rebellion of slaves like Nathaniel Turner and Denmark Vesey, the uproar of John Brown's raid on Harper's Ferry, the excitement at Abraham Lincoln's Emancipation Proclamation, and the pride of African American soldiers marching off to war.[44] Different from African American intellectuals earlier in the century who emphasized achievement as the path to social change, these artists embraced defiant figures and events in which African Americans rose up in arms against oppression and injustice. They also called attention to revolutionaries and common African American soldiers whose efforts were downplayed, or overlooked altogether, in mainstream narratives of the Civil War but whose heroism African Americans had long revered.

In 1938 Jacob Lawrence devoted a series of thirty-two panels to the life of Frederick Douglass, the Maryland slave who escaped from bondage to emerge as a powerful voice for abolition and democracy during the Civil War.[45] Painted in vividly colored casein tempera, a centuries-old medium that captures the historical significance of its subject, Lawrence's series celebrates Douglass' resilience in the face of adversity and highlights the breadth of his accomplishments as an orator, writer, newspaper editor, and statesman.

The work also highlights his efforts to recruit men to join the 54th Massachusetts, a regiment that modeled for Lawrence and his contemporaries a trailblazing spirit of fortitude in the face of racial discrimination (fig. 9). The panel presents three crossed bayonets in the foreground that rise up from the soil to pierce the sky. Rendered in rich colors, bold lines, and flat, geometric forms that characterize Lawrence's style, the scene conveys both the surge of battle and the silence of death that war leaves behind. Douglass himself is not pictured, nor is there any indication of a speech or broadside soliciting African American men to enlist in the Union army.

Rather, the panel illustrates the impact of Douglass' call to arms on generations of African Americans. Unlike Saint-Gaudens' relief, in which the soldiers of the 54th rest their bayonets on their shoulders, Lawrence's image depicts the weapons in an active and defining role. Rising upward in the center of the composition, the bayonets symbolize what Douglass called the "gallant rush" of African American Civil War soldiers. "Only a moderate share of sagacity was needed to see that the arm of the slave was the best defense against the arm of the slaveholder," he wrote in his enlistment editorial. "Hence…with every exulting shout of victory raised by the slaveholding rebels…

9

Fig. 9 Jacob Lawrence, *The Frederick Douglass Series*, 1938–1939, panel no. 26, "The North and South were at war.... The 54th and 55th colored regiments were mustered." Collection of the Hampton University Museum, Hampton, Virginia

Fig. 10 "The Attack on Fort Wagner—The Stormers Advancing Under Fire," *Harper's Weekly*, August 8, 1863

I urge you to fly to arms, and smite with death the power that would bury the Government and your Liberty in the same hopeless grave."[46]

Comparison to an engraving published in *Harper's Weekly* in 1863 suggests that the specific charge Lawrence refers to in this panel is the one led by the 54th at Fort Wagner (fig. 10). Both views feature a triangular surge of bayonets in the foreground, the diagonal coastline of Charleston Harbor in the middle ground, and the crest of a wave on the horizon. In the background, a series of serrated lines — a jagged, yellow tree in Lawrence's panel and lightning bolts in the *Harper's* view — cut through both ominous skies.

The tension of battle in this image gives way to triumph in the final panel of Lawrence's series. Once again, the artist depicts the coastal landscape, but he replaces the bayonets and tree with an American flag and flower to convey Douglass' rise to citizenship. By calling upon the 54th to honor African American soldiers' participation in the Civil War, which Douglass helped make possible, Lawrence reminds contemporary viewers of the history of African American revolt against injustice and inspires them to fight for civil rights with the same resolve.

With the United States' entry into the Second World War in 1941, the question of African American civic equality took on a new tenor. Not only were African American soldiers still required to serve in separate regiments, they were fighting for liberties abroad to which they themselves were not entitled at home. It was within this context that in 1943, William J. Thompkins, recorder of deeds in Washington, DC, commissioned a mural devoted to the "valor" and "soldiership" of the 54th Massachusetts for his office's headquarters in the nation's capital (fig. 11).[47]

At the time, the Department of the Treasury's section of the fine arts, which was established in 1934 as part of the New Deal, was overseeing the decoration of hundreds of government buildings, including several in Washington, DC. Thompkins, a seasoned politician and longtime supporter of President

10

Franklin D. Roosevelt, used his government savvy to procure section funds for a new building for the Recorder of Deeds office to house administrators and the property titles they oversaw in one location. The design included a decorative program that featured portraits of past recorders as well as seven murals that celebrated the contribution of African Americans to the nation in time of war and to scientific progress. Thompkins devoted one of the two central murals to "the death of Colonel Shaw at Fort Wagner."[48]

Thompkins likely selected this subject in part to honor the first African American recorder of deeds, Frederick Douglass, who was appointed to the position in 1881. Douglass' assignment established the office as one of a handful of federally appointed positions open to African Americans until well into the twentieth century. The post thus became synonymous with African American achievement, which Thompkins sought to memorialize during his tenure in office.

In its patronage, design, and location, the Recorder of Deeds mural marks a pivotal demonstration of cultural autonomy in the history of artistic responses to the 54th. Within months of the assault on Fort

11

Wagner in 1863, the African American community in Charleston had attempted to erect a monument to honor the regiment. Yet fear of a hostile response among Southerners for whom the Confederate loss was still an open wound brought the project to a standstill.[49] African American painters and sculptors celebrated the troop in their art in the late nineteenth century, and African Americans in Boston were instrumental in bringing about the Shaw Memorial. But it was not until Thompkins' mural commission that an African American patron of the arts successfully brought to fruition a large-scale public art work that celebrated the courage and sacrifice of the regiment, and of the some 180,000 African Americans who fought in the Civil War.

The design of the mural infuses earlier representations of the regiment with new poignancy that reflects the increasing momentum of the "long civil rights movement" after the Second World War. Created by Carlos Lopez, a Spanish American artist then working as an "artist correspondent" for the Department of War's art advisory committee, the composition was selected through a national mural competition for "its sheer conviction of statement, simplicity of treatment and moving spiritual content."[50] In the center of a loosely organized triptych, a torrent of soldiers rises in a pyramid of blue uniforms, expressive faces, gesturing hands, and crisscrossed bayonets and swords. A possible representation of Sergeant Carney, whose tattered clothes convey both the mayhem of battle and his willingness to fight for freedom against all odds, tightly grips the broken staff that keeps the flag aloft. Beneath him, a soldier takes aim at the enemy through the sight of his bayonet; another covers his eyes with his hand and throws his head back in dismay. In the foreground, two soldiers tend to a dying Shaw, who is reverently laid to rest among his fallen comrades.

The Recorder of Deeds depiction of the 54th signaled a coming sea change in the struggle for civil rights. Situated in a federal building as part of a decorative program devoted to African American achievement, and funded by the Roosevelt administration, the first presidency to acknowledge African Americans as an integral voting constituency, the mural amounted to a bold political statement. Most provocative is its unprecedented focus on the actions and sentiments of the regiment's African American soldiers. Shaw no longer strides above the troop, as he does in nineteenth-century prints of the assault on Fort Wagner by firms like Currier & Ives (pl. 41), nor does he remain distinct from his men, as in Saint-Gaudens' memorial. Rather, the young colonel lies dying on the ground, still central to the scene but shrouded by his soldiers, who finally become protagonists in the tragic drama. Completed at a time when black stereotypes still dominated popular culture, Thompkins' celebration of African Americans' vital

Fig. 11 Carlos Lopez, *The 54th Massachusetts Regiment, under the Leadership of Colonel Shaw in the Attack on Fort Wagner, Morris Island, South Carolina, in 1863*, 1943, mural at the Recorder of Deeds building, Washington, DC. From the Carol M. Highsmith "This is America!" Collection at the Library of Congress

role in the nation's history marked a declaration of cultural emancipation. In addition, the longstanding tradition of African American military service illustrated in the Recorder of Deeds murals challenged the continued segregation of the armed forces. Such public outcries against institutionalized racial prejudice prompted the military to integrate its servicemen officially in 1948.[51]

The boldness of the Recorder of Deeds decorative program is all the more apparent when considered in light of the events that were held to honor the centennial of the Civil War between 1961 and 1965. These commemorations across the country — coinciding with the apogee of the civil rights movement — tended to glorify the war as an epic battle for restoration and national unity, rather than recount a more complex story that might, it was thought, fuel already simmering racial tension across the country.[52] Instead, the many national and regional events all but ignored African Americans' participation in the conflict and skirted, or denied outright, discussions of slavery as its underlying cause. The opinion expressed by one author in 1964 that "in the war slavery was to die an incidental death" typified views of the period.[53]

A few centennial events did celebrate African American Civil War soldiers. Margaret Burroughs, founder of the DuSable Museum, organized an exhibition in Chicago in 1963 to celebrate a century of African American progress since the Emancipation Proclamation.[54] Sidney Kaplan, then a professor at University of Massachusetts at Amherst, mounted an exhibition on *The Portrayal of the Negro in American Painting* at Bowdoin College in Maine in 1964.[55] Yet these occasions were the exceptions that proved the rule.

REPRESENTING THE MEMORY OF THE 54TH

By the early 1970s Americans had grown deeply skeptical of quixotic versions of history. The racial violence of the previous decade and, more recently, the Watergate scandal, Richard Nixon's resignation, and the Vietnam War had made many people wary of patriotic sentiment and had primed them for more incisive narratives of the nation's past. Public military and civic monuments, which dotted the American landscape, made ready subjects for artists for whom the changing guise of national memory was a chief concern. Of the countless memorial sculptures that graced town squares and city plazas across the country, perhaps none offered artists a more cogent embodiment of Americans' regard for their history during this dispirited decade than the Shaw Memorial.

For photographer Lee Friedlander, Saint-Gaudens' singular work offered a way to capture the current American slant on symbols of patriotism and military valor (fig. 12). Shot at an angle, his photograph shows the monument sandwiched between a tree in the foreground and a stand of apartment buildings along Boston Common. While the figure of Shaw on horseback stands in the center of the image, as he does in Saint-Gaudens' composition, he and his soldiers are cast in shadow by the afternoon sun. One of the squat, marble eagles framing the bronze relief takes the spotlight instead. The 54th thus appears to fall dutifully in line behind a new, avian commander, who, with wings back and chest puffed, proudly leads the troop through the twentieth-century wilds of downtown Boston.

Friedlander included his view of the Shaw Memorial in *The American Monument*, a book he produced in collaboration with Richard Benson and Leslie George Katz in 1976, coincidentally the year of the American Bicentennial. The volume features photographs of memorial sculptures located "in town squares and civic nooks and crannies across the nation," as Benson described them.[56] Made over the better part of a decade, the photographs create a portrait of the American social landscape, much like the photographic essays of Walker Evans and Robert Frank had done in the 1930s and 1950s.[57] Rather than venerate the nation's monuments "as relics in isolation," Katz noted in his afterword, Friedlander shows them as part of the everyday experience of our

12

surroundings.⁵⁸ They stand near grocery stores and are crisscrossed by power lines; pigeons rest on them; nearby signs give them new meanings. Sometimes we only catch a glimpse of them out of the corner of an eye. Such skewed perspectives of monuments, like Friedlander's oblique view of the Shaw Memorial, convey national myths with new biases and leave us questioning the reality of events that have become the stuff of legend.

While working with Friedlander on *The American Monument*, Benson collaborated with Katz and writer Lincoln Kirstein to produce a book of his own photographs of the Shaw Memorial, *Lay This Laurel* (1973). Different from Friedlander's witty take on the monument, Benson's photographs offered both a loving portrait and a woeful lament of Saint-Gaudens' bronze, "in a time," wrote Kirstein, "when military heroism [was] suspect and a thousand images of melodramatic violence [had] polluted the subject."⁵⁹

The eighteen photographs of the Shaw Memorial in *Lay This Laurel* evoke the experience of viewing the sculpture in situ. The first image shows the monument frontally on the edge of Boston Common. As we turn the pages, Benson's views bring us ever closer to Saint-Gaudens' relief until its surrounding context and marble entablature disappear beyond the photographic frame. We are left to focus on Saint-Gaudens' embodiments of the 54th: the drummer boys, the older soldiers, the younger ones, the cast of Shaw on horseback, and the troops who march behind their commander (pls. 72–75). Through Benson's richly detailed, black-and-white images, it is as if we were watching the regiment — cast in bronze — march down Beacon Street on a late spring afternoon in 1863. While the richness and texture of the photographs stir us to envision the past, they also shock us out of our reverie by bringing into relief the monument's badly worn surface.

Fig. 12 Lee Friedlander, "Robert Gould Shaw and the First Black Volunteer Regiment, Boston, Massachusetts," 1976, from *The American Monument* (1976). The Smithsonian American Art Museum, Museum purchase through the Lusita L. and Franz H. Denghausen Endowment, Margery and Edgar Masinter, Kevin and Lisa McGovern, and Bernie Stadiem

When it was published in 1973, *Lay This Laurel* brought readers face to face with the nation's current regard for its heritage. After nearly three-quarters of a century of New England weather, and more recent years of neglect, Saint-Gaudens' bronze had fallen into piteous disrepair. Green corrosion streaked the faces of Shaw and his men. Shaw's sword had been broken off at the hilt. A bare electric light fixture crowned the marble cornice like a gaudy jewel.

The book aimed in part to familiarize "young Americans, patriots, art lovers and others" with Saint-Gaudens' monument to the 54th, as Kirstein notes in his essay. In this regard, it updated earlier photographs of the Shaw Memorial that intended above all to disseminate an image of the sculpture, a work of art in a fixed place, to a wider audience. Such reproductions tended to show the relief from a frontal view and centered within the image. This was precisely the way "one should photograph sculptures," according to the late-nineteenth-century theorist Heinrich Wölfflin, who published his landmark treatise on the relationship between photography and sculpture in 1896.[60] One year later, Saint-Gaudens unveiled his memorial in Boston. He also commissioned photographers to produce images of the sculpture that adhered to these criteria, as we see hanging above the mantelpiece in Hine's African American family portrait (pl. 71).[61]

Benson's photographs, like Friedlander's, do far more than simply distribute a likeness of Saint-Gaudens' sculpture to audiences outside of Boston. They harness the particular qualities of the camera — cropping, camera angle, isolation of details, and lighting — to comment on current perceptions of Saint-Gaudens' bronze and offer insight into Americans' memory of the nation's history. In reproductions as velvety as butterfly wings, Benson's images brought viewers face to face with the sullied surface of Saint-Gaudens' sculpture and prompted them to question their own concern, or indifference, for the future of the nation's past. His photographs also revealed what the Boston monument did not commemorate: the identities of the African Americans who served in the 54th Massachusetts. While Shaw is clearly recognizable, and the poems originally engraved on the marble entablature praised the colonel specifically, the names of the African American soldiers who fell at Fort Wagner were never inscribed on the sculpture. In response to this oversight, Benson and Kirstein used War Department records assembled by Captain Luis F. Emilio, who served in the regiment and wrote its history, to list the soldiers who were wounded, missing, or killed at Fort Wagner in *Lay This Laurel*. The book thus marks a crucial effort to broaden perceptions of the monument to include Shaw as well as the African American soldiers who fought alongside him. It also serves as a reminder that the bravery of the "Fifty-Fourth and…other black regiments in a national history often dominated by shameful events," wrote Kirstein, "form an episode that gives cause for pride."[62]

For the generation of artists who emerged in the 1980s and 1990s, however, the failure to acknowledge the identities of African Americans in narratives of the nation's history gave cause for lament. Determined to bring their stories to light, Carrie Mae Weems produced a photographic series that honored and called attention to the anonymous African Americans who had been the unknown, even unwilling subjects of historic and popular photographs. *From Here I Saw What Happened and I Cried* (1995–1996) features more than thirty images that Weems appropriated or, as scholar Cherise Smith suggests, "rescued" from other sources.[63] One of these is Benson's photograph of the unnamed drummer boy in the Shaw Memorial (pl. 73). While he, like his comrades, appears as a distinct individual, he nonetheless represents an anonymous type, the drummer boy, whose leading role in the bronze relief has rarely been acknowledged.

In Weems' series, Benson's portrait of Saint-Gaudens' common soldier takes on a new, iconic identity (pl. 77). As she did with each image, Weems altered Benson's photograph by changing its presentation: she zoomed in on the soldier's profile, circled him in a black mat and frame, and colored the image red. She then mounted the photograph behind glass etched with the caption from a new and different story: "Restless through the longest winter you marched and marched and marched." By representing Saint-Gaudens' bronze in this manner, Weems assigns to the African American soldier the role typically given to Shaw: to embody the 54th and honor the thousands of other African American soldiers who fought for emancipation.

In this regard, Weems takes her cue from Jacob Lawrence, who symbolized the 54th not with an image of its celebrated colonel, but by representing the crossed bayonets of the regiment's African American soldiers on the battlefield. For Lawrence and other protagonists of the Harlem Renaissance, art had the power to help right the current injustices of racism.

For Weems, art highlights the persistence of ethnically based prejudice in American society to question how much progress has really been made. She presents Saint-Gaudens' common soldier not only as a focal point of a work of art but also as a target seen through the rounded sight of an enemy rifle. The red hue signals both his bloodshed on the battlefield and the anger that failure to commemorate his death for so many years has caused. The streaks of tarnish on his cheek, which Benson depicts as a cry to preserve a beloved monument, become tears of outrage for the generations of African Americans whose heroism and sacrifice remain unsung.

Weems has remarked about photography: "I'm not so much stuck on the medium as I am on what I can do with it."[64] Exploring the many meanings of Saint-Gaudens' memorial, and the equally numerous untold narratives of the 54th and other African American soldiers, she adapted an image from Benson's Shaw Memorial series once again in *The Hampton Project* (2000). The installation incorporates digitized reproductions of historic photographs that have been printed on diaphanous, cloth banners. Hanging from the ceiling at different angles and intervals throughout the room, the photographs create a visual maze that leads viewers through what Weems has called "the tangled web of history."[65] Large-scale portraits of Hampton Institute students, some of which were made by Frances Benjamin Johnston for the 1900 Paris Exposition, intermingle with photographs that depict the institution of slavery and its legacy of racial prejudice in the twentieth century.

In Weems' provocative commentary on race relations, social norms, and education within the United States, members of the 54th Massachusetts assume the role of pioneers in the struggle for African American civil rights. They also symbolize the African American Civil War soldiers whose determination inspired Samuel Chapman Armstrong to establish Hampton Institute after the war as a way to edify the country's newly emancipated population. While Weems' project questions the validity of Armstrong's philosophy, it also suggests that education remains a powerful tool to combat the ignorance of prejudice and shore up the ideals of democracy.

Weems, like Benson and Friedlander, represents one of the most famous markers of the Civil War to comment on how we remember—or forget—the nation's past. Photographer William Earle Williams, in contrast, probes the nature of historical memory by focusing on unmarked, often overlooked sites that are rich in significance for African American Civil War soldiers. Williams began taking photographs of Civil War memorial sites for a project on Gettysburg in the late 1980s. Among the many monuments to the Civil War dead, he noticed a glaring absence of statues or plaques commemorating the thousands of African American soldiers who participated in the conflict.[66] To bring to light and honor their important presence in this defining moment in American history, Williams set out to create a comprehensive visual record of prominent locations where African American soldiers trained, fought, and lost their lives to advance a Union victory in the Civil War.

Williams' *Unsung Heroes: African American Soldiers in the Civil War* (2007) includes a series of photographs that restore to the landscape of Civil War memory the places where the 54th Massachusetts earned its place in history. One image, titled *Folly Beach Looking towards Morris Island* (1999), shows all that remains today of Fort Wagner: a single lighthouse rising from the sea against a pale, gray sky (pl. 80). Years of waves have eroded the once formidable stronghold that defended Charleston, washing away the battleground where the 54th fought so valiantly to eradicate the institution of slavery and transform American society.

Williams has remarked that bringing to light the contemporary landscape of places where so much blood was shed helps "dispel the myth that blacks were given their citizenship and rights after the Civil War without having fought for and earned them."[67] His photograph of Fort Wagner returns to contemporary iconography of the Civil War a site that is no longer visible. Its intimate scale invites contemplation of the quiet seascape, which has submerged the site of such clamorous violence. Its range of soft grays calls to mind period photographs of Civil War battlefields and ravaged townscapes by George Barnard, Mathew Brady, Timothy O'Sullivan, and others. Yet in Williams' view, the barracks and corpses that once covered the ground have been washed away by the sea, leaving behind only a single, guiding light. As we gaze across the horizon in Williams' photograph, we are compelled to imagine the soldiers of the 54th when they first arrived on the coast of South Carolina, brimming with courage and the possibility of change to come. The memory of their determination to bring about that change remains an inspiration for us all.

Commemorating Black Soldiers:
The African American Civil War Memorial
in Washington, DC

*"This was the biggest thing
that ever happened in my life.
I felt like a man with a uniform on
and a gun in my hand."*

—ELIJAH MARRS, 1885

RENÉE ATER

MONUMENTS HELP INDIVIDUALS and communities remember the past and preserve important historical events, heroes, personal or collective triumphs, even moments of conflict. Marking the landscape in highly visible ways, monuments are located in front of civic buildings, in town squares, in plazas and parks, in cemeteries and memorial gardens, and in specially designated areas set aside for remembrance and tribute. People visit such spaces for private reflection or public commemoration. Monuments can offer redemption, recognition, pride, and belonging. But the past sometimes meets the present uneasily, reflecting varied interpretations of whose history matters. Thus public monuments can also arouse intense anger, feelings of exclusion, as well as dissension among communities, local governments, and special interest groups. People throw paint on monuments, scribble graffiti across their surfaces, physically destroy them, attempt to reroute mainstream narratives, hold protest rallies to call attention to omissions and distortions of the past and present.

Many monuments force public conversations about what is important to communities and to the nation. They galvanize public opinion in unpredictable ways. They are not static: each individual, neighborhood, and new generation encounters and interprets the meaning in ways that are as fluid as time and space. Although people may become desensitized to the significance of monuments in their daily lives, those who build them often start from a storehouse of deep emotion and want to celebrate or correct some aspect of history — glorifying or reinventing the past, or revealing a part of it that has remained unacknowledged.[1]

The commission and creation of the African American Civil War Memorial (1998) in Washington, DC (fig. 1), offer insights into both monument building and shared remembrance and commemoration in relation to public space. As an active "site of memory," this memorial sought to rectify the nation's failure to recognize African American participation in the American Civil War and to encourage visitors to extract new meaning from the past.[2] It now stands in the nation's capital as a significant commemoration of the Civil War, acknowledging the active participation of African American men in restoring the nation. It also relates to other Civil War monuments in Washington, DC — including three equestrian statues arrayed along Vermont Avenue and Thomas Ball's *Freedmen's Memorial to Abraham Lincoln* (*Emancipation Group*) (1876) on Capitol Hill. And while the African American Civil War Memorial took some inspiration from Augustus Saint-Gaudens' Memorial to Robert Gould Shaw and the 54th Massachusetts Regiment (1897), one of the preeminent monuments of the Civil War (see p. 82, fig. 1; pl. 65), it also gave the artist who created it a chance to rethink the content and interpretation put forward a century before. The resulting memorial places African American men at the forefront of the story of American freedom, recognizes their contributions to the young nation, and highlights their presence, commitment, and strength. It gives material witness to the real names and units of the United States Colored Troops and represents their bravery and loyalty despite the trauma of slavery, racism, and the denigration of black manhood during the nineteenth century.

Significantly, the architects and design committee chose to place the African American Civil War Memo-

1

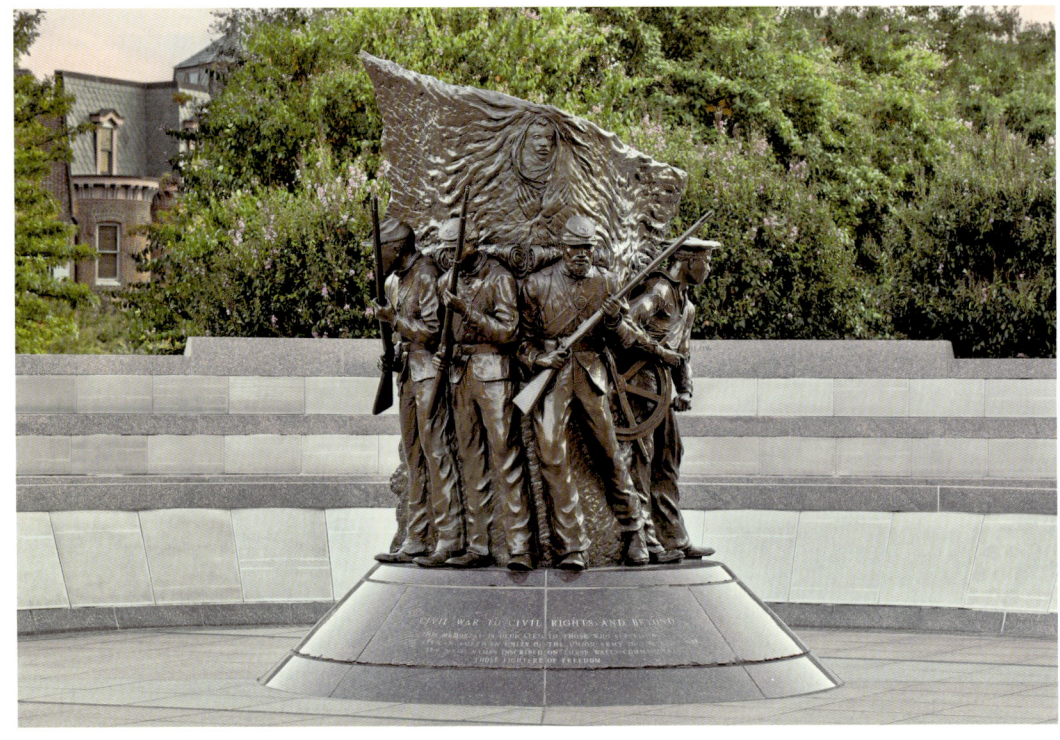

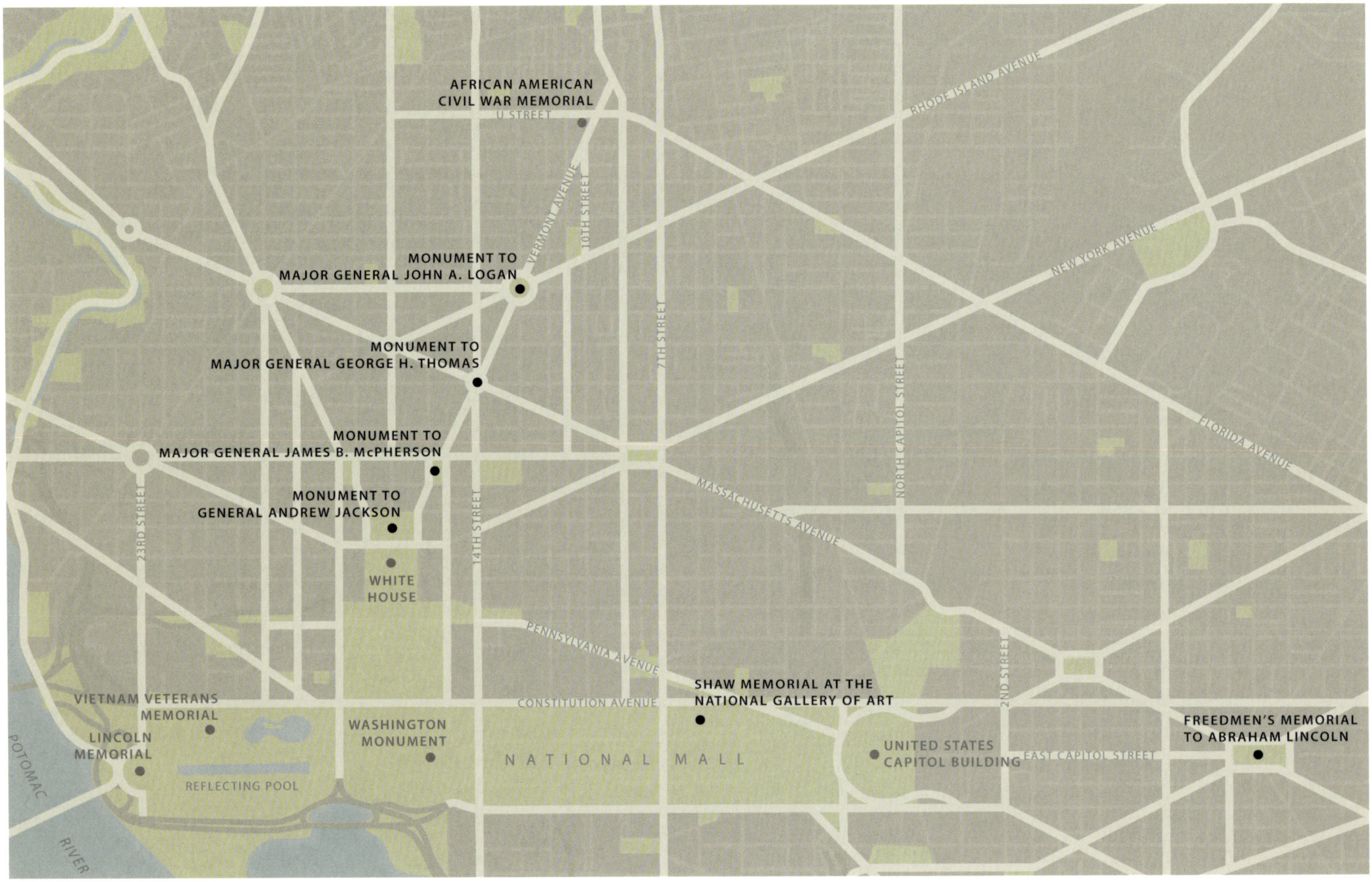
AFRICAN AMERICAN
CIVIL WAR MEMORIAL
U STREET
RHODE ISLAND AVENUE
VERMONT AVENUE
10TH STREET
MONUMENT TO
MAJOR GENERAL JOHN A. LOGAN
NEW YORK AVENUE
7TH STREET
MONUMENT TO
MAJOR GENERAL GEORGE H. THOMAS
NORTH CAPITOL STREET
FLORIDA AVENUE
MONUMENT TO
MAJOR GENERAL JAMES B. McPHERSON
MASSACHUSETTS AVENUE
MONUMENT TO
GENERAL ANDREW JACKSON
23RD STREET
14TH STREET
WHITE
HOUSE
PENNSYLVANIA AVENUE
2ND STREET
VIETNAM VETERANS
MEMORIAL
CONSTITUTION AVENUE
SHAW MEMORIAL AT THE
NATIONAL GALLERY OF ART
FREEDMEN'S MEMORIAL
TO ABRAHAM LINCOLN
LINCOLN
MEMORIAL
WASHINGTON
MONUMENT
UNITED STATES
CAPITOL BUILDING
EAST CAPITOL STREET
POTOMAC
NATIONAL MALL
REFLECTING POOL
RIVER

2

Fig. 1 The African American Civil War Memorial, with Ed Hamilton's *Spirit of Freedom*, 1998, Washington, DC. National Park Service

Fig. 2 Map of Washington, DC, showing the African American Civil War Memorial in relation to other monuments in the nation's capital

rial outside the monumental core of the National Mall (fig. 2). Located at the convergence of Vermont Avenue with 10th and U Streets NW, the new memorial occupies an extended, triangular urban space, which is landscaped on the east side and adjacent to the historic Prince Hall Masonic Temple on the west. The plaza is composed of rose and gray granite, laid out in an array of squares and rectangles that are bisected by angled lines that form a regular pattern of large isosceles triangles. At the center of the plaza and resting on a two-foot-high granite base, the nine-foot-tall bronze *Spirit of Freedom* by Ed Hamilton depicts three African American infantrymen and one sailor. On the reverse of the semicircular sculpture, a multigenerational family gathers around a soldier who stands ready to depart for war. Etched on the surface of the granite base are the words, "Civil War to Civil Rights and Beyond." A series of four curved and progressively higher granite walls form a mirroring semicircular niche immediately behind the sculpture. On this composite "Wall of Honor," 157 burnished stainless steel plaques are engraved with the names of more than two hundred thousand African American soldiers and sailors as well as their white officers. Carved near the top of the outermost wall are the words of Frederick Douglass, the nineteenth-century abolitionist: "Who would be free themselves must strike the blow. Better even die free than to live slaves."[3]

ENVISIONING THE MEMORIAL

On July 2, 1991, the Council of the District of Columbia passed a resolution that endorsed the creation of an African American Civil War Memorial. A month later Representative Eleanor Holmes Norton presented a resolution in the House of Representatives to authorize the government of the District of Columbia to establish a memorial to honor African American soldiers of the Union army in the Civil War. At a meeting on August 8, 1991, city politicians, educators, and black leaders envisioned the memorial as "a way to claim the black soldier's rightful place in American history, provide inspiration for a new generation of youth, and help to revive the U Street corridor."[4] The United States Senate and House of Representatives passed Joint Resolution 320 on October 14, 1992, authorizing the government of the District of Columbia "to establish a memorial on Federal land in the District of Columbia or its environs to honor African-Americans who served with Union forces during the Civil War." No federal funds were allocated for the project, and the public law stated clearly that the government of the District of Columbia was "solely responsible for payment, from official funds or charitable donations."[5]

Under the leadership of Frank Smith Jr., then a Ward 1 city councilman, the African American Civil War Memorial Freedom Foundation was formed in 1992 to raise the necessary monies to realize the memorial. In partnership with the Washington Metropolitan Area Transit Authority, the DC Commission on the Arts and Humanities, the National Planning Commission, the National Park Service, and the National Archives and Records Administration, the foundation eventually raised $2.6 million from public and private sources to landscape the site, construct the Wall of Honor, and commission *Spirit of Freedom*.[6]

Washington architects Paul S. Devrouax and Edward D. Dunson Jr. designed the site for the African American Civil War Memorial, transforming the unwieldy triangular site in front of the U Street/Cardoza Metrorail station into a broad and attractive plaza for commemorative activities and community gatherings. They set the two-toned plaza back from the street and Metrorail station and placed the semicircular niche at the narrowest point of the triangle to allow easy access and direct engagement with the Wall of Honor and *Spirit of Freedom*. And they specified crepe myrtle trees and plantings at the corner of U Street and along Vermont Avenue to provide greenery at a busy city intersection.

With its long side parallel to Vermont Avenue, the memorial lines up with three significant Civil War bronze equestrian monuments in the city: Major General John A. Logan (1901) at Logan Circle; Major General George Henry Thomas (1876) at Thomas

3

Circle; and Major General James Birdseye McPherson (1876) at McPherson Square (see fig. 2). All three generals face south atop massive bronze horses, seemingly on a perpetual march of conquest. Vermont Avenue ends at Lafayette Square and H Street NW, immediately in front of the White House. At the center of that square is an equestrian statue of General Andrew Jackson (1853) with an inscription on the base that reads, "Our Federal Union It Must Be Preserved." This quotation, taken from Jackson's toast at a Democrat Party dinner honoring Thomas Jefferson's birthday on April 13, 1830, related to the South Carolina nullification crisis of the early 1830s.[7] Whether or not a visitor is fully aware of the geography, architects Devrouax and Dunson exploited the city's monument tradition by locating the African American Civil War Memorial in relation to these older hero statues. Yet they also added a new element to their space, orienting the new memorial to the north — the symbolic place of freedom.

The Wall of Honor is an essential component of the African American Civil War Memorial, inspired by Maya Lin's Vietnam Veterans Memorial (1982), with its two black granite walls inscribed with the names of 58,272 men and women who died in that war. "This listing of names," according to scholar Marita Sturken, "creates an expanse of cultural memory, one that could be seen as alternately subverting, rescripting, and contributing to the history of the Vietnam War as it is being currently written."[8] The planners of the African American Civil War Memorial wished to commemorate the men who served in the United States Colored Troops in a similar fashion, using their names to rewrite Civil War history. In collaboration with the National Archives and Records Administration, the foundation retrieved 209,145 names from the compiled service records of the Bureau of Colored Troops. Each stainless steel plaque lists the names alphabetically within each regiment, starting with the men from the 1st Regiment, United States Cavalry (fig. 3). Permanently inscribed in the burnished steel, the names bring into presence the thousands of African American men who served in the Union army. The names are also points of reference for descendants to delve deeper into genealogy and history, and they are physical reminders of the loyalty these men showed to the Union cause and the nation.

The African American Civil War Memorial Freedom Foundation and architects considered locations on the National Mall but chose a site significant to the African American community: the historic U Street district and the Shaw neighborhood, one of the city's oldest.[9] Beginning in the 1860s, the

Fig. 3 Detail of the "Wall of Honor" from the African American Civil War Memorial with quotation from Frederick Douglass

neighborhood shifted from a mostly rural area to a thriving urban core. Several Union army camps and hospitals were located there, including Camp Barker, Wisewell Barracks and Hospital, and Campbell Hospital, which attracted formerly enslaved men and women (contrabands) who sought shelter and safety within the city's boundaries.[10] During the late nineteenth and early twentieth centuries, the area became a thriving center for African American intellectual, cultural, and civic life. The neighborhood's name, adopted in the 1960s, derived from the local junior high school named for Robert Gould Shaw, the leader of the all-black 54th Massachusetts Volunteer Infantry.

In October 1992 the DC Commission on the Arts and Humanities issued a call for proposals, directed specifically to African American artists, for a commemorative figurative statue for the African American Civil War Memorial. By December 1992 the commission along with the foundation and the architects had narrowed their selection down to four sculptors: Eddie Dixon, Ed Hamilton, Jerome Meadows, and James Earl Reid. The architects were primarily concerned with finding "an artist who would work as part of the design team to insure that the sculptural element will be integrated into the overall design."[11] On May 26, 1993, Dixon, Hamilton, Meadows, and Reid gave formal presentations of their work, showing examples of their previous public monuments and discussing their proposed memorials for the U Street site. Unable to decide between Dixon and Hamilton, the commission invited both artists to return to Washington, DC, in July 1993. To enhance the presentation of his sculpture, Hamilton placed his maquette within a scale model of the memorial plaza.[12] His plaster maquette featured four Union soldiers and two sailors standing at parade rest, with the figures emerging from a semicircular wall, its concave side shielding members of a family.

On the strength of this model, Hamilton won the contract for the project in a unanimous vote. The commission wrote Hamilton in August 1993, stating: "[the design team] felt that your proposal combined their interests and concerns in a manner and style that would be appropriate for the memorial. They commented that your work displayed a profound unity in placing representatives from the armed forces on the outer side of the semicircle, essentially protecting a family on the inner circle. The selection committee agreed that this conveys the sense that they 'were fighting for the protection of their families from the slave trade, unjust treatment, and equal protection under the law.'" The commission specifically commented on the style of Hamilton's design as well, saying: "your proposed work goes beyond many of the other memorials and monuments in Washington through the use of the bas relief semicircle. They agreed that it was an original and unique approach. Its relationship to the walls of the memorial where the names will be placed is also very important."[13] Sixteen months later the commission awarded Hamilton an "Arts in Public Spaces" grant to realize a "permanent art in public spaces installation" for the African American Civil War Memorial.[14]

In commissioning Hamilton to create the central figurative statue for the memorial plaza, the selection committee had found a sculptor well versed in the art of public monuments. Hamilton was responsible for several important public artworks, including the Booker T. Washington Memorial (1984) at Hampton University in Hampton, Virginia; the Joe Louis Memorial (1987) for Cobo Hall and Arena in Detroit, Michigan; and the Amistad Memorial (1992) in New Haven, Connecticut. Born in 1947, Hamilton grew up in Louisville, Kentucky. He is a graduate of the Art Center School (later known as the Louisville School of Art and eventually absorbed by the University of Louisville). Hamilton writes that he was interested in creating three-dimensional objects from a young age and discovered sculpture upon entering the Art Center School: "I walked into the sculpture studio and caught sculpting fever. I saw modeling tools and smelled the clay. I felt an inner glow that spread throughout my body. Somehow I knew sculpting would allow me to use all my creative energies and I was hooked. Sculpture to me was physical. It had dimension. An artist can't fake form in three-dimen-

4

5

sions. Suddenly it all made sense and clicked with the way I viewed objects."[15]

Upon graduation in 1969, Hamilton found employment teaching art at a local high school and later at the community college. A chance meeting in 1973 with Louisville sculptor Jeptha Bernard "Barney" Bright changed the course of Hamilton's career. Bright hired Hamilton as a full-time assistant to work with him on several local commissions, including the River Horse (1973) and the Louisville Clock (1976). Hamilton's work with Bright expanded his sculptural skills and knowledge of the dynamics of public art. After his apprenticeship with Bright ended in 1977, Hamilton established his own studio, sculpting liturgical pieces for Catholic churches in the Louisville area and working on a series entitled "Junkology" in which he used scavenged pieces of steel, tin, rock, feathers, chicken and fish bones, and other materials to create abstract sculptures.[16] When Hamilton received the commission for the Booker T. Washington Memorial in 1983, he returned to creating large-scale sculpture and began a career as a full-time builder of monuments.

Hamilton commenced work on *Spirit of Freedom* in the fall of 1995, modifying his design to include three soldiers who grip the barrels of their rifled muskets and one sailor who holds a ship's wheel (fig. 4). He began the process by fashioning a cardboard frame to establish the scale of the memorial and making paper forms of each of the figures to determine their overall relation to one another. Over several months, he replaced the cardboard frame with a metal frame made from water pipes onto which he applied water-based clay, pushing and moving the wet material to create swirls and undulations suggestive of movement. He then modeled the life-size bodies of the soldiers in high relief, making them "appear as if they were walking out of the wall of clay." Hamilton paid careful attention to the details of physiognomy and focused on their hands. The faces are a fusion of the faces of black men he knew growing up around Louisville. One depicts a bearded older man (fig. 5), who seems a more experienced soldier leading the two younger men into battle. Hamilton wanted "their faces, hands, and feet to be real enough to touch." While sculpting the individual faces, he played the

Fig. 4 Ed Hamilton, *Spirit of Freedom*, 1998, bronze, 9 ½ feet high

Fig. 5 Detail of bearded soldier from Hamilton's *Spirit of Freedom*

Fig. 6 West Point Monument (Norfolk African American Civil War Memorial), 1909–1920, West Point Cemetery, Norfolk, Virginia

Fig. 7 Colored Soldiers Monument (Kentucky African American Civil War Veterans Monument), 1924, Green Hill Cemetery, Frankfort, Kentucky

soundtrack from *Glory*, the epic Civil War movie that immortalized the bravery of the 54th Massachusetts Regiment at the Battle of Fort Wagner; both its original score by James Horner and the voices of the Boys Choir of Harlem inspired his work.[17]

In finalizing his design, Hamilton was aware of two earlier memorials dedicated solely to deceased African American troops: the West Point Monument (1909–1920) in West Point Cemetery in Norfolk, Virginia; and the Colored Soldiers Monument (1924) in Greenhill Cemetery in Frankfort, Kentucky. The West Point Monument (fig. 6 and pl. 78) is a large granite shaft supporting a bronze statue of Sergeant William Harvey Carney, a native of Norfolk, member of the 54th Massachusetts Regiment, and the first African American to be awarded the Medal of Honor (see pl. 69). The statue is surrounded by the graves of one hundred African American men who served in the American Civil War and the Spanish-American War. The Colored Soldiers Monument (fig. 7) is a gray limestone tapered plinth inscribed with the names of 142 African American men from central Kentucky who served in the Civil War. Early efforts at remembering the United States Colored Troops, these two monuments have fallen into obscurity in their respective locations.

Instead of the memorial form of the obelisk, Hamilton's multifigure statue focuses intently on the details of the uniform and rifled musket. To ensure historical accuracy, the artist purchased William C. Davis' *The Fighting Men of the Civil War* (1989), a large book filled with photographs of Union and Confederate soldiers and illustrations of uniforms, weapons, and a range of personal items. He obtained a copy of William A. Gladstone's *Men of Color* (1993), and his daughter gave him a subscription to *Civil War Times*.[18] He also read Frederick Douglass' Philadelphia speech from 1863, which maintained that the Union uniform held the potential for transformation and for building self-confidence. In reference to the Emancipation Proclamation and the new right of African American men to fight in the Union army, Douglass

6

7

stated: "Never since the world began was a better chance offered to a long enslaved and oppressed people. The opportunity is given to us to be men. With one courageous resolution we may blot out the handwriting of ages against us. Once let the black man get upon his person the brass letter, U.S., let him get an eagle on his button, and a musket on his shoulder and bullets in his pocket, there is no power on earth that can deny that he has earned his right to citizenship."[19]

Wearing the United States Army uniform was an important moment for African American soldiers, and Hamilton wanted to capture the dignity of the uniformed men in his *Spirit of Freedom*. According to historian Joseph T. Glatthaar, "The uniform was a tacit recognition of their importance to the country and to the war effort, as well as a chance to demonstrate to the white race that they could stand on their own and contribute significantly to the United States in its time of need."[20] Wearing the Union blue symbolized this fight for self-emancipation and signaled the personal investment of African Americans to end slavery in the United States.

African American soldiers' government-issued rifles were also associated with this real change in status. One popular song from the period, sung by the 8th United States Colored Infantry, emphasized the connection between arming African American men and manhood:

They look like men, they look like men,
They look like men of war,
All arm'd and dressed in uniform,
They look like men of war.[21]

Once African American men joined the Union army, the uniform and rifle became essential markers of their manhood and citizenry.

Hamilton took careful note of this pride and belonging through his attention to the uniforms and rifles in *Spirit of Freedom*. He clothed his soldiers in the blue wool uniform of the Union army, rendering with precision the fatigue blouse, a light wool coat with four brass buttons, and the wool trousers with inset stripes. Each man wears a forage cap — a hat with a flat round top and leather visor — and blackened leather boots with thick leather soles and heels (see fig. 8). Hamilton included other important details: the leather sling with the leather cartridge box, the eagle breastplate attached to the center of the sling (see fig. 9), the U.S. brass buckle on the wide leather belt, the leather cap box attached to the right side of the belt, and the scabbard for the bayonet, which hung on the belt at a soldier's left hip. The soldiers also wear tin canteens draped to their left side.

On the back of each soldier, Hamilton modeled the Union-issued knapsack that held personal belongings and a rolled blanket tied in place at the top. He made a mold of a reproduction .58 caliber 1861 Springfield rifled musket borrowed from a re-enactor in the 54th Massachusetts Regiment, as he wanted to render the firearms "true" to those the army would have issued to the United States Colored Troops. Each soldier strides forward and carries this Springfield rifled musket pointing outward, hammer cocked at the ready.

The sailor is rendered with equal veracity. He wears the federal navy "flat hat" made of dark blue wool and the blue wool frock and trousers. With his hands on a ship's wheel, he stands with his legs wide apart as if balancing himself against the water's movement. At his feet rest three rows of small cannon balls.[22]

In the concave arc of the reverse of the statue, Hamilton shaped in low relief six members of a multigenerational family, interconnected through touch and glance (fig. 10). To the left, a young wife holds a newborn in her arms, her head held high and eyes closed in reflection or perhaps in fear at the potential loss of her spouse. Hamilton used the features of his wife, Bernadette, and the hands of his daughter as models for this figure. The woman's soldier husband, fully dressed in his Union uniform and resting the butt of his rifle on the ground, stands beside her and extends his right arm behind her to hold her steady. Two young children hold hands: a girl grasps tightly her burlap doll, and a boy reaches across to his grandmother.

Fig. 8 Detail of soldier from *Spirit of Freedom* by Ed Hamilton

Fig. 9 Detail of Union eagle breastplate from Hamilton's *Spirit of Freedom*

Fig. 10 Reverse of Hamilton's *Spirit of Freedom*

8

9

10

The grandparents mirror the position of the young husband and wife, with the grandfather holding his son's left wrist and the grandmother staring stoically forward. Just out of the fields, the latter wears a cotton bag draped on her left shoulder and a necklace of cowry shells indicating her connection to Africa.[23]

The family group is integral to *Spirit of Freedom* — the wife, children, and grandparents are the reason the soldier is heading to the battlefield. Hamilton hints at the sacrifices such families made during the Civil War through the closed eyes of the wife and long-suffering expressions of the grandparents. Many African American families faced particular hardships when their men went to war, especially around the issue of equal and timely pay for black soldiers. Some women followed their husbands to the front lines, working as laundresses and cooks in camps. Many stayed behind and continued to work the land, growing crops and supporting themselves and their children. Still others fled to towns and cities working as maids, seamstresses, and day laborers.[24] At the end of the twentieth century Hamilton wanted visitors to be deeply aware of these sacrifices and emphasized both the soldiers' and their families' perseverance in the face of the overwhelmingly difficult conditions surrounding the war.

Once Hamilton had finished the figures for the monument, he turned to the bare space above the soldiers' heads. Some years earlier, in 1991, he had stopped in Boston to see Saint-Gaudens' *Memorial to Robert Gould Shaw and the 54th Massachusetts Regiment*, also known as the Shaw Memorial. In his words, he was "blown away" by the powerful scene of marching black soldiers and the angelic figure floating above them, though he felt the soldiers were subordinated to the figure of Shaw riding high above the regiment on his horse. Wanting to fill the blank space in his own sculpture, Hamilton recalled Saint-Gaudens' memorial as the "face of a protector emerged" in his mind. He conceived the image of a shrouded winged figure whose face tilts upward with closed eyes and whose crossed hands rest at the chest (fig. 11). As Hamilton worked to resolve the placement of this figure, his

11

former pastor visited his studio to discuss the emerging spiritual nature of the memorial. She suggested that Hamilton read Psalm 91:4: "He will cover you with his pinions, and under his wings you will find refuge; his faithfulness is a shield and buckler." Once Hamilton read this passage, he felt confident that he had realized his vision and that the figure with closed eyes unified his concept for the sculpture: not as an angel of death, but as an angel of protection leading the soldiers into battle.[25]

RESPONDING TO THE PAST

The full significance of Hamilton's sculpture comes into focus when compared to Thomas Ball's *Freedmen's Memorial to Abraham Lincoln* (1876) and Saint-Gaudens' Shaw Memorial (1897). The African American Civil War Memorial is in dialogue with these nineteenth-century memorials, with both their representations

Fig. 11 Detail of the "Spirit of Freedom" from *Spirit of Freedom* by Ed Hamilton

Fig. 12 Thomas Ball, *Freedmen's Memorial to Abraham Lincoln* (*Emancipation Group*), 1876, bronze, Lincoln Park, Washington, DC

and their content. The most noted and notorious sculpture to commemorate emancipation, Ball's memorial is installed in Lincoln Park and aligned with East Capitol Street, which leads directly to the Capitol Building. Free African Americans raised the monies to pay for the monument, first conceived by committee in 1866 and completed a decade later, but they had no say in its conceptualization. The work was the most visible attempt in public sculpture to capture the ideals of the Emancipation Proclamation. Yet it failed miserably and served as the antithetical model of emancipation.

Ball subordinated a partly dressed African American male to the fully clothed Abraham Lincoln (fig. 12). Although based on a portrait of a former slave named Archer Alexander, the image is one of obsequiousness, with the liberated black male crouching at Lincoln's feet and encumbered by broken manacles still attached to his wrists. Lincoln stands tall and erect, his right hand holding the Emancipation Proclamation, his left bestowing freedom on the former slave. Ball depicted Lincoln as the noble and commanding head of the nation, while he showed the African American male as a noncitizen, uncultured and childlike, stripped of his dignity and potency. The monument was ultimately not about emancipation but about domination and the continued paternalistic power of the white nation.[26] Ball's statue visually anchored the park until the National Council of Negro Women commissioned a statue of Mary McLeod Bethune for the east end of the park in the mid-1970s, changing the focus from Ball's statue to the modern rendering of the well-known African American educator.

If Hamilton's *Spirit of Freedom* stands in stark contrast to Ball's *Freedmen's Memorial*, its relationship to Saint-Gaudens' work is more complicated, reflecting both his admiration for and his criticism of the earlier memorial. Hamilton appreciated the powerful emotional charge and material beauty of the Shaw Memorial and the way Saint-Gaudens captured the psychological drama of men marching to their deaths in time of war. Saint-Gaudens conveyed this drama through his modeling of the physiognomies of the infantrymen (although the faces were idealized likenesses of anonymous models in his New York studio) and faithful rendering of the soldiers' Union uniform. Hamilton, too, created idealized portraits of African American men for his *Spirit of Freedom* and depicted them in accurately detailed Union uniforms and weapons. He seemed to make a visual connection between the bearded older man who marches in front of Shaw's horse and his own bearded man. In both the Shaw Memorial and Hamilton's *Spirit of Freedom*, the somber expression and greater maturity of this figure add gravitas to the portrayal of the African American soldier.[27]

Yet Hamilton also believed that Saint-Gaudens' sculpture emphasized the disparity between the white officer, Shaw, sitting high atop his horse and the African American soldiers striding below him. From the beginning, Hamilton envisioned a memorial that focused exclusively on African American

12

soldiers and sailors rather than the white officers who led them, reversing the narrative content of Saint-Gaudens' memorial. Equally important in considering the relationship between the two memorials is that they occupy radically different public spaces. Saint-Gaudens' memorial resides on Boston Common facing the Massachusetts State House, the oldest park in the United States, an important civic location for the nation, and a marker of Boston's Brahmin identity.[28] The architects and planners of the African American Civil War Memorial consciously placed it within the context of U Street and the Shaw neighborhood, affirming African American identity in the context of a historic black section of the city. The Shaw neighborhood is not the grand, sedate green of Boston Common, but a bustling urban district filled with apartment buildings, restaurants, and theaters. Importantly, visitors to Washington, DC, can now go to the National Gallery of Art to see the plaster cast of the Shaw Memorial as well (see pl. 65). Separated by only a few miles, the two memorials offer viewers an opportunity to consider the way in which two artists, separated by one hundred years, responded visually to African American participation in the Civil War.

In its final form, *Spirit of Freedom* stands nine feet high and curves six feet along its horizontal axis. Integrating the traditional soldier monument with an evocation of family and the embodiment of an abiding spirit, Hamilton's memorial to the United States Colored Troops is about the strength of character of African American men who volunteered to do battle in the Civil War, and it presents the cohesiveness of the African American family even in times of duress. It is also about motion and coming change. Influenced deeply by the French sculptor Auguste Rodin's fluid handling of his materials, giving expressive rendering of the psychological state of his subjects, Hamilton pushed the clay with his hands to suggest wind, movement, and the ethereal propelling the men forward. His soldiers are protected by the righteous presence of his angel and thus able to fight for freedom to ensure the end of centuries of enslavement.

REMEMBERING AND COMMEMORATING THE PAST

At the end of the Civil War, the role of African American soldiers and sailors in the war faded from public memory. Weeks after the surrender of Robert E. Lee and the Confederate army at Appomattox, Virginia, the Grand Review of the Armies took place in Washington, DC, celebrating the Union victory. On May 23 and May 24, 1865, approximately 150,000 men of the Army of Tennessee, the Army of Georgia, and the Army of the Potomac marched up Pennsylvania Avenue to great fanfare and passed a reviewing stand in front of the White House with President Andrew Johnson and his cabinet in attendance. As historian Stuart McConnell writes, "The Grand Review was the visual embodiment of a reunified nation." Yet this event excluded African Americans. Not one of the 166 regiments of the United States Colored Troops was invited to participate. The only African Americans involved in the Grand Review, McConnell notes, were "pick and shovel brigades" or former slaves used as comic relief.[29] In the post–Civil War era, former African American soldiers faced discrimination and violence, fighting for pensions and recognition of their service.[30]

In 1913, as the fiftieth anniversary of the Battle of Gettysburg approached, profound differences crystallized between how blacks and whites remembered the war. In a move intended to amalgamate an official account of the Civil War, both southern and northern whites celebrated reconciliation and white solidarity. But they ignored slavery and emancipation as critical to the meaning of the war. A national amnesia set in, with people willfully forgetting the service of African American soldiers. This move to a reconciliationist memory of the Civil War was exemplified in the celebration at Gettysburg from July 1 to 4, 1913. Funded and supported by the federal government, Union and Confederate veterans participated in ceremonies that emphasized the Civil War as a battle of brothers that forged greater national unity. Organizers actively excluded African American veterans from the reunion and refused to acknowledge their importance to the outcome of the Civil War, ultimately ensuring the whitewashing of this history. The fiftieth anniversary of the Battle of Gettysburg was a segregated event, with African Americans on the periphery, employed as laborers and camp workers.[31]

Not until seventy-six years later with the film *Glory* (1989) did a popular art form give mass audiences a glimpse of the role of African American soldiers in the Civil War. It was both this film — despite its historical inaccuracy and romantic storytelling — and the profound erasure from historical memory of the service of black soldiers in the war that awakened citizens to the need for the African American Civil War Memorial. At the dedication of *Spirit of Freedom* in 1998, Frank Smith Jr., the founding director of the African American Civil War Museum, stated, "I consider it a grave oversight in American history that very little is known about the heroic contribution of these brave soldiers in ending slavery and keeping this country united under one flag."[32] The historical suppression of the role of African Americans in the Civil War is tied to racism, the battle for equal rights, and attitudes of white supremacy in the nineteenth and early twentieth centuries. And the social organization of forgetting and exclusion was the impetus for the new memorial.[33] African Americans did not forget the United States Colored Troops, but the rest of the nation paid little attention to their military service. Only with Benjamin Quarles' *The Negro in the Civil War* (1953) and Dudley Taylor Cornish's *The Sable Arm: Negro Troops in the Union Army, 1861–1865* (1956) did historians begin to acknowledge the significance of African Americans to the American Civil War. Yet many years and scholarly books later, the general public still does not have true understanding of the war or of African Americans' participation in it.

Historical amnesia also extends to what we see in public spaces. If monuments signal the importance of historical events and individuals, then the absence of certain populations in monumental form implies that they are unworthy of public representation. Many monuments in American cities and towns are focused solely on white male military and political leaders, "illustrious men" and their great deeds. Others are dedicated to perceived high points in U.S. history — marble and bronze statues that stress the ideals of heroism, freedom, and democracy. Writing about the monumental core of the National Mall, historian Kirk Savage argues: "Public monuments are an inherently conservative art form. They obey the logic of the last word, the logic of closure.... Traditionally, this means that monuments strip the hero or event of historical complexities and condense the subject's significance to a few patriotic lessons frozen for all time. Washington's monuments, in this conception, promise to immerse visitors in the 'essential' America, the 'soul of the nation.'"[34] With the African American Civil War Memorial, a long-ignored chapter of American history is reinserted into the landscape of the nation's capital. Visitors and residents of the city are asked to expand their understanding of the past and broaden their perceptions of national identity.

As a site of memory, the African American Civil War Memorial encourages people to take part in public acts of commemoration in the plaza. Historian Jay Winter writes in his work on World War I monuments: "Commemoration at sites of memory is an act arising out of a conviction, shared by a broad community, that the moment recalled is both significant and informed by a moral message."[35] Under the auspices of the Sons and Daughters of the United States Colored Troops, a group chartered to augment the African American Civil War Memorial Freedom Foundation's mission, several commemorative events occur throughout the year: wreath-laying ceremonies on Martin Luther King Jr. Day, Memorial Day, the Fourth of July, and Veterans Day; the Buffalo Thunder annual Memorial Day ceremony; and a national candle-lighting ceremony held in November.[36] At some events, African American Civil War reenactors and current military servicemen participate along with the public. These acts of commemoration are often related to the "moral message" of remembering the contributions of all African American servicemen and women, not just the United States Colored Troops during the Civil War. They are acts of profound acknowledgment and deep emotion in the public sphere.

The African American Civil War Memorial recognizes African Americans who have served their country despite the ongoing battle for emancipation, freedom, and civil rights, and it celebrates their bravery and loyalty within the context of the family and the nation. Importantly, the memorial exists in tandem with the African American Civil War Museum housed across Vermont Avenue in the historic Grimke Building. Through permanent exhibits and educational activities, including a wide-ranging series of lectures, the museum offers a historical overview of enslavement to freedom. It preserves artifacts, archival documents, photographs, and music that remind visitors of the integral role African American soldiers and sailors have played in the Civil War and beyond. The African American Civil War Memorial and Museum bring together the past and present in powerful ways. Visitors can search for the names of their ancestors on the Wall of Honor and find further information in the National Park Service's Civil War Soldiers and Sailors System database and in the National Archives' Bureau of Colored Troops Records, which collect documents and photographs that provide a physical reminder of African American presence in history. With a careful balance between heroic ideal and everyday concerns, the African American Civil War Memorial reinvigorates the meaning of the American Civil War within the memorial landscape of Washington, DC.

PLATES 57 – 80

THE LEGACY OF THE
54TH MASSACHUSETTS REGIMENT

"Art...outlasts the fevered voices, the civil
and military strivings, in mineral potency,
serenity and silence."

— LINCOLN KIRSTEIN, "LAY THIS LAUREL," 1973

57

Augustus Saint-Gaudens

EARLY STUDY OF THE ALLEGORICAL FIGURE
FOR THE SHAW MEMORIAL

late 1880s, plaster, 10 × 37 (25.4 × 94)
U.S. Department of the Interior, National Park Service,
Saint-Gaudens National Historic Site, Cornish, New Hampshire
Washington only

58

Augustus Saint-Gaudens

PRELIMINARY SKETCH FOR SHAW MEMORIAL

1883, plaster, 16⅛ × 15¼ (41 × 38.7)
U.S. Department of the Interior, National Park Service,
Saint-Gaudens National Historic Site, Cornish, New Hampshire
Washington only

59

Augustus Saint-Gaudens

STUDY HEAD OF A BLACK SOLDIER

1883/1893, plaster, 6 × 4⅞ (15.1 × 12.4)
U.S. Department of the Interior, National Park Service,
Saint-Gaudens National Historic Site, Cornish, New Hampshire
Washington only

60

Augustus Saint-Gaudens

STUDY HEAD OF A BLACK SOLDIER

1883/1893, plaster, 6¼ × 5½ (15.9 × 14)
U.S. Department of the Interior, National Park Service,
Saint-Gaudens National Historic Site, Cornish, New Hampshire
Washington only

61

Augustus Saint-Gaudens

STUDY HEAD OF A BLACK SOLDIER

1883/1893, plaster, 5 × 5¾ (12.7 × 14.6)

U.S. Department of the Interior, National Park Service,
Saint-Gaudens National Historic Site, Cornish, New Hampshire

Washington only

#

62

Augustus Saint-Gaudens

STUDY HEAD OF A BLACK SOLDIER

1883/1893, plaster, 6⅛ × 4⅞ (15.6 × 12.4)
U.S. Department of the Interior, National Park Service,
Saint-Gaudens National Historic Site, Cornish, New Hampshire
Washington only

63

Augustus Saint-Gaudens

STUDY HEAD OF A BLACK SOLDIER

1883/1893, plaster, 5⅞ × 5¼ (14.8 × 13.2)
U.S. Department of the Interior, National Park Service,
Saint-Gaudens National Historic Site, Cornish, New Hampshire
Washington only

LEGACY

64

Augustus Saint-Gaudens

STUDY HEAD OF A BLACK SOLDIER

1883/1893, plaster, 7⅞ × 4¾ (20 × 12.1)
U.S. Department of the Interior, National Park Service,
Saint-Gaudens National Historic Site, Cornish, New Hampshire
Washington only

65

Augustus Saint-Gaudens

SHAW MEMORIAL

1900, patinated plaster,
145¼ × 206½ × 34 (368.9 × 524.5 × 86.4)
U.S. Department of the Interior,
National Park Service,
Saint-Gaudens National Historic Site,
Cornish, New Hampshire
Washington only

66

Ringwalt & Brown

VIEW OF TRANSPARENCY, IN FRONT OF HEADQUARTERS OF SUPERVISORY COMMITTEE FOR RECRUITING COLORED REGIMENTS, CHESTNUT STREET, PHILADELPHIA, IN COMMEMORATION OF EMANCIPATION IN MARYLAND, NOVEMBER 1, 1864

c. 1864, woodcut print in four colors, 12 3/8 × 8 1/2 (31.5 × 21.6)
Library of Congress, Rare Book and Special Collections Division

67

Unknown photographer

WILLIAM H. CARNEY

c. 1887, gelatin silver print 5¼ × 3⅞ (13.4 × 9.8)

Carl J. Cruz Collection

68

CONGRESSIONAL MEDAL OF HONOR,
AWARDED TO SERGEANT WILLIAM H. CARNEY, CO. C,
54TH MASS. INF., FOR GALLANTRY AT FORT WAGNER, S.C.,
JULY 18, 1863 (obverse/reverse)
issued 1900, bronze and silk, 3¾ × 2⅛ (9.3 × 5.3)
Carl J. Cruz Collection

69

James E. Reed

WILLIAM H. CARNEY

c. 1901–1908, gelatin silver print, 5½ × 3¾ (13.8 × 9.3)
Moorland-Spingarn Research Center, Howard University

70

Curtis & Cameron Publishers

SHAW MEMORIAL

1897, photogravure, 16 3/8 × 20 1/8 (41.6 × 51.1)
U.S. Department of the Interior, National Park Service,
Saint-Gaudens National Historic Site, Cornish, New Hampshire

LEGACY

71

Lewis Hine

BLACK FAMILY BY FIREPLACE,
FROM THE SERIES "SOUTHERN NEGROES"

c. 1920, gelatin silver print, 4⅝ × 6⅜ (11.8 × 16.2)
Collection of George Eastman House
Washington only

141

72

Richard Benson

ROBERT GOULD SHAW MEMORIAL

1973, pigmented inkjet print, 2008, 12 × 15¼ (30.5 × 38.7)
National Gallery of Art, Gift of Susan and Peter MacGill

LEGACY

73

Richard Benson

ROBERT GOULD SHAW MEMORIAL

1973, pigmented inkjet print, 2008, 15 3/8 × 12 (38.9 × 30.5)
National Gallery of Art, Gift of Susan and Peter MacGill

74

Richard Benson

ROBERT GOULD SHAW MEMORIAL

1973, pigmented inkjet print, 2008, 10¼ × 13 (26 × 32.9)
National Gallery of Art, Gift of Susan and Peter MacGill

LEGACY

75

Richard Benson

ROBERT GOULD SHAW MEMORIAL

1973, pigmented ink jet print, 2008, 13 × 10 ¼ (32.8 × 26.1)
National Gallery of Art, Gift of Susan and Peter MacGill

76

Carrie Mae Weems

RESTLESS AFTER THE LONGEST WINTER YOU MARCHED
& MARCHED & MARCHED, FROM
"FROM HERE I SAW WHAT HAPPENED AND I CRIED"
1995–1996, chromogenic print with etched text on glass,
26½ × 22¾ (67.3 × 57.8)
Courtesy of the artist and Jack Shainman Gallery, New York

77

Carrie Mae Weems

DETAIL FROM THE SHAW MONUMENT,
FROM "THE HAMPTON PROJECT"

2000, digital photograph on muslin cloth and canvas,
59 ½ × 47 ½ (151.1 × 120.7)
Collection of Williams College Museum of Art, Williamstown, Massachusetts,
Museum purchase, Kathryn Hurd Fund

Caption by William Earle Williams
for his photograph
Sergeant Carney Monument, Norfolk, Virginia, 2004
(pl. 78)

James Fuller, a veteran of the 1st Colored Cavalry and Norfolk's first African American Councilman, led the effort to erect this monument and for the establishment of this section of Elmwood Cemetery known as West Point as a burial ground for Norfolk's African American citizens. The Civil War soldier depicted in the memorial statue is Norfolk native William Carney of the 54th Massachusetts Voluntary Infantry. Carney was in the lead column in the attack on Ft. Wagner on July 18, 1863. When the color bearer fell dead, Carney, despite being severely wounded, saved the flag from being captured. He was the first African American soldier to receive the Medal of Honor for his exceptional bravery in battle.

LEGACY

78

William Earle Williams

SERGEANT CARNEY MONUMENT, NORFOLK, VIRGINIA, 2004

2004, gelatin silver print, 9 ½ × 7 ½ (24.1 × 19.1)

National Gallery of Art, Charina Endowment Fund

149

79

William Earle Williams

FOLLY BEACH, SOUTH CAROLINA, 1999

1999, gelatin silver print, 7 ½ × 7 ½ (19.1 × 19.1)
National Gallery of Art,
Mary and Dan Solomon Fund

LEGACY

80

William Earle Williams

FOLLY BEACH LOOKING TOWARDS MORRIS ISLAND, 1999

1999, gelatin silver print, 7½ × 7½ (19.1 × 19.1)
National Gallery of Art,
Purchased as the Gift of the Gallery Girls

ROSTER OF THE 54TH MASSACHUSETTS REGIMENT

COMPILED BY LINDSAY HARRIS, ZOË SAMELS, NICOLE STRIBLING, AND MEGAN SWEENEY

Following are the names of more than 1,500 soldiers and officers who served with the 54th Massachusetts Regiment at some point between March 1863 and April 1865.[1] The men's age, place of origin, profession at enlistment, rank, and company are also provided if known. Most mustered in and out with the rank of private, but fifty-two were promoted to sergeant and two rose to become sergeants major—the highest rank then possible for an African American soldier.

The 54th Massachusetts Regiment was divided into eleven companies (A through K). About a quarter of the men were Massachusetts residents; others came from both Union and Confederate states as well as a handful of foreign countries. The average age at enlistment was twenty-four: the youngest gave his age as sixteen; the oldest as forty-seven.[2] Most of the black soldiers were farmers and laborers, while many of the white officers, including Colonel Robert Gould Shaw, abandoned their college studies or professional careers to join the Union army.

If known, an individual's fate at Fort Wagner on July 18, 1863, is listed as wounded, killed, missing and presumed dead, or survived. If it could be confirmed that a soldier was not present at Fort Wagner for any reason (such as discharged, transferred, deserted, captured, killed, or not yet mustered in before July 18, 1863), he is listed here as "(not present)."

We have made every effort to ensure the accuracy of the names and personal data presented and have provided only information that could be confirmed in primary sources.[3] It bears noting that Civil War military and pension records constituted the bulk of available archival materials, and that these records themselves were transcribed from oral communications and handwritten copies.[4]

Adams, Jacob, 39, Lenox, MA, laborer, private, Co. A, survived

Addison, David (alt.: Adason), 25, Sheffield, MA, laborer, private, Co. A (not present)

Addison, George, 26, Elmira, NY, barber, private, Co. E, survived

Addison, Henry, 25, Shippensburg, PA, mason, private, Co. K, survived

Adgurson, James M., 22, Milton, MA, farmer, private, Co. F (not present)

Aikens, William H., 26, Boston, MA, laborer, private, Co. A, wounded July 18, 1863, at Ft. Wagner

Albert, Henry, 42, Boston, MA, farmer, private, Co. A, killed July 18, 1863, at Ft. Wagner

Alexander, George, 18, Syracuse, NY, farmer, private, Co. H, survived

Allen, James, 26, Lafayette, IN, brakeman (?), private, Co. A, captured July 18, 1863, at Ft. Wagner

Allen, John W., 23, Logan County, OH, laborer, private, promoted to corporal, Co. G, survived

Allen, William, 25, VA, farmer, private, transferred to 55th Mass. (not present)

Allison, Charles, 36, Rehoboth, MA, farmer, private, Co. C, survived

Allison, George, 22, Philadelphia, PA, farmer, private, Co. B, missing July 18, 1863, after Ft. Wagner; supposed killed

Ampey, Isom, 21, Newport, IN, farmer, private, Co. K, survived

Ampey, Thomas R., 26, Newport, IN, laborer, private, Co. K, killed July 18, 1863, at Ft. Wagner

Anderson, Elijah, 30, Philadelphia, PA, stevedore, private, Co. B, survived

Anderson, Emery, 23, Burlington, VT, laborer, private (not present)

Anderson, James, 33, Chester County, PA, laborer, private, Co. G, wounded July 18, 1863, at Ft. Wagner

Anderson, John, 18, Carlisle, PA, baker, private, Co. G, survived

Anderson, John, 19, Lancaster, PA, shoemaker, private, Co. D, survived

Anderson, John H., 32, Chelsea, MA, barber, private, Co. C, wounded July 18, 1863, at Ft. Wagner

Anderson, John W., 32, Chester, PA, farmer, private, Co. D, survived

Anderson, Joseph, 18, Hartford, CT, farmer, private, transferred to 55th Mass. (not present)

Anderson, Lewis, 30, KY, laborer, private, Co. G, wounded July 18, 1863, at Ft. Wagner

Anderson, Solomon E., 34, West Chester, PA, farmer, private, Co. B, captured July 18, 1863, at Ft. Wagner

Anderson, Washington, 25, Chicago, IL, farmer, private, Co. H, survived

Anderson, William, 24, Xenia, OH, steward, private, Co. E, missing July 18, 1863, after Ft. Wagner

Annick, John H., 20, Toronto, Canada, waiter, private, Co. E, survived

Anthony, Francis, 25, Rutland, VT, laborer, private, Co. D (not present)

Appleton, John W.M., 30, Boston, MA, clerk (?), 2nd lieutenant, promoted to major, wounded July 18, 1863, at Ft. Wagner

Appleton, Thomas L., 21, Brighton MA, salesman (?), 2nd lieutenant, promoted to captain, Co. B, survived

Archer, Sylvester, 20, Binghampton, NY, farmer, private, Co. F, survived

Armstrong, George A., 22, Philadelphia, PA, barber, private, promoted to corporal, Co. B (not present)

Armstrong, Wesley R., 39, Horseheads, NY, blacksmith, private, Co. F, wounded July 18, 1863, at Ft. Wagner

*__Arnum, Charles H.,__ 21, Littleton, MA, teamster, private, Co. E (not present) [pl. 25]

Artis, Elias, 30, Shelby County, OH, farmer, private, Co. D, wounded July 18, 1863, at Ft. Wagner

*Asterisks indicate illustrations in catalogue.

Artist, Joseph, 23, Urbana, OH, laborer, private, Co. K, survived

Asberry, Joseph, 22, Oberlin, OH, farmer, private, Co. F, survived

Asbury, Thomas, 25, Dayton, OH, cook, private, Co. I, survived

Ashport, Lemuel A., 18, South Bridgewater, MA, farmer, private, Co. I (not present)

Atkins, Charles G., 21, Mount Morris, NY, boatman, private, Co. G, survived

Atlee, Abner, 25, Morristown, PA, farmer, private, Co. I, survived

Augustus, Charles, 30, Ypsilanti, MI, blacksmith, private, promoted to corporal, Co. I, missing July 18, 1863, after Ft. Wagner

Bailey, David, 22, Philadelphia, PA, laborer, private, Co. B, missing July 18, 1863, after Ft. Wagner; supposed killed

Baker, George, 30, Montrose, PA, laborer, private, Co. C, survived

Baldwin, William, laborer, private

Ball, Thomas, 21, Boston, MA, private, transferred to 55th Mass. (not present)

Ballard, Jacob, 29, Philadelphia, PA, farmer, private, Co. B, survived

Ballou, Owen, 23, Harrisburg, PA, farmer, private, promoted to corporal, Co. E, survived

Bancroft, John, 26, Stoughton, MA, shoemaker, private, Co. A, wounded July 18, 1863, at Ft. Wagner

Baptist, Benjamin D., 20, Mount Pleasant, OH, plasterer, private, Co. K, survived

Barcas, Ezekiel L., 36, Philadelphia, PA, brickmaker, private, Co. B, survived

Barker, John L., 28, Oberlin, OH, farmer, private, promoted to sergeant, Co. G, wounded July 18, 1863, at Ft. Wagner

Barks, William T., 23, Montrose, PA, moulder, private, promoted to corporal, Co. D, survived

Barnes, William, 20, Mercersburg, PA, laborer, private, Co. I, survived

Barquet, Joseph H., 40, Galesburg, IL, mason, private, Co. H, survived

Barrett, Isaac, 19, Urbana, OH, farmer, private, Co. E, wounded July 18, 1863, at Ft. Wagner

Barrett, William, 20, Salem, OH, laborer, private, Co. K, survived

Barrows, John, 30, Washington, NC, steward, private, transferred to 55th Mass. (not present)

Barton, Lot Lee, 27, Chatham Four Corners, NY, farmer, private, Co. C, survived

Barton, Thomas, 27, Chatham Four Corners, NY, seaman, private, Co. A (not present)

Bass, John, 20, Columbus, OH, laborer, private, Co. I, survived

Bassett, Almon H., 20, Pittsfield, MA, served as 2nd lieutenant, survived

Bateman, Charles, 18, Northampton, MA, farmer, private, Co. H (not present)

Batson, John, 20, Peachbottom, PA, laborer, private, Co. G, survived

Battis, John, 25, Boston, MA, sailor, private, Co. E (not present)

Battles, Robert Henry, 38, Dedham, MA, hostler/smith, private, Co. G (not present)

Bayard, Joseph, 28, Lockport, NY, turnkey, private, Co. K, wounded and captured July 18, 1863, at Ft. Wagner

Beach, Samuel, 29, Hingham, MA, laborer, private, transferred to 55th Mass. (not present)

Beatenbough, Andrew (alt.: Betenbough), 23, Hamilton, OH, carpenter (?), private, Co. I, survived

Beatty, Jones, 20, New Lisbon, OH, laborer, private, Co. I, survived

*__Becker, Theodore J.,__ 32, physician (?), private, served as hospital steward, survived [p. 14, fig. 7]

Bell, Charles, 19, Boston, MA, servant, private, Co. F (not present)

Bell, Charles H., 20, Albany, NY, waiter, private, promoted to corporal, Co. E, survived

Bell, Henry, 22, Binghampton, NY, laborer, private, Co. E, survived

Bell, Nathaniel, 23, Carlisle, PA, laborer, private, Co. I, survived

Bell, Samuel, 26, New York, NY, hostler, private, promoted to corporal, Co. E (not present)

Bell, William, 21, Carlisle, PA, brickmaker, private, Co. I, survived

Bennett, Horace B., 25, Middletown, PA, farmer, private, promoted to sergeant, Co. F, survived

Bennett, William, 17, Jackson County, TN, private (not present)

Benson, John, 30, brickmaker, private, Co. D (not present)

Benton, Andrew, 28, waiter, private, promoted to sergeant, Co. A, missing July 18, 1863, after Ft. Wagner

Benton, Anthony, 19, Hudson, NY, laborer, private, Co. A, survived

Benton, Nelson R., 28, Catskill, NY, laborer, private, Co. C, wounded July 18, 1863, at Ft. Wagner

*****Benton, Samuel J.,** 18, New York, NY, waiter, private, Co. A, survived [pl. 32]

Berry, Elijah, 19, Lancaster, PA, laborer, private, Co. D (not present)

Berry, Joseph S., 22, Franklin County, PA, laborer, private, Co. D, survived

Berry, Samuel, 23, West Chester, PA, farmer, private, Co. A, survived

Betts, Thomas, 19, Columbus, OH, waiter, private, Co. I, survived

Beverly, Thomas, 21, Columbus, OH, laborer, private, Co. I (not present)

Biddle, Eli G., 17, Boston, MA, painter, private, Co. A, wounded July 18, 1863, at Ft. Wagner

Bird, Levi, 37, Pittsfield, MA, laborer, private, Co. A, survived

Blackburn, John, 20, New Bedford, MA, laborer, private, Co. C (not present)

Blackburn, John W., 18, New Bedford, MA, laborer, private, Co. C, survived

Blakes, Lemuel (alt.: Samuel), 21, West Chester, PA, farmer, private, Co. B (not present)

Body, Charles, 28, Lancaster County, PA, laborer, private, Co. G, missing July 18, 1863, after Ft. Wagner

Bond, Benjamin M., 38, Boston, MA, cook, private, Co. B (not present)

Bond, Frederick L., 22, Binghampton, NY, teamster, private, promoted to corporal, Co. E, wounded July 18, 1863, at Ft. Wagner

Bond, John H., 19, Binghampton, NY, farmer, private, Co. F, survived

Bond, William H., 19, laborer, private, Co. E, survived

Bosley, Joseph E., 30, Worcester, MA, laborer, private, Co. B, survived

Boss, Caleb, 19, Boston, MA, sailor, private, Co. D (not present)

Boulden, John A., 27, Cleveland, OH, saddler (?), private, promoted to corporal, Co. G, wounded July 18, 1863, at Ft. Wagner

Bounds, Robert, 20, Hudson, NY, farmer, private, Co. A, survived

Bowman, Thomas, 27, Cincinnati, OH, trader, private, promoted to sergeant, Co. I, survived

Bowser, Charles, 18, Middletown, PA, laborer, private, Co. F, survived

Boyd, Milton Taylor, 33, Chester County, PA, farmer, private, Co. B (not present)

Boyer, Frank, 19, Elmira, NY, farmer, private, Co. F, survived

Boyer, James, 21, New Bedford, MA, seaman, private (not present)

Brace, Peter, 18, St. Albans, VT, laborer, private, Co. E (not present)

Braddish, Elisha, 31, Woodstock, VT, laborer, private, Co. K (not present)

Bradford, John, 21, Harrisburg, PA, laborer, private, Co. I, survived

Bradley, Daniel, 20, Philadelphia, PA, brickmaker, private, Co. B, survived

Bradley, Jeremiah, 34, South Adams, MA, farmer, private, Co. B (not present)

Brady, Randolph, 24, Hamilton, OH, shoemaker, private, promoted to corporal, Co. I, missing July 18, 1863, after Ft. Wagner

Brady, William, 21, Salem, OH, barber, private, Co. K, killed July 18, 1863, at Ft. Wagner

Branson, Alexander, 21, Philadelphia, PA, barber, private, Co. B, survived

Branson, Samuel, 21, Philadelphia, PA, shoemaker, private, Co. B, survived

Brewster, Henry S., 21, Boston, MA, shoemaker, private, Co. C, survived

Bridge, Watson W., 26, Wilbraham, MA, clerk (?), lieutenant, promoted to captain, Co. F, survived

Bridgham, Charles B., 22, Buckfield, MA, student (?), asst. surgeon, promoted to 1st lieutenant/asst. surgeon, survived

Bridgham, Thomas S., 26, Buckfield, ME, lawyer (?), 2nd lieutenant, promoted to 1st lieutenant, Co. C (not present)

Briggs, Charles E., 30, Boston, MA, physician (?), surgeon, promoted to major and surgeon (not present)

Briggs, Chauncey, 20, Castleton, VT, farmer, private, Co. D (not present)

Briggs, Royal, 18, Rutland, VT, barber, private, Co. D (not present)

Briggs, William M., 21, Albany, NY, waiter, private, Co. E, wounded July 18, 1863, at Ft. Wagner

Bright, Alfred, discharged after December 1863

Brittania, Lorenzo (alt.: Brittanio), 34, New Bedford, MA, seaman, private, Co. I (not present)

Broadwater, William, 23, Havre de Grace, MD, mariner, private, Co. E (not present)

Broady, George, 28, Battle Creek, MI, laborer, private, Co. H, wounded July 18, 1863, at Ft. Wagner

Bronson, David, 20, Berryville, PA, laborer, private, Co. K, wounded July 18, 1863, at Ft. Wagner

Brooks, James J., 23, Bellows Falls, VT, farmer, private, Co. H (not present)

Brooks, John H., 36, Philadelphia, PA, waterman, private, Co. B, missing July 18, 1863, after Ft. Wagner; supposed killed

Brooks, William H., 28, Rutland, VT, laborer, private, Co. H (not present)

*****Brown, Abraham F.,** 30, Toronto, Canada, sailor, private, Co. E (not present) [pls. 23, 24]

Brown, Charles, 23 (22?), Boston, MA, farmer, private, Co. E (not present)

Brown, Charles, 23, Sunberry, PA, farmer, private, Co. E, survived

Brown, Charles, private, transferred to 55th Mass.

Brown, David, 35, Reading, PA, laborer, private, Co. H, survived

Brown, David, 39, Eastern Shore, MD, private, transferred to 55th Mass. (not present)

Brown, Fielding C., 23, Lebanon, OH, barber, private, promoted to 1st sergeant, Co. G, survived

Brown, George, 16, Chicago, IL, laborer, private, Co. H, survived

Brown, George, 20, West Chester, PA, farmer, private, Co. B, survived

Brown, Henry, 19, Hollidaysburg, PA, farmer, private, Co. B, survived

Brown, Henry, 37, Toledo, OH, laborer, private, Co. K, survived

Brown, Isaac, 21, Pittsburgh, PA, waiter, private, Co. K, survived

Brown, James, 33, Bardstown, KY, laborer, private, Co. F, survived

Brown, James E., 26, Oberlin, OH, laborer, private, Co. F, survived

Brown, Jessie H., 23, West Chester, PA, farmer, private, Co. B, wounded and captured July 18, 1863, at Ft. Wagner

Brown, John, 25, Fort Erie, Canada, sailor, private, Co. F, survived

Brown, John, 32, Zanzibar, Africa, private, transferred to 55th Mass. (not present)

Brown, John, private, transferred to 55th Mass.

Brown, John A., 18, Steubenville, OH, farmer, private, Co. F, survived

Brown, John H., 19, Kalamazoo, MI, farmer, private, Co. I, survived

Brown, John S., 18, Worcester, MA, laborer, private, Co. A, survived

Brown, Joseph, 35, Cazenovia, NY, laborer, private, Co. E, survived

Brown, Morris, 22, West Chester, PA, wagoner, private, Co. B, missing July 18, 1863, after Ft. Wagner; supposed killed

Brown, Nathan, 23, Bryan, OH, cook, private, Co. E (not present)

Brown, Peter, 21, MI, farmer, private, transferred to 55th Mass. (not present)

Brown, Robert, 21, Castleton, VT, laborer, private (not present)

Brown, Thomas A., 44, Harrisburg, PA, laborer, private, Co. E (not present)

Brown, William, 19, Detroit, MI, sailor, private, Co. E, survived

Brown, William H., 22, Wilberforce, OH, farmer, private, promoted to corporal, Co. K, survived

Brown, William R., 26, Elmira, NY, laborer, private, promoted to corporal, Co. F, survived

Brummzig, George, 20, Mercersburg, PA, laborer, private, Co. I, survived

Buchanan, James, 22, New Bedford, MA, laborer, served as corporal, Co. C, survived

Buck, Henry George, 22, Philadelphia, PA, laborer, private, Co. B, survived

Buck, William W., 31, Lebanon, CT, private (not present)

Bump, Austin S., served as 1st lieutenant

Bundy, George L., 23, Worcester, MA, barber, private, promoted to sergeant, Co. A, wounded July 18, 1863, at Ft. Wagner

Burch, William A., 25, New York, NY, waiter (?), private, Co. E, survived

Burdoo, Silas, 37, Woodstock, VT, farmer, private, Co. H (not present)

Burgess, Thomas E., 22, Mercersburg, PA, carpenter, private, Co. I, wounded July 18, 1863, at Ft. Wagner

Burgess, William, 20, Mercersburg, PA, laborer, private, Co. K, wounded July 18, 1863, at Ft. Wagner

Burgess, William H., 25, Mercersburg, PA, laborer, private, Co. K, wounded July 18, 1863, at Ft. Wagner

Burghardt, Henry F., 21, North Lee, MA, mason, private, Co. A, killed July 18, 1863, at Ft. Wagner

Burkett, Elisha, 35, Newport, IN, farmer, private, Co. H (not present)

Burns, John, 21, Bath County, KY, laborer, private, Co. D (not present)

Burns, John, 34, Bowling Green, MO, laborer, private, Co. H, survived

Burns, Robert, 21, private (not present)

Burrell, Sylvester, 19, Lancaster County, PA, laborer, private, Co. D, survived

Burton, Reuben, 38, Rutland, VT, farmer, private (not present)

Bush, Henry, 26, Baltimore, MD, seaman, private, Co. D (not present)

*****Bush, James W.,** 20, Xenia, OH, student, private, promoted to 1st sergeant, Co. K, survived [pl. 28]

Butler, Albert, 27, Peekskill, NY, engineer, private, Co. K, survived

Butler, Daniel, brush maker, private

Butler, David, 29, Welsh Run, PA, tanner, private, Co. I, survived

Butler, George, 23, Harrisburg, PA, laborer, private, Co. E, survived

Butler, George, 29, Peekskill, NY, hostler, private, Co. H (not present)

Butler, George, laborer (?), private, Co. E (not present)

Butler, Joseph, 25, Harrisburg, PA, laborer, private, Co. D, survived

Butler, Morris, 19, Mount Holly, NY, laborer, private, Co. E, captured July 18, 1863, at Ft. Wagner

Butler, Richard, 24, Franklin County, PA, farmer, private, Co. D, survived

Butler, Wm., 22, Boston, MA, farmer, private, Co. D (not present)

Byard, Robert, 26, St. Albans, VT, laborer, private, Co. C, survived

Cain, William, 18, Xenia, OH, laborer, private, Co. G, survived

Calaman, Joseph, 20 (30?), Trenton, NJ, laborer, private, Co. E, survived

Caldwell, Charles, 21, Baltimore, MD, private, transferred to 55th Mass. (not present)

Caldwell, James, 19, Battle Creek, MI, blacksmith, private, Co. H (not present)

Caldwell, Reuben, 22, Galesburg, IL, laborer, private, Co. H, survived

Campbell, Joseph R., 23, New Bedford, MA, caulker, corporal, Co. C, missing July 18, 1863, after Ft. Wagner

Canady, Barker, 23, East Stoughton, MA, farmer, private, Co. F (not present)

Cannon, Henry, 41, seaman, private, Co. D (not present)

Cardorone, Donald, 21, Valparaiso, Chile, seaman, private, transferred to 55th Mass. (not present)

*****Carney, William H.,** 22, New Bedford, MA, seaman, private, promoted to sergeant, Co. C, wounded July 18, 1863, at Ft. Wagner [pls. 67, 69; p. 6, fig. 2; p. 18, fig. 11]

Carraway, John, 30, Newbern, NC, tailor, private, Co. A (not present)

Carrington, Evan, private, Co. E (not present)

Carroll, Samuel, 26, Nashville, TN, barber, private, promoted to corporal, Co. K, survived

Carroll, William, 22, Harrisburg, PA, laborer, private, Co. F, survived

Carson, Arthur, 25, Mercersburg, PA, laborer, private, Co. K, survived

Carson, George, 21, Mercersburg, PA, laborer, private, Co. I, survived

Carter, Henry J., 20, Lenox, MA, stonecutter, private, promoted to sergeant, Co. G, survived

Carter, Jacob, 26, Syracuse, NY, barber, private, Co. E, wounded July 18, 1863, at Ft. Wagner

Carter, Levi, 38, Elmira, NY, laborer, private, Co. F, survived

Cass, Isaiah, 24, Woodford, KY, laborer, private, Co. C, survived

Cassell, Charles C., 32, Baltimore, MD, stoveworker, private, transferred to 55th Mass. (not present)

Cassell, John M., 42, Baltimore, MD, barber, private, transferred to 55th Mass. (not present)

Cebolt, William, 27, New Bedford, MA, farmer, private, Co. D (not present)

Cezar, Garnet G., 18, Buffalo, NY, porter, sergeant, promoted to sergeant, Co. D, wounded July 18, 1863, at Ft. Wagner

Champion, John Battis, 22, Dominique, WI, laborer, private, Co. K (not present)

Champlin, David H., 28, Hingham, MA, laborer, private, promoted to corporal, Co. B (not present)

Champlin, Dennis V., 23, Amherst, MA, laborer, private, transferred to 55th Mass. (not present)

Champlin, Jason, 30, Shutesbury, MA, farmer, private, Co. K (not present)

Chaney, Cato, 34, Carthagena, OH, farmer, private, Co. D, wounded July 18, 1863, at Ft. Wagner

Charles, George T., 24, Richmond, IN, barber, private, Co. E, survived

Charlton, Henry C., 21, Cincinnati, OH, boatman, private, Co. I, wounded July 18, 1863, at Ft. Wagner

Chase, Jacob C., 22, Philadelphia, PA, tinsmith, private, transferred to 55th Mass. (not present)

Chipman, Charles G., 22, Salem, MA, clerk (?), 2nd lieutenant, promoted to captain, Co. D (not present)

Christy, Jacob, 19, Mercersburg, PA, laborer, private, Co. I, wounded July 18, 1863, at Ft. Wagner

Christy, Joseph, 16, Mercersburg, PA, woodcutter, private, Co. I, survived

Christy, Samuel, 23, Mercersburg, PA, laborer, private, Co. I, survived

Christy, William, 21, Mercersburg, PA, laborer, private, Co. I, survived

Churchman, John, 19, Carthagena, OH, laborer, private, Co. K, survived

Clark, Andrew, 30, Chester County, PA, laborer, private, Co. D, killed July 18, 1863, at Ft. Wagner

Clark, Charles, 18, South Framingham, MA, farmer, private, Co. G, wounded July 18, 1863, at Ft. Wagner

Clark, George H., 40, Sandwich, MA, laborer, private, Co. H (not present)

Clark, Isaac Jefferson, 23, Philadelphia, PA, farmer, private, Co. B, survived

Clark, John W. H., 27, Boston, MA, laborer, private, Co. H, survived

Clark, Lewis, 19, Lebanon, OH, laborer, private, Co. C, survived

Clark, Theodore, 21, Savannah, GA, laborer, private, transferred to 55th Mass. (not present)

Clark, Thomas, 27, Frankfort, KY, teamster, private, Co. G, survived

Clayton, Samuel, 18, Mount Holly, NY, laborer, private, Co. E, survived

Cleveland, Abram, 21, Syracuse, NY, laborer, private, Co. E, survived

Cleveland, James, 18, Cincinnati, OH, farmer, private, Co. G, survived

Clifford, George, 26, Martinsburg, VA, brickmaker, private, promoted to corporal, Co. H, survived

Clow, John I., 37, Stockbridge, MA, laborer, private, Co. B (not present)

Coatney, Rodolphus, 18, Green County, OH, farmer, private, Co. C, survived

Coburn, George E., 41, Boston, MA, laborer, private, Co. D, survived

Cogswell, George E., 18, Laconia, NH, farmer, private, Co. D, missing July 18, 1863, after Ft. Wagner

Coker, George W., 18, Brownsville, MI, laborer, private, Co. H, survived

Cole, James, 19, Oxford PA, farmer, private, Co. B, wounded July 18, 1863, at Ft. Wagner

Cole, Josiah, 19, Chester County, PA, farmer, private, Co. B, survived

Cole, Philip, 19, Middletown, PA, laborer, private, promoted to corporal, Co. F, survived

Cole, William, 27, Middletown, PA, laborer, private, Co. F, survived

Coleman, George B., 28, Salem, MA, barber, private, transferred to 55th Mass. (not present)

Coleman, James, 20, Adrian, MI, farmer, private, Co. G, wounded July 18, 1863, at Ft. Wagner

Coleman, John, 19, Adrian, MI, farmer, private, Co. G, wounded July 18, 1863, at Ft. Wagner

Coleman, Samuel, 37, Cincinnati, OH, laborer, private, Co. I, survived

Coleman, William, 18, private, Co. G

Collins, John H. W., 22, Chicago, IL, printer, private, promoted to sergeant, Co. H, wounded July 18, 1863, at Ft. Wagner

Conant, John H., 22, Brighton, MA, 2nd lieutenant, promoted to 1st lieutenant, Co. A (not present)

Conaway, Shedrick (alt.: Shederick), 19, Cleveland, OH, waiter, private, promoted to sergeant, Co. G, survived

Cook, William, 22, Huntington, PA, brickmaker, private, Co. G, survived

Cooper, George, 23, Windsor, Canada, cook, private, Co. G, survived

Cooper, Lloyd, 27, Cincinnati, OH, laborer, private, Co. K, survived

Cooper, Peter S., 27, Medford, MA, brickmaker, private, Co. F, survived

Cooper, Thomas F., 26, West Chester, PA, laborer, private, Co. B, wounded July 18, 1863, at Ft. Wagner

Cooper, Watson, 18, Medfield, MA, servant, private, Co. A, survived

Cornish, Alford, 18, Binghampton, NY, painter, private, promoted to corporal, Co. F, survived

Cornish, John, 36, Springfield, MA, laborer, private, Co. C, survived

Cornish, Russell, 27, Hartford, CT, waiter, private (not present)

Cotton, Asa, 21, Xenia, OH, farmer, private, promoted to sergeant, Co. K, survived

Counsel, George, 26, West Chester, PA, laborer, private, Co. B (not present)

Cousens, Joseph E., 40, Newton, MA, carpenter (?), 2nd lieutenant, promoted to captain, Co. E (not present)

Cousins, William, 18, Niles, MI, farmer, private, Co. I, survived

Covington, Evans, 30, Newburyport, MA, barber, private, Co. E (not present)

Cowen, George, 22, Oxford, OH, barber, private, Co. I, survived

Craft, Samuel, 20, Naponock, NY, boatman, private, Co. D (not present)

Cragg, Robert, 22, Mercer County, OH, farmer, private, Co. D, survived

Craig, Henry, 47, Cincinnati, OH, boatman, private, Co. K, killed July 18, 1863, at Ft. Wagner

Craig, Noah, 28, New Bedford, MA, seaman, private, Co. C, survived

Cranch, George W., 18, student (?), 2nd lieutenant, promoted to 1st lieutenant, Co. B (not present)

Crawford, Joshua, 35, Peekskill, NY, laborer, private, Co. E (not present)

Creamer, Charles L., 18, Syracuse, NY, laborer, private, Co. E, wounded July 18, 1863, at Ft. Wagner

Croger, George A., 29, Elmira, NY, laborer, private, promoted to corporal, Co. F, survived

Crooks, Joseph, 34, Valparaiso, Chile, mariner, private, transferred to 55th Mass. (not present)

Crosier, Silas, 18, Bristol, VT, farmer, private, Co. K (not present)

Croslear, Edward A., 26, Sheffield, MA, laborer, private, Co. B (not present)

Cross, Jerome B., 29, Richmond, VA, upholsterer, private (not present)

Cross, Martin B., 31, Catskill, NY, barber, private, promoted to sergeant, Co. A, wounded July 18, 1863, at Ft. Wagner

Crossler, Chauncy, 33, Norfolk, CT, farmer, private, Co. F, survived

Crozier, Eugene, 21, Bristol, VT, farmer, private, Co. A, survived

Crozier, Nelson, 25, Lincoln, VT, laborer, private, Co. A, survived

Crozier, Oscar James, 20, Philadelphia, PA, hostler, private, Co. B (not present)

Cuff, Thomas, 21, Mercersburg, PA, quarryman, private, Co. I, survived

Cummings, Aaron, 22, York County, PA, laborer, private, Co. G, survived

Cunningham, Charles, 19, Middletown, PA, farmer, private, Co. F, survived

Cunningham, Ferdinand, 19, Mount Holly, NY, farmer, private, Co. F, survived

Cunningham, William A., 20, Montgomery, NY, boatman, private, Co. G, survived

Curry, Josephus, 20, Washington, PA, farmer, private, Co. G, killed July 18, 1863, at Ft. Wagner

Curtis, Bishop E., 23, private, Co. H (not present)

Cutler, George R., 22, Boston, MA, hostler, private, Co. A, survived

Dadford, Thomas, 34, Harrisburg, PA, barber, private, Co. F (not present)

Dandridge, James, 26, Winchester, PA, waiter, private, Co. G (not present)

Daniels, Pleasant, 21, Memphis, TN, drayman, private, Co. K, survived

Darks, Charles H., 18, Mercersburg, PA, farmer, private, Co. K, survived

Darks, Edward, 25, Mercersburg, PA, farmer, private, Co. K, survived

Davenport, James, 33, Brookline, MA, laborer, private, Co. I (not present)

Davis, Anthony, 26, Jackson, LA, farmer, private, Co. G, wounded July 18, 1863, at Ft. Wagner

Davis, Edward, 20, Harrisburg, PA, moulder, private, Co. E, survived

Davis, Enoch, 27, East Troy, NY, laborer, private, Co. C, survived

Davis, Frank, 18, Elmira, NY, laborer, private, Co. F (not present)

Davis, James, 18, Columbia, PA, laborer, private, Co. D, survived

Davis, Jefferson H., 20, Boston, MA, private, Co. K (not present)

Davis, Jeremiah, 33, Philadelphia, PA, farmer, private, promoted to corporal, Co. B, survived

Davis, John, 19, Galesburg, IL, laborer, private, Co. H, survived

Davis, John E., 28, Niagara, NY, farmer, private, Co. D (not present)

Davis, John H., 22, Chicago, IL, waiter, private, promoted to corporal, Co. H, survived

Davis, Thomas, 23, Oswego, NY, sailor, private, Co. D, wounded July 18, 1863, at Ft. Wagner

Davis, William, 19, Canada, waiter, private, transferred to 55th Mass. (not present)

Davis, William, 35, Elmira, NY, laborer, private, Co. F (not present)

Davis, William A., 38, St. Albans, VT, barber, private, Co. F (not present)

Day, Robert M., 20, Philadelphia, PA, laborer, private, Co. B, survived

Day, Solomon, 26, Washtenaw, MI, cook, private, Co. G, survived

Dean, Anthony A., 33, Cleveland, OH, cook (?), private, Co. E, wounded July 18, 1863, at Ft. Wagner

Debois, Jacob, 24, Belleville NJ, waiter, private, transferred to 55th Mass. (not present)

Decker, John, 23, Syracuse, NY, laborer, private, Co. E, survived

Deforest, Andrew, 19, Syracuse, NY, waiter (?), private, promoted to sergeant, Co. E, wounded July 18, 1863, at Ft. Wagner

Delaney, Toussaint L.O., 18, Chatham, Canada, student, private, Co. D, survived

Delevan, George, 41, New Bedford, MA, laborer, served as corporal, Co. C, wounded July 18, 1863, at Ft. Wagner

Deming, Orin, 21, Monston, VT, laborer, private, Co. A, survived

Demory, Francis, 35, New Bedford, MA, waiter, private, Co. C, survived

Demus, Charles M., 18, Harrisburg, PA, laborer, private, Co. G (not present)

Demus, David, 22, Mercersburg, PA, farmer, private, Co. K, wounded July 18, 1863, at Ft. Wagner

Demus, George, 18, Mercersburg, PA, farmer, private, Co. K, survived

Dennis, Henry, 27, Ithaca, NY, barber, private, promoted to corporal, Co. H (not present)

Depp, Stephen, 33, Lebanon, OH, farmer, private, Co. C, survived

Derrick, Benjamin, 36, Cooperstown, NY, farmer, private, Co. F, survived

Dexter, Benjamin F., 21, Cambridge, MA, laborer (?), served as 2nd lieutenant, Co. C, survived

Dexter, Thomas, 20, Plymouth, MA, laborer, private, Co. C (not present)

Dickerson, Wesley, 38, Burbon County, KY, farmer, private (not present)

Dickinson, John W., 30, Galesburg, IL, teamster, private, Co. H (not present)

Dickson, Anderson (alt.: Alex), 19, Muscatine, IA, farmer, private, Co. B, survived

Disbrow, Theodore, 30, laborer (?), private, Co. E, survived

Dixon, Henry A., 21, Boston, MA, mason, private, Co. A, survived

Dixon, John W., 22, West Chester, PA, farmer, private, Co. B, survived

Dogan, Francis, 21, Springfield, OH, servant, private, Co. I (not present)

Dolby, Cyrus, 31, Fairhaven, VT, farmer, private, Co. D (not present)

Dorsey, George W., 24, Adrian, MI, laborer, private, Co. F, survived

Dorsey, Thomas, 23, Harrisburg, PA, laborer, private, Co. I, survived

Dorsey, William, 35, Cleveland, OH, waiter, private, Co. H (not present)

Douglass, Charles H., 23, Toronto, Canada, laborer, private, Co. I, survived

Douglass, Charles R., 19, Rochester, NY, printer, private, Co. F, survived

Douglass, John, 23, West Chester, PA, farmer, private, Co. B, survived

*****Douglass, Lewis H.,** 22, Boston, MA, laborer, private, promoted to sergeant major, Co. F, wounded July 18, 1863, at Ft. Wagner [pls. 21, 46]

Dover, John H., 18, Buffalo, NY, confectioner, private, promoted to sergeant, Co. D, survived

Downing, James, 26, New Bedford, MA, barber, private, Co. C, survived

Draper, Charles, 18, Philadelphia, PA, drummer, private, Co. B, survived

Dugan, George W., 44, Concord, MA, farmer, private, Co. A, missing July 18, 1863, after Ft. Wagner

Duggin, Frank, 20, Washington, DC, private, transferred to 55th Mass. (not present)

Duncan, Justin M., 19, Chester, MA, laborer, private, Co. A, survived

Duncan, Lorenzo S., 21, Hinsdale, MA, farmer, private, Co. A, survived

Duncan, Orrin, 30, Lanesboro, MA, seaman, private, transferred to 55th Mass. (not present)

Duncan, Samuel, 22, Franklin County, OH, sailor, private, Co. G, survived

Dunlap, Cyrus, 25, Pittsburgh, PA, laborer, private, Co. K, survived

Duren, Charles M., 21, Cambridge, MA, clerk (?), 2nd lieutenant, promoted to 1st lieutenant/adjutant, Cos. F,D (not present)

Dustin, Moses N., 33, Canterbury, VT, farmer, private, Co. D (not present)

Easley, David, 26, private, Co. H (not present)

Easton, James H., 20, Newport, RI, laborer, private, Co. C, survived

Ebbitts, William H.H., 22, Worcester, MA, yeoman, private, Co. F (not present)

Edgerly, William, 20, Lancaster County, PA, laborer, private, Co. D, killed July 18, 1863, at Ft. Wagner

Edmands, Benjamin B., 39, Brookline MA, potter (?), 2nd lieutenant, promoted to 1st lieutenant, Cos. F,H (not present)

Edrington, William, 21, Centerville, IN, laborer, private, Co. K, survived

Edwards, John, 25, Boyle County, TX, private (not present)

Edwards, John, 30, Philadelphia, PA, laborer, private, Co. C, survived

Ellender, George, 33, York County, PA, laborer, private, Co. G, wounded July 18, 1863, at Ft. Wagner

Elletts, James (alt.: Eletts), 27, Hollidaysburg, PA, laborer, private, Co. B, captured July 18, 1863, at Ft. Wagner

Elletts, Samuel (alt.: Eletts), 18, Hollidaysburg, PA, farmer, private, Co. B, survived

Ellis, Charles L., 30, Hyannis, MA, barber, private, Co. D (not present)

Ellis, George J.F., 19, Providence, RI, hostler, private, Co. A, missing July 18, 1863, after Ft. Wagner

Ellis, Henry, 18, Cincinnati, OH, hackman, private, Co. G, survived

Ellis, Jefferson, 19, Poughkeepsie, NY, boatman, private, promoted to corporal, Co. F, survived

Ellis, William, 24, Cincinnati, OH, railroading, private, promoted to corporal, Co. G, wounded July 18, 1863, at Ft. Wagner

Emerson, Edward B., 17, Pittsfield, MA, student (?), 2nd lieutenant, promoted to captain, Cos. A,D,E, survived

*****Emilio, Luis F.,** 17, Salem, MA, student (?), 2nd lieutenant, promoted to captain, Co. E, survived [pls. 35, 36]

Endicott, Henry C., 19, Plymouth, MA, waiter, private, Co. I (not present)

Ennis, Stephen, 25, Montrose, PA, musician, private, Co. C, survived

Esau, Albert E., 23, Warren, MA, seaman (?), private, Co. E (not present)

Etheridge, Andrew J., 18, Kishwaukee, IL, laborer, private, Co. H, survived

Evans, Albert, 28, Springfield, OH, machinist, private, Co. D, killed July 18, 1863, at Ft. Wagner

Evans, George, 22, Xenia, OH, barber, private, Co. G, survived

Evans, Richard, 34, Xenia, OH, barber, private, Co. G, wounded July 18, 1863, at Ft. Wagner

Everson, William H., 19, Albany, NY, laborer, private, Co. E, survived

Everson, William S., 22, New York, NY, farmer, private, Co. K (not present)

Evins, Joseph (alt.: Evans), 22, Green County, OH, plasterer, private, Co. C, survived

Fairchild, Lewis L., 40, Greenfield, MA, farmer (?), private, Co. H (not present)

Fairchild, Lewis L., 40, New Milford, CT, farmer, private, transferred to 55th Mass. (not present)

Farmer, George, 39, Unionville, PA, farmer, private, promoted to corporal, Co. B, survived

Ferman, John (alt.: Firman), 21, Philadelphia, PA, boot bringer, private, Co. D, survived

Ferris, John R., 27, Great Barrington, MA, laborer, private, Co. B (not present)

Field, Henry A., 36, Xenia, OH, painter, private, promoted to corporal, Co. K, survived

Finess, Jacob, 21, Rochester, NY, teamster, private (not present)

Finnemore, Charles A., 27, Amherst, MA, farmer, private, Co. C, survived

Fisher, Albanus S., 32, Norristown, PA, laborer, private, promoted to sergeant, Co. I, survived

Fisher, Benjamin, 19, Newbern, NC, waiter, private, Co. E, survived

Fisher, George, 25, Cumberland County, PA, farmer, private, Co. D, wounded July 18, 1863, at Ft. Wagner

Fleetwood, Lewis A., 21, New Bedford, MA, laborer, private, Co. C, wounded July 18, 1863, at Ft. Wagner

Fletcher, David S., 20, New Bedford, MA, hostler, private, promoted to corporal, Co. C, wounded July 18, 1863, at Ft. Wagner

Fletcher, Francis H., 22, Salem, MA, clerk, private, promoted to sergeant, Co. A, survived

Fletcher, Isaac, 23, VA, laborer, private, transferred to 55th Mass. (not present)

Fletcher, Merrick, 43, farmer, private, Co. C, survived

Flora, Samuel, 29, Fort Monroe, VA, farmer, private, transferred to 55th Mass. (not present)

Floyd, Thomas, 20, Cincinnati, OH, barber, private, Co. K, survived

Foot, Abram, 22, Spencer, NY, farmer, private, Co. F, survived

Ford, Joseph, 21, Boston, MA, laborer, private, Co. A, missing July 18, 1863, after Ft. Wagner

Ford, Samuel, 26, Lancaster, PA, laborer, private, Co. K, killed July 18, 1863, at Ft. Wagner

Foster, Charles, 22, Society Island, private (not present)

Foster, Moses, 19, Pittsfield, MA, farmer, private, Co. A, survived

Foster, Richard M., 26, Troy, NY, laborer, served as corporal, Co. C, survived

Fountain, James W., 44, Essex, MA, barber, private, transferred to 55th Mass. (not present)

Foutz, Luke, 28, Denver, CO, laborer, private (not present)

Fowler, William, 25, Battle Creek, MI, cook, private, Co. I, wounded July 18, 1863, at Ft. Wagner

Fowlis, William, 20, Champaign, OH, railroading, private, Co. G, survived

Francis, William A., 30, Albany, NY, waiter (?), private, Co. E, survived

Franklin, Eli, 32, Pittsfield, MA, laborer, private, Co. C, wounded July 18, 1863, at Ft. Wagner, died of wounds July 31, 1863

Franklin, Stephen, 40, Dayton, OH, blacksmith, private, Co. G, survived

Freeland, Milo J., 22, Sheffield, MA, laborer, private, Co. A, survived

Freeman, Aaron N., 36, Ferrisburg, VT, hostler, private, Co. K (not present)

Freeman, Abraham, 29, Groton, MA, private, transferred to 55th Mass. (not present)

Freeman, Coydan (alt.: Coyden), 23, Burlington, VT, laborer, private, Co. H (not present)

Freeman, Cyrus, 36, Springfield, MA, laborer, private, Co. C, survived

Freeman, Isaiah, 24, Freehold, NJ, laborer, private, promoted to sergeant, Co. F, survived

Freeman, James, 22, Columbus, OH, farmer, private, Co. I, missing July 18, 1863, after Ft. Wagner

Freeman, John H., 37, Middlebury, VT, farmer, private (not present)

Freeman, Leander, 20, Burlington, VT, laborer, private, Co. H (not present)

Freeman, Theophilus D., 40, South Brookfield, MA, barber, private, Co. F (not present)

Freeman, Thomas, 29, Boston, MA, upholsterer, private, promoted to corporal, Co. H, survived

Freeman, Warren F., 18, Scituate, MA, farmer, private, Co. H (not present)

Freeman, William H., 22, South Scituate, MA, farmer, private, Co. H (not present)

Freeman, William T., 25, Lower Chanceford, PA, farmer, private, Co. F, survived

Fuller, John C., 21, Woodstock, VT, farmer (?), private, Co. K (not present)

Furlong, Wesley, 24, New Bedford, MA, steward, served as sergeant, Co. C, survived

Furman, James, 22, Boston, MA, barber (?), private, Co. E (not present)

Gaines, Alexander, 20, Pittsfield, MA, porter, private, Co. K (not present)

Gaines, John W., 20, Homestead, NJ, laborer, private, Co. F, wounded July 18, 1863, at Ft. Wagner

Gaines, Noah, 34, Haddonfield, NY, laborer, private, Co. I, missing July 18, 1863, after Ft. Wagner

Gallas, Joseph, 27, Philadelphia, PA, stevedore, private, Co. B, wounded July 18, 1863, at Ft. Wagner

Galloway, Silas, 26, Carlisle, PA, laborer, private, promoted to corporal, Co. H, survived

Gamrell, Charles S., 25, Springfield, OH, painter, private, Co. H (not present)

Gardiner, Ira W., 26, Penn Yan, NY, cook, private, Co. D, survived

Gardner, Ralph, 23, Great Barrington, MA, laborer, private, promoted to corporal, Co. A, captured July 18, 1863, at Ft. Wagner

Garner, George H., 28, Marlboro, MA, barber, private, Co. B, survived

Garnet, Hiram, 20, Galesburg, IL, laborer, private, Co. H, survived

Garrison, Alexander, 25, New York, NY, farmer, private, Co. F, survived

Garrison, Silas, 20, Chatham, Canada, painter, private, Co. A, missing July 18, 1863, after Ft. Wagner

Garrison, William, 25, Chambersburg, PA, laborer, private, Co. G, wounded July 18, 1863, at Ft. Wagner

Gayton, Walter, 18, barber, private, Co. E (not present)

Gibbs, George, 23, Boston, MA, laborer, private, Co. B, survived

Gibbs, William, 18, VA, farmer, private, transferred to 55th Mass. (not present)

Gibson, Joshua, 21, Detroit, MI, seaman (?), private, Co. E, survived

Gibson, Martin, 18, Taunton, MA, waiter, private, Co. A, survived

Gibson, William, 29, Paxton, MA, yeoman, private, Co. F (not present)

Gillespie, Peter, 20, Chicago, IL, laborer, private, Co. H, wounded July 18, 1863, at Ft. Wagner

Gilman, Martin, 23, Chambersburg, PA, farmer, private, Co. D, wounded July 18, 1863, at Ft. Wagner

Gladden, Henry, 21, Greenwich, NY, farmer, private, promoted to corporal, Co. C, survived

Glasgow, Abraham, 26, Unionville, PA, farmer, private, promoted to corporal, Co. B, survived

Glasgow, London, 22, Unionville, PA, farmer, private, Co. B, missing July 18, 1863, after Ft. Wagner; supposed killed

Glazier, Abraham, 18, Catskill, NY, farmer, private, Co. A, wounded July 18, 1863, at Ft. Wagner

Goff, Charles, 22, Springfield, OH, carpenter, private, Co. H, wounded July 18, 1863, at Ft. Wagner

*__Gomar, Richard,__ 17, Battle Creek, MI, laborer, private, Co. H, survived [pl. 34]

Gooding, James H., 26, New Bedford, MA, seaman, sergeant, demoted to corporal, Co. C, survived

Goodman, Richard D., 20, Elmira, NY, farmer, private, Co. F, survived

Goodwin, John, 25, Fredericktown, MD, farmer, private, Co. G, survived

*__Gooseberry, John,__ 25, St. Catharines, Canada, sailor, private, served as musician, Co. E (not present) [pl. 30]

Gordon, Daniel, 34, Burlington, VT, private, Co. K (not present)

Gover, Franklin, 19, Great Barrington, MA, farmer, private, Co. A, survived

Grace, James W., 29, New Bedford, MA, merchant (?), 2nd lieutenant, promoted to captain, Co. A, survived

Grant, George, 20, Philadelphia, PA, farmer, private, Co. B, captured July 18, 1863, at Ft. Wagner

Grant, John T. (not present)

Gray, Jesse, 30, Harrisburg, PA, laborer, private, Co. E, survived

Gray, John, 22, Poughkeepsie, NY, farmer, private, Co. F, survived

*__Gray, William H.W.,__ 38, New Bedford, MA, seaman, served as 1st sergeant, Co. C, wounded July 18, 1863, at Ft. Wagner [p. 11, fig. 6]

Graytons, Walter, 18, New York, NY, private, Co. E (not present)

Greeley, Howard, 18, Corinth, VT, farmer, private, Co. F (not present)

Green, Alexander F., 41, Philadelphia, PA, barber, private, Co. D (not present)

Green, Alfred, 26, Hollidaysburg, PA, farmer, private, Co. B, captured July 18, 1863, at Ft. Wagner

Green, Amos B., 23, Sheeban, PA, seaman, private, Co. D (not present)

Green, Benjamin, 21, Oberlin, OH, engineer, private, Co. I, survived

Green, Frank W., 17, Woburn, MA, laborer, Co. K (not present)

Green, Franklin, 17, Harrisburg, PA, laborer, private, Co. D, survived

Green, George W., 18, Pittsfield, MA, laborer, private, Co. I (not present)

Green, Henry, 22, Worcester, MA, laborer, private, transferred to 55th Mass. (not present)

Green, James W., 21, Sheeban, PA, seaman, private, Co. D (not present)

Green, John, 31, Carlisle, PA, laborer, private, Co. H, survived

Green, John A., 18, Brooklyn, NY, laborer, private, Co. D, survived

Green, John A., 21, NH, farmer, private, transferred to 55th Mass. (not present)

Green, John S., 25, Carlisle, PA, laborer, private, Co. H, survived

Green, John W., 19, Montrose, PA, farmer, private, Co. C, survived

Green, Joseph Henry, 16, Boston, MA, laborer, private, Co. A, survived

Green, Louis (alt.: Lewis), 22, Philadelphia, PA, laborer, private, Co. C, survived

Green, Peter, 21, Montrose, PA, farmer, private, Co. C, survived

Greene, Charles E., 23, Providence, RI, laborer, served as corporal, Co. C, survived

Grey, Solomon, 21, Woodstock, Canada, laborer, private, Co. A (not present)

Griffin, Samuel, 22, Philadelphia, PA, brickmaker, private, promoted to corporal, Co. D, wounded July 18, 1863, at Ft. Wagner

Grimes, Romeo, 34, Newbern, NC, laborer, private, Co. G, survived

Grinnage, Benjamin (alt.: Grimmidge), 18, Canada, farmer, private, Co. G, wounded July 18, 1863, at Ft. Wagner

Grinton, William H., 21, Chicago, IL, butcher, Co. E, survived

Groomer, Edward, 19, Hudson, NY, seaman, private, Co. A, survived

Grover, William, 18, Hartford, CT, farmer (?), private, Co. E, survived

Gunn, Benjamin I., 30, Columbia County, NY, farmer, private, Co. C, survived

Gunn, Titus M., 22, Columbia County, NY, farmer, private, Co. C, survived

Haines, William, 19, Schuylkill, PA, boatman, private, Co. G, survived

Hales, Henry, 24, Chicago, IL, laborer, private, Co. H, wounded July 18, 1863, at Ft. Wagner

Hall, Aaron C., 33, Exeter, NH, laborer, private, Co. B (not present)

Hall, Amos, 24, Oxford, OH, farmer, private, promoted to sergeant, Co. I, survived

Hall, Edward, 21, Exeter NH, laborer, private, transferred to 55th Mass. (not present)

Hall, Elias, 26, Boston, MA, laborer, private, Co. A, survived

Hall, George Henry, 20, Philadelphia, PA, farmer, private, Co. B, survived

Hall, James A., 21, Detroit, MI, chair maker, private, promoted to sergeant, Co. E, survived

Hall, James Henry, 38, Philadelphia, PA, barber, private, promoted to corporal, Co. B, survived

Hall, John, 34, Lenox, MA, sailor, private, Co. D, survived

Hall, Joseph Lee, 19, New Bedford, MA, laborer, private, Co. C, missing July 18, 1863, after Ft. Wagner

Hall, Robert F., 23, private, Co. H (not present)

Hall, William, 26, Lima, OH, engineer, private, Co. D, survived

Hall, William D., 20, Exeter, NH, yeoman, private, Co. B, survived

Hallenbeck, John J., 23, Jersey City, NJ, laborer, private, Co. A, survived

*****Hallett, Charles O.,** 22, Brookline, MA, clerk (?), served as 2nd lieutenant, Cos. B,E (not present) [pl. 37]

Hallowell, Edward N., 20, Medford, MA, merchant (?), captain, promoted to colonel, wounded July 18, 1863, at Ft. Wagner

Hallowell, Joseph F., 32, Marshall County, MO, laborer, private, Co. D, survived

*****Hallowell, Norwood P.,** 24, Cambridge, MA, student (?), served as lieutenant colonel, survived [pl. 39]

Halmus, Benjamin, 28, Albany, NY, waiter, private, Co. E, survived

Halstead, James W., 18, Farmington, CT, farmer, private, promoted to corporal, Co. A, survived

Hamilton, Alfred, 18, Yates County, NY, farmer, private, Co. G, survived

Hamilton, Frank, 40, Hinsdale, MA, farmer, private, Co. A, survived

Hamilton, Frank, 22, Hinsdale, MA, farmer, private, Co. A, survived

Hamilton, Henry, 24, Pittsfield, MA, farmer, private, Co. K (not present)

Hamilton, James, 20, Jackson, MS, farmer, private, transferred to 55th Mass. (not present)

Hamilton, Napoleon, 24, Ypsilanti, MI, farmer, private, Co. I, survived

Hamilton, Paul, 19, Pittsfield, MA, laborer, private, Cos. A,D (not present)

Hamilton, Thomas, 30, Buffalo, NY, seaman (?), private, Co. A, wounded July 18, 1863, at Ft. Wagner

Hammond, Alexander, 23, Philadelphia, PA, laborer, private, promoted to corporal, Co. B, survived

Hankerson, Charles, 23, Burlington, NJ, waiter, private, Co. D, survived

Harder, Peter H., 22, Columbia County, NY, laborer, private, Co. C, survived

Harding, Cornelius, 41, Utica, NY, barber, private, Co. G, survived

Harding, David, 22, Detroit, MI, brickmaker, private, promoted to corporal, Co. F, survived

Hardy, Charles, 20, Philadelphia, PA, laborer, private, promoted to corporal, Co. B, captured July 18, 1863, at Ft. Wagner

Harmon, William, 24, Selina, MI, farmer, private, Co. I, survived

Harper, Henry, 22, Obrine County, TN, blacksmith, private (not present)

Harper, John W., 23, Zanesville, OH, barber, private, promoted to corporal, Co. K, survived

Harris, Alfred, 28, Detroit, MI, sailor, private, Co. E, missing July 18, 1863, after Ft. Wagner

Harris, Charles, 23, New York, NY, laborer, private, Co. A, survived

Harris, Fleming, 18, Chicago, IL, laborer, private, Co. H, survived

Harris, Hill, 26, Jackson, LA, farmer, private, promoted to corporal, Co. G, survived

Harris, John, 18, Candor, PA, farmer, private, Co. D, survived

Harris, John C., 20, Sheffield, MA, farmer, private, Co. B (not present)

Harris, John H., 38, Abington, MA, farmer, private, Co. A, survived

Harris, Moses, 22, Lancaster, PA, laborer, private, Co. K, survived

Harrison, Charles H., 19, New Bedford, MA, laborer, private, Co. C, survived

Harrison, Isaiah, 19, Mercersburg, PA, laborer, private, Co. I, survived

Harrison, John F., 18, Buffalo, NY, sailor, private, Co. D (not present)

Harrison, John H., 21, New Bedford, MA, laborer, private, Co. C, survived

Harrison, Samuel, 45, Pittsfield, MA, clergyman (?), served as chaplain (not present)

Harrison, William Henry, 22, Battle Creek, MI, teamster, private, Co. H, killed July 18, 1863, at Ft. Wagner

Harrison, William Henry, 35, Chicago, IL, laborer, private, Co. H (not present)

Harrison, William Henry, 36, Philadelphia, PA, farmer, private, Co. B, survived

Harrison, Wm. H., 23, Paris, ME, laborer, private, Co. A, survived

Hart, Christopher C., 23, Springfield, OH, waiter, private, Co. E, survived

Hart, George, 21, Rutland, VT, laborer, private, Co. G (not present)

Hartwell, Alfred S., 26, Natick, MA, student (?), served as captain, Co. D, survived

Hasbrook, James H., 18, Catskill, NY, laborer, private, promoted to corporal, Co. C, wounded July 18, 1863, at Ft. Wagner

Haskell, James F., 21, Warner, NH, farmer, private, Co. D, survived

Hawkins, Isaac S., 29, Medina, NY, sailor, private, Co. D (not present)

Hayes, George, 20, Wilmington, NC, carpenter, private, Co. F, survived

Hayes, Nathan E., 44, Rutland, VT, teamster, private, Co. H (not present)

Hazard, Austin E., 32, Woodstock, VT, butcher, private, Co. B (not present)

Hazard, Horace, 28, Townsend, MA, barber, private, Co. D (not present)

Hazard, Nahum G., 33, Townsend, MA, teamster, private, transferred to 55th Mass. (not present)

Hazard, Solomon, 22, West Chester, PA, farmer, private, Co. B, survived

Hazard, Theodore, 20, Boylston, MA, cook, private, Co. D (not present)

Hazard, William, 23, New York, NY, farmer, private, Co. K, survived

Hazzard, Adrastus, 18, Groton, MA, farmer, private, Co. F, survived

Hazzard, Henry, 19, Shirley, MA, laborer, private, Co. D (not present)

Hazzard, James, 30, Woodstock, VT, gardener, private, Co. G (not present)

Hazzard, Oliver E., 35, Townsend, MA, laborer, private, Co. D (not present)

Hazzard, Samuel, 24, Nova Scotia, Canada, seaman, private, transferred to 55th Mass. (not present)

Hedgepeth, John, 23, Clinton County, OH, farmer, private, promoted to corporal, Co. G, wounded July 18, 1863, at Ft. Wagner

Helmon, Preston (alt.: Helman), 30, Leoni, MI, carpenter, private, promoted to corporal, Co. E, survived

Hemmenway, Alexander, 28, Worcester, MA, barber, private, promoted to 1st sergeant, Co. F, survived

Henderson, John, 23, Townsend, MA, cook, private, Co. D (not present)

Henderson, Samuel, 21, Upper Darby, PA, private, transferred to 55th Mass. (not present)

Henderson, William, 22, Woodstock, CT, laborer, private, Co. H, survived

Henderson, William H., 28, Quincy, IL, laborer, private, Co. K, survived

Henry, Alexander, 25, Syracuse, NY, laborer, private, Co. E, survived

Henry, Thomas, 28, West Indies, cook, private (not present)

Henry, William, 19, Fort Erie, Canada, hostler, private, Co. F, survived

Henson, Cornelius, 22, New Bedford, MA, laborer, private, Co. C, captured July 18, 1863, at Ft. Wagner

Henson, John, 20, Coatesville, PA, laborer, private, Co. C, survived

Herbert, Phillip, 41, VA, laborer, private, transferred to 55th Mass. (not present)

Hercules, Lewis, 21, West Chester, PA, farmer, private, Co. B, survived

Hersey, Samuel E., 23, Churchville, NY, laborer, private, Co. E, survived

Heuston, Joseph, 21, Cincinnati, OH, drayman, private, Co. K, survived

Hewett, James, 21, Xenia, OH, farmer, private, promoted to sergeant, Co. K, survived

Hewett, Thomas, 19, Xenia, OH, farmer, private, promoted to corporal, Co. K, survived

Hicks, Henry J., 23, Cambridge, MA, shoemaker, private, Co. C, survived

Higgins, Thomas, 22, New Brunswick, NJ, waiter, private, Co. F, wounded July 18, 1863, at Ft. Wagner

Higginson, Francis L., 21, Boston, MA, served as 1st lieutenant, Cos. F,I, survived

Hight, James, 21, Philadelphia, PA, teamster, private, Co. B, survived

Hill, Alexander, 32, Hudson, NY, laborer, private, Co. A, wounded July 18, 1863, at Ft. Wagner

Hill, Charles M., 18, Plymouth, MA, waiter, private, Co. H (not present)

Hill, William, 19, Philadelphia, PA, teamster, private, Co. B, survived

Hill, William F., 18, Sherborne, MA, farmer, private, Co. A, captured July 18, 1863, at Ft. Wagner

Hilton, Leroy, 28, Pittsburgh, PA, farmer, private, promoted to corporal, Co. E, wounded July 18, 1863, at Ft. Wagner

Hines, Edward, 20, Norfolk, CT, jobber, private, Co. A, killed July 18, 1863, at Ft. Wagner

Hockins, Henry E., 19, Cresson, PA, laborer, private, Co. I, survived

Hogan, Benjamin, 25, Mercer County, OH, farmer, private, Co. D, killed July 18, 1863, at Ft. Wagner

Hoke, Bromily, 18, Montgomery County, NY, laborer, private, Co. G, survived

Holloway, Charles M., 24, Wilberforce, OH, student, private, promoted to corporal, Co. K (not present)

Holmes, Charles, 20, Hamilton, Canada, waiter, private, transferred to 55th Mass. (not present)

Holmes, George, 31, Elmira, NY, laborer, private, Co. F, wounded July 18, 1863, at Ft. Wagner

Holmes, Joseph R., 21, Cincinnati, OH, farmer, private, Co. G, wounded July 18, 1863, at Ft. Wagner

Homans, William H., 26, Malden, MA, 2nd lieutenant, promoted to captain, Cos. A,C, wounded July 18, 1863, at Ft. Wagner

Homes, Philip, 20, Chambersburg, PA, hostler, private, Co. H, survived

Hooper, Henry N., 28, Roxbury, MA, Major, promoted to lieutenant colonel (not present)

Hoose, Edward, 21, Dalton, MA, farmer, private, Co. B (not present)

Hopkins, Peter, 20, Philadelphia, PA, farmer, private, Co. D, wounded July 18, 1863, at Ft. Wagner

Horton, Chauncey B., 20, Newton, NJ, farmer, private, promoted to corporal, Co. G, survived

Howard, Charles, 26, Carlisle, PA, waiter, private, promoted to corporal, Co. I, survived

Howard, James, 19, Philadelphia, PA, farmer, private, Co. B, survived

Howard, Leander, 20, Oberlin, OH, farmer, private, Co. G, wounded July 18, 1863, at Ft. Wagner

Howard, Robert, 18, Carlisle, PA, laborer, private, Co. H, survived

Howard, Willard, 25, Boston, MA, salesman (?), 2nd lieutenant, promoted to captain, Cos. H,I, survived

Hubbard, George, 23, Galesburg, IL, laborer, private, Co. H, survived

Hulsey, Ira E., 25, Chatham Four Corners, NY, laborer, private, Co. C, missing July 18, 1863, after Ft. Wagner

Hunter, Alexander, 28, Cleveland, OH, laborer, private, Co. H, survived

Hunter, James, 38, blacksmith, private, Co. D (not present)

Hunter, Samuel, 36, Fairhaven, VT, farmer, private, Co. D (not present)

Hurdle, Robert H., 20, Falmouth, MA, farmer, private, Co. B (not present)

Hurley, Nathaniel, 19, Rochester, NY, laborer, private, Co. E, captured July 18, 1863, at Ft. Wagner

Hutchings, James A., 22, Trenton, NJ, waiter, private, Co. E, survived

Jackson, Abraham A., 24, Great Barrington, MA, hostler, private, Co. A, survived

Jackson, Charles, 23, Ghent, NY, farmer, private, Co. C, survived

Jackson, Charles, 18, Monterey, MA, laborer, private, promoted to corporal, Co. B (not present)

Jackson, Elmer H., 19, Troy, NY, laborer, private, Co. A, survived

Jackson, Francis, 23, Rockingham, VT, laborer (?), private, Co. I (not present)

Jackson, Francis J., 18, Great Barrington, MA, laborer, private, Co. C, survived

Jackson, Franklin, 37, Northampton, MA, farmer, private, Co. K (not present)

Jackson, George, 19, Harrisburg, PA, laborer, private, Co. I, survived

Jackson, George, 30, Northampton, MA, laborer, private, Co. E, wounded July 18, 1863, at Ft. Wagner

Jackson, George F., 20, Binghampton, NY, laborer, private, Co. E, survived

Jackson, Henry P., 32, Rutland, VT, laborer, private, Co. G (not present)

Jackson, Horace, 29, Glens Falls, NY, boatman, private, Co. G, survived

Jackson, James H., 19, Adrian, MI, barber, private, Co. D (not present)

Jackson, James H., 18, Great Barrington, MA, waiter, private, Co. A, wounded and missing July 18, 1863, at Ft. Wagner

Jackson, James L., 18, Columbia, NY, laborer, private, Co. C, survived

Jackson, James W. (not present)

Jackson, John H., 22, Troy, NY, laborer, private, Co. C, survived

Jackson, Levi, 18, Oxford, OH, laborer, private, Co. I, survived

Jackson, Levi H., 20, Great Barrington, MA, waiter, private, Co. C, survived

Jackson, Matthias, 18, Dutchess County, NY, laborer, private, Co. C, survived

Jackson, Moses, 24, Grand Rapids, MI, barber, private, Co. E, survived

Jackson, Samuel, 20, Hudson, NY, hostler, private, Co. C, survived

Jackson, Samuel D., 32, Pittsfield, MA, farmer, private, Co. B (not present)

Jackson, Sandford, 33, Amherst, MA, farmer, private, Co. A, wounded July 18, 1863, at Ft. Wagner

Jackson, Simon A., 22, Haddam, CT, coaster, private, Co. F, survived

Jackson, Thomas, 21, Lenox, MA, farmer, private, Co. A, survived

Jackson, William, 32, Rutland, VT, teamster, private, Co. D (not present)

Jackson, William, 22, farmer, private (not present)

Jackson, Wm. N., 21, Hudson, NY, farmer, private, Co. A, survived

James, Garth W., 18, Concord, MA, student (?), 1st lieutenant/adjutant, promoted to captain, Co. C, wounded July 18, 1863, at Ft. Wagner

James, Henry, 23, Foxborough, MA, laborer, private, Co. F (not present)

James, John, 22, Dominique, West Indies, private (not present)

Jameson, James, 24, Syracuse, NY, barber, private, Co. H, survived

Jarvis, George, 18, Sheffield, MA, laborer, private, Co. A, survived

Jarvis, George W., 24, Greenfield, MA, hairdresser, private, Co. A, survived

Jay, George, 19, Oxford PA, farmer, private, Co. B (not present)

Jay, Wesley, 26, Oxford PA, farmer, private, Co. B, survived

Jay, William, 22, Oxford PA, farmer, private, Co. B, survived

Jefferson, Benjamin F., 21, South Bend, OH, hostler, private, Co. C, survived

Jeffrey, Nathan C., 18, Rochester, NY, laborer, private, Co. D, survived

Jeffries, Walter A., 38, Cincinnati, OH, laborer, private, promoted to sergeant, Co. H (not present)

Jennings, Frank N., 20, Hadley, MA, farmer, private, Co. H (not present)

Jennings, Wm., 44, farmer, private, Co. C, survived

Jennings, Wm. H., 22, Amherst, MA, farmer, private, Co. C, survived

Jewett, Charles, 33, Millbury, MA, farmer (?), 2nd lieutenant, promoted to 1st lieutenant, Co. K (not present)

Jewett, Richard H.L., 28, Boston, MA, engineer (?), 1st lieutenant, promoted to captain, Co. K, wounded July 18, 1863, at Ft. Wagner

Johnson, Alexander, 19, Buckland, MA, student (?), served as 2nd lieutenant, Co. F, survived

Johnson, Alexander, 34, Elmira, NY, laborer, private, promoted to 2nd lieutenant, Co. F, survived

*****Johnson, Alexander H.,** 16, New Bedford, MA, seaman, served as musician, Co. C, survived [pl. 31]

Johnson, Augustus, 21, Philadelphia, PA, farmer, private, Co. B, survived

Johnson, B. S., 21, Mount Morris, NY, blacksmith, private, Co. F, survived

Johnson, Charles F., 20, Chicago, IL, farmer, private, Co. H, survived

Johnson, Charles H., 19, Warren, MA, barber, private, promoted to corporal, Co. F, wounded July 18, 1863, at Ft. Wagner

Johnson, Clayton, 18, West Chester, PA, farmer, private, Co. B, survived

Johnson, David, 22, Detroit, MI, farmer, private, Co. I, survived

Johnson, Edward, 33, Evansville, IN, laborer, private, Co. G (not present)

Johnson, Frederick, 25, Boston, MA, hairdresser, private, promoted to sergeant, Co. C, survived

Johnson, George, 22, West Chester, PA, laborer, private, Co. I (not present)

Johnson, George A., 20, Detroit, MI, harness maker, private, promoted to sergeant, Co. E, survived

Johnson, George W., 21, Philadelphia, PA, farmer, private, Co. B, survived

Johnson, Henry, 22, Montrose, PA, laborer, private, Co. C, survived

Johnson, Isaac, 22, South Reading, MA, farmer, private, Co. C, survived

Johnson, James P., 21, Owego, NY, barber, private, Co. F, survived

Johnson, John, 22, Chicago, IL, laborer (?), private, Co. H, survived

Johnson, John, 23, Philadelphia, PA, teamster (?), private, Co. H, survived

Johnson, John E., 20, Harrisburg, PA, barber, private, Co. E, survived

Johnson, John H., 23, Worcester, MA, upholsterer, private, Co. H (not present)

Johnson, John Henry, 16, Lanesville, VA, laborer, private, Co. D, survived

Johnson, Joseph, 36, Hamilton, OH, laborer, private, Co. I, wounded July 18, 1863, at Ft. Wagner

Johnson, Joseph C., 31, Chicago, IL, farmer, private, Co. H, survived

Johnson, Moses, 28, Philadelphia, PA, laborer, private, Co. B, survived

Johnson, Nathaniel H., 24, Sheffield, MA, carpenter (?), private, Co. A, survived

Johnson, Norman, 22, Sheffield, MA, farmer, private, Co. A, survived

Johnson, Peter, 26, Martha's Vineyard, MA, seaman, private, Co. I (not present)

Johnson, Peter B., 29, Springfield, MA, turner, private, Co. A, missing July 18, 1863, after Ft. Wagner

Johnson, Ralph, 25, Carroll County, MD, laborer, private, Co. D, survived

Johnson, Samuel, 21, Montrose, PA, farmer, private, Co. C, missing July 18, 1863, after Ft. Wagner

Johnson, Stanley, 18, Mercersburg, PA, farmer, private, Co. I, wounded July 18, 1863, at Ft. Wagner

Johnson, Thomas, 20, Detroit, MI, sailor, private, Co. E, survived

Johnson, Thomas A., 39, Detroit, MI, farmer, private, promoted to sergeant, Co. G, survived

Johnson, Wheeler, 26, Rockingham, VT, cook, private, Co. G (not present)

Johnson, William, 21, Baltimore, MD, sailor, private, Co. K, survived

Johnson, William, 29, Montrose, PA, farmer, private, Co. C, survived

Johnson, William H., 34, Brunswick, ME, seaman (?), private, Co. I (not present)

Jones, Alexander, 23, Pittsburgh, PA, waiter, private, promoted to corporal, Co. D, survived

Jones, Edward L., 23, Boston, MA, clerk (?), 1st lieutenant, promoted to captain, Co. D, wounded July 18, 1863, at Ft. Wagner

Jones, Henry E., 19, Lanesborough, MA, farmer, private, Co. A, survived

Jones, James R., 33, Albany, NY, barber, private, promoted to sergeant, Co. E, survived

Jones, Joseph, 19, Coatesville, PA, farmer, private, Co. C, survived

Jones, Robert, 20, Lancaster County, PA, laborer, private, served as musician, Co. D, survived

Jones, Robert J., 20, Hamilton, OH, farmer, private, promoted to corporal, Co. I, survived

Jones, Samuel, 19, Pittsfield, MA, laborer, private, Co. I (not present)

Jones, William, 32, Indianapolis, IN, porter, private, Co. H, wounded July 18, 1863, at Ft. Wagner

Jones, William, 17, Mount Pleasant, OH, farmer, private, Co. G, survived

Jones, William, 45, Sheffield, MA, laborer, private, Co. B (not present)

Jones, William, 22, West Chester, PA, farmer, private, Co. K, survived

Jones, William Henry, 44, Richmond, VA, trader, private, Co. A, survived

Jones, Willis, 35, Detroit, MI, laborer, private, Co. F (not present)

Jordan, Wiley, 29, Mercer County, OH, engineer, private, Co. D, survived

Joy, Charles F., 19, Brighton, MA, clerk (?), 2nd lieutenant, promoted to captain, Co. F (not present)

Kane, Charles, 28, Buffalo, NY, laborer, private, Co. A, wounded July 18, 1863, at Ft. Wagner

Kane, Robert, 21, Lancaster County, PA, laborer, private, promoted to corporal, Co. D, survived

Keith, William, 38, Mercersburg, PA, farmer, private, Co. K, survived

Kelley, James A., 23, St. Josephs MI, barber, private, Co. E, survived

Kelley, James E., 19, Poughkeepsie, NY, farmer, private, Co. F, survived

Kelly, Daniel (alt.: Kelley), 19, Poughkeepsie, NY, farmer, private, Co. F, killed July 18, 1863, at Ft. Wagner

Kelly, William D., 19, New Bedford, MA, laborer, private, promoted to corporal, Co. C, survived

Kelsey, Louis J., 19, Detroit, MI, farmer, private, Co. E, wounded July 18, 1863, at Ft. Wagner

Kelson, Joseph, 22, Peru, laborer, private, Co. A, survived

Kennard, William, 20, Lancaster County, PA, farmer, private, Co. D, survived

Kenney, Samuel, 39, Motticksville, PA, blacksmith, private, promoted to corporal, Co. F, wounded July 18, 1863, at Ft. Wagner

King, Amos, 43, Fulton County, NY, farmer, private, Co. G, survived

King, Anthony L. (alt.: Antony), 18, Newbern, NC, gentleman, private, transferred to 55th Mass. (not present)

King, George, 30, Toledo, OH, laborer, private, Co. K, survived

King, Henry, 37, Boston, MA, bricklayer, private, Co. G, survived

King, Henry, 27, Carlisle, PA, laborer, private, Co. H (not present)

King, John, 21, Farmington, CT, sailor, private, Co. E, wounded July 18, 1863, at Ft. Wagner

King, Oliver W., 24, Delaware, MD, laborer, private, Co. G, survived

Kirk, Henry, 22, Galesburg, IL, laborer, private, Co. H, wounded and captured July 18, 1863, at Ft. Wagner

Knowles, Alfred H., 21, Orleans MA, plumber (?), 2nd lieutenant, promoted to 1st lieutenant, Co. A (not present)

Knox, Norman, 20, Utica, NY, boatman, private, Co. G, survived

Knox, Thomas E., 21, Hollidaysburg, PA, barber, private, Co. D, survived

Krunkleton, Cyrus, 19, Mercersburg, PA, farmer, private, Co. K (not present)

Krunkleton, James, 19, Mercersburg, PA, farmer, private, Co. K, wounded July 18, 1863, at Ft. Wagner

Krunkleton, Wesley, 24, Mercersburg, PA, farmer, private, Co. K, survived

Krunkleton, William 21, Mercersburg, PA, farmer, private, Co. K, survived

Lamb, Marshall, 19, Newbury, SC, laborer (?), private, Co. A, missing July 18, 1863, after Ft. Wagner

Lane, James, 22, Buffalo, NY, laborer, private, Co. H, survived

Lane, Milton, 31, Carlisle, PA, laborer, private, Co. H, wounded July 18, 1863, at Ft. Wagner

Langley, John N., 25, Rutland, VT, farmer, private, Co. D (not present)

Langley, Lewis, 40, Ferrisburg, VT, farmer, private, Co. K (not present)

Langley, Loudon S., 24, Rutland, VT, farmer, private, Co. B (not present)

Langley, Newell C., 36, Ferrisburg, VT, farmer, private, Co. F (not present)

Lawrence, Robert, 28, New Bedford, MA, laborer, private, Co. C, survived

Lawrence, Thomas, 18, Xenia, OH, farmer, private, Co. G, survived

Laws, William, 19, Philadelphia, PA, sailor, private (not present)

Lawson, Jesse, 31, Franklin, PA, farmer, private, Co. K, survived

Leader, John, 20, Reading, PA, boatman, private, Co. E, survived

Leatherman, John, 24, Ypsilanti, MI, seaman, private, Co. H (not present)

Lee, Alfred, 20, Philadelphia, PA, farmer, private, Co. B, wounded July 18, 1863, at Ft. Wagner

Lee, Arthur B., 29, Charleston, SC, harness maker, private, promoted to commissary sergeant, Co. A (not present)

Lee, Benjamin F., 19, South Scituate, MA, shoemaker, private, Co. G (not present)

Lee, George H., 21, New Bedford, MA, hostler, served as sergeant, Co. C, survived

Lee, Harrison, 21, New Bedford, MA, laborer, private, Co. D (not present)

Lee, John, 35, Harrisburg, PA, laborer, private, Co. I (not present)

Lee, Joseph, 21, Brownville, PA, farmer, private, Co. G, survived

Lee, Manuel, 22, Buffalo, NY, laborer, private, Co. H, survived

Lee, Philip, 21, Worcester, MA, yeoman, private, Co. E (not present)

Lee, William, 23, Columbus, OH, farmer, private, Co. I, survived

Lee, William H., 35, Hagerstown, MD, farmer, private (not present)

Lee, William R., 38, Cleveland, OH, weaver, private, Co. F, wounded July 18, 1863, at Ft. Wagner

Leighton, Samuel, 41, New Bedford, MA, laborer, corporal, Co. C, wounded July 18, 1863, at Ft. Wagner

Lenox, Charles W., 38, Watertown, MA, barber, private, promoted to sergeant, Co. A, survived

Leonard, Andrew W., 21, Charlestown, MA, clerk (?), 2nd lieutenant, promoted to 1st lieutenant, Co. K (not present)

Lew, Zimri, 36, Dracut, MA, laborer, private, transferred to 55th Mass. (not present)

Lewis, Alfred, 26, Spartanburg, IN, laborer, private, promoted to corporal, Co. K, survived

Lewis, Augustus, 20, Shippensburg, PA, laborer, private, Co. H, killed July 18, 1863, at Ft. Wagner

Lewis, Daniel D.H., 21, Richmond, IN, laborer, private, Co. K, survived

Lewis, Douglas, 18, Chatham Four Corners, NY, laborer, private, Co. A, survived

Lewis, George, 23, Richmond, IN, barber, private, Co. K, survived

Lewis, George

Lewis, George F., 28, Cambridgeport, MA, laborer, private, Co. C, wounded July 18, 1863, at Ft. Wagner

Lewis, Lorenzo T., 19, Dearborn, MI, woodman, private, Co. I, survived

Lewis, Richard, 19, Lincoln County, KY, laborer, private (not present)

Lightfoot, William, 33, VA, laborer, private (not present)

Lipscomb, George, 23, Cincinnati, OH, boatman, private, promoted to sergeant, Co. I, survived

Little, Thomas, 26, Windsor, VT, farmer, private, Co. H (not present)

Little, William, 18, Chambersburg, PA, laborer, private, Co. D, survived

Littlefield, Henry W., 20, Milton, MA, clerk (?), 2nd lieutenant, promoted to 1st lieutenant, Cos. H,G, survived

Livingstone, Franklin R., 19, Hudson, NY, seaman, private, Co. A, wounded July 18, 1863, at Ft. Wagner

Lloyd, Charles, 20, Utica, NY, laborer, private, Co. G, survived

Lloyd, Thomas, 20, Chester County, PA, farmer, private, Co. D, killed July 18, 1863, at Ft. Wagner

Lloyd, William, 25, Boston, MA, sailor, private, Co. D, killed July 18, 1863, at Ft. Wagner

Locard, Lewis J., 37, Blairsville, PA, boatman, private, Co. K (not present)

Logan, Samuel, 23, Rock Castle, KY, teamster, private (not present)

Lomack, Samuel, 24, Columbus, OH, laborer, private, Co. K, survived

Long, Henry, 35, Harrisburg, PA, laborer, private, Co. B, survived

Lopeman, Charles H., 19, Reading, PA, boatman, private, Co. E, missing July 18, 1863, after Ft. Wagner

Lott, John, 18, barber, private, Co. C, wounded July 18, 1863, at Ft. Wagner, died of wounds Mar. 30, 1864

Louis, Anderson (alt.: Lewis), 30, KY, laborer, private, Co. G, wounded July 18, 1863, at Ft. Wagner

Lowe, Francis, 20, Cleveland, OH, cook, private, Co. F, killed July 18, 1863, at Ft. Wagner

Lowe, John, 26 (24?), Detroit, MI, barber, private, promoted to sergeant, Co. E, survived

Lowry, Joseph, 21, Urbana, OH, farmer, private, Co. E, survived

Lucas, George, 28, Buffalo, NY, laborer, private, Co. D, survived

Lukes, Edwin, 28, Steugen County, NY, boatman, private, Co. D (not present)

Lushay, George, 21, New York, NY, teamster, private, Co. A (not present)

Lyons, James, 34, Hollidaysburg, PA, farmer, private, promoted to corporal, Co. B, survived

Lyons, John, 19, Chicago, IL, laborer, private, Co. F, survived

Lyons, Robert, 21, Mercersburg, PA, farmer, private, promoted to corporal, Co. I, missing July 18, 1863, after Ft. Wagner

Madison, Leonard E., private, Co. A

Madrey, George, 19, Hamilton, OH, farmer, private, Co. I, survived

Magill, Benjamin, 30, Grove, PA, farmer, private, Co. C (not present)

Mahan, Jesse, 22, Xenia, OH, blacksmith, private, Co. K, wounded and missing July 18, 1863, at Ft. Wagner

Maimi, Menomine L., 28, Philadelphia, PA, private, survived

Malery, William (alt.: Malory), 21, Denver, CO, teamster, private (not present)

Manuel, William L.G., 17, Lowell, MA, barber, served as musician, Co. F, survived

Marshall, Henry B., 45, Brooklyn, NY, laborer, private, Co. C, survived

Martin, James M., 43, Cambridge, MA, cook, private, Co. A, survived

Martin, William, 19, West Indies, sailor, private, Co. G (not present)

Mason, Charles, 22, Detroit, MI, mason, private (not present)

Mayhew, Answell W. (Alt: Ansell W. Mayhwe), private, Co. D

Mayho, Varnall W. (alt.: Mayo), 29, Oxford Granville County, NC, laborer, private, Co. I, wounded July 18, 1863, at Ft. Wagner

Mayhugh, Isaiah, 19, Christiane, PA, farmer, private, Co. I (not present)

McClellan, William, 21, Detroit, MI, cook, private, Co. F, survived

McCloud, James, 21, St. Thomas, WI, sailor, private, Co. C, survived

McCormick, Andrew, 24, Green County, AR, farmer, private (not present)

McCowan, David, 24, Morning Sun, OH, laborer, private, Co. K, survived

McCowan, George T. (alt.: McCorwan), 23, Richmond, IN, farmer, private, Co. K, survived

McCowan, Pleasant, 19, Richmond, IN, laborer, private, promoted to corporal, Co. K, survived

McCrawford, William, 21, Washington, DC, waiter, private (not present)

McCullar, Moses, private, Co. K

McCullar, Thomas, 22, Mercersburg, PA, farmer, private, Co. K, survived

McDermott, William, 22, Cambridge, MA, farmer (?), 2nd lieutenant, promoted to 1st lieutenant, Cos. K,I (not present)

McJohnson, Robert, 27, Preble County, OH, laborer, private, Co. K, survived

McLane, Charles, 21, St. Albans, VT, private, transferred to 55th Mass. (not present)

McNally, James, 21, Brattleboro, VT, farmer, private, Co. I (not present)

McNelly, private, Co. I

McPherson, Alvus, 37, Oxford, OH, laborer, private, Co. I, survived

McPherson, John, 23, Harrisburg, PA, laborer, private, Co. D, survived

McQuorn, Charles (alt.: McQueen), 19, bricklayer (?), private, Co. E (not present)

Meades, Thomas, 28, Rappahannock, VA, private (not present)

Meads, Andrew, 21, Chambersburg, PA, laborer, private, Co. D, survived

Means, Emsley B., 19, Abington, MA, farmer, private, Co. I (not present)

Meeks, Joseph W., 20, Springfield, OH, shoemaker (?), private, Co. E, survived

Mero, Andrew H., 27, Rutland, VT, laborer, private, Co. B (not present)

Mero, Charles, 22, Rutland, VT, laborer, private, Co. I (not present)

Mero, Edward H., 19, Woodstock, VT, farmer, private, Co. B (not present)

Mero, Sylvester, 19, Woodstock, VT, farmer, private, Co. B (not present)

Merriman, George, 22, West Chester, PA, farmer, private, promoted to sergeant, Co. B (not present)

Merritt, William, 21, Hudson, NY, laborer, private, Co. A, survived

Middleton, Samuel, 23, Catskill, PA, farmer, private, Co. C, survived

Milbury, Augustus, 26, Boston, MA, hostler, private, Co. K (not present)

Miller, Andrew, 39, Elmira, NY, blacksmith, private, Co. F, survived

Miller, John, 38, Allegheny City, PA, seaman, private, Co. G, survived

Miller, John, 25, Philadelphia, PA, barber, private, Co. B, survived

Miller, John A., 18, Goshen, NY, laborer, private, Co. F, survived

Miller, Theodore, 19, Montgomery County, NY, teamster, private, Co. G, survived

Miller, William, 27, Cambridge, MA, seaman, private, Co. A, survived

Milliman, Jeremiah, 23, Saratoga County, NY, boatman, private, promoted to corporal, Co. G, survived

Mills, Edward, 22, New York, NY, waiter, private, Co. E, wounded July 18, 1863, at Ft. Wagner

Mills, James H., 23, Bradford, NY, laborer, private, Co. D, killed July 18, 1863, at Ft. Wagner

Milner, Martin, 33, Chicago, IL, farmer, private, Co. H, survived

Milton, William P., 24, Columbus, OH, farmer, private, Co. I, wounded July 18, 1863, at Ft. Wagner

Miner, Thomas, transferred to 55th Mass.

Mitchell, Edward, 20, New York, NY, laborer, private, Co. C (not present)

Mitchell, Hamilton, 25, Boston, MA, hostler, private, Co. E (not present)

Mitchell, Perry, farmer, private, transferred to 55th Mass.

Mitchell, Thomas

Mitchell, William, 22, Oberlin, OH, farmer, private, Co. F, survived

Moles, Samuel, 23, Middletown, PA, laborer, private, Co. F, wounded July 18, 1863, at Ft. Wagner

Monde, Aristide, 24, New Orleans, LA, machinist, private, Co. I (not present)

Monroe, George C., 20, Littleton, MA, laborer, private, Co. C, survived

*****Monroe, Henry A.,** 13, New Bedford, MA, laborer, private, served as musician, Co. C, survived [pl. 29]

Monroe, Lewis G. (alt.: Louis), 35, Toledo, OH, blacksmith, private, Co. K, survived

Montgomery, John H., 28, Hillsboro, MD, laborer, private, Co. I, wounded July 18, 1863, at Ft. Wagner

Montgomery, John W., laborer, private, transferred to 55th Mass.

Moore, David, 30, Richmond, PA, laborer, private, Co. K, survived

*****Moore, David Miles,** 16, Elmira, NY, laborer, private, served as drummer, Co. H, survived [p. 16, fig. 8]

Moore, George H., 21, Boston, MA, farmer, private, Co. D (not present)

Moore, John W., 22, Dundas, Canada, gunsmith, private, Co. D, survived

Moore, William, 24, Edgartown, MA, farmer, private, Co. F (not present)

More, Edward, 36, Sheffield, MA, laborer, private, Co. B (not present)

Morehouse, Stephen W., 21, Boston, MA, waiter, private, Co. E (not present)

Morey, Benjamin, farmer, private, transferred to 55th Mass.

Morgan, Colonel, 19, Cincinnati, OH, tobacconist, private, Co. K, missing July 18, 1863, after Ft. Wagner

Morgan, Eden G., 19, Albany, NY, laborer, private, Co. E

Morgan, John, 24, Cincinnati, OH, tobacconist, private, promoted to sergeant, Co. G, wounded July 18, 1863, at Ft. Wagner

Morgan, Joseph, 21, Reading, PA, boatman, private, Co. E, survived

Morris, George, 22, Philadelphia, PA, sailor, private, promoted to corporal, Co. B, survived

Morris, James

Morris, Moses, 27, Lancaster, PA, porter, private, promoted to corporal, Co. D, wounded July 18, 1863, at Ft. Wagner

Morris, William Henry, 22, New Bedford, MA, sailor, private, Co. K (not present)

Morse, George, 26, Fayetteville, PA, blacksmith, private, Co. I, survived

Morse, William H., 23, Chicago, IL, mechanic, private, Co. H, survived

Moshroe, George W., 33, Elmira, NY, laborer, private, Co. F, captured July 18, 1863, at Ft. Wagner

Munroe, James, 27, Kalamazoo, MI, laborer, private, promoted to sergeant, Co. H, wounded July 18, 1863, at Ft. Wagner

Munroe, Peter F., farmer, private, transferred to 55th Mass.

Murphy, Charles, 18, Detroit, MI, boatman, private, Co. I, survived

Murphy, Francis H., 18, Hudson, NY, teamster, private, Co. C, survived

Murray, Horace W., 32, Harrisburg, PA, laborer, private, Co. I (not present)

Murray, James, 24, Lafayette, VA, laborer, private (not present)

Myers, Francis, 23, Paterson, NJ, laborer, private, Co. K, wounded July 18, 1863, at Ft. Wagner

Myers, John, 33, Oxford, OH, teamster, private, Co. I, survived

Myers, William, 22, Washington, DC, waiter, private, Co. G, missing July 18, 1863, after Ft. Wagner

Naylor, Benjamin, 18, Montrose, PA, mechanic, private, Co. C, survived

Neal, Samuel, 24, Philadelphia, PA, farmer, private, Co. B, wounded July 18, 1863, at Ft. Wagner

Nelson, Charles E., 21, Bristol, VT, farmer, private, Co. I (not present)

Nelson, Daniel, 20, Montrose, PA, mechanic, private, Co. C, survived

Nelson, James, 24, Chatham, Canada, cook, private, Co. D, survived

Nelson, James, 28, Warbeck, PA, farmer, private, Co. F, survived

Nelson, Richard, 44, laborer, private, Co. C, survived

Nelson, Robert, 19, Niles, MI, laborer, private, Co. K, survived

Nesbitt, William W., 20, Altoona, PA, barber, private, promoted to corporal, Co. D, survived

*****Netson, William J.,** 27, Niagara, NY, private, served as musician, Cos. E,K, survived [pl. 27]

Nettle, John H., 27, Boston, MA, blacksmith, private, Co. A, wounded July 18, 1863, at Ft. Wagner

Newby, James R., 19, New London, CT, laborer, private, Co. E, survived

Newell, Robert R., 19, Philadelphia, MA, student, 2nd lieutenant, promoted to captain, Co. B (not present)

Newport, Erastus, 32, Monson, MA, farmer, private, Co. B (not present)

Newport, Fitz Henry, 26, Hardwick, MA, laborer, private (not present)

Newton, Stephen, 18, New Haven, CT, waiter, private, Co. D, killed July 18, 1863, at Ft. Wagner

Nicholas, Lemuel, 24, Philadelphia, PA, shoemaker, private, Co. B, survived

Nichols, Harrison, 26, Oberlin, OH, farmer, private, Co. G, missing July 18, 1863, after Ft. Wagner

Nichols, John, 26, Concord, MA, seaman, private, Co. A (not present)

Nichols, John, 26, Haiti, seaman, private, transferred to 55th Mass. (not present)

Niles, William H., 21, Kingston, RI, seaman, private, Co. G (not present)

Noe, Charles, 26, Springfield, MA, teamster, private, promoted to corporal, Co. A, survived

Nokes, Jeremiah, 42, Monterey, MA, laborer, private, Co. K (not present)

Norman, Henry, 20, Concordville, PA, farmer, private, promoted to sergeant, Co. F, survived

Nutt, William, 26, Natick, MA, shoemaker (?), served as 2nd lieutenant, Co. F (not present)

Oaky, John, 24, Columbia, PA, laborer, private, Co. G, survived

Oliver, James, 25, Salem County, NJ, waiter, private, promoted to corporal, Co. D, survived

Oliver, Wm. H., 20, Springfield, MA, trader, private, Co. A (not present)

O'Neil, John, 24, Buffalo, NY, cook, private, Co. D, survived

Ormsbee, John E., 18, Rutland, VT, laborer, private, Co. B (not present)

Owans, John, transferred to 55th Mass.

Owen, Clark, 19, Mansfield, KS, farmer, private, Co. F, survived

Owen, William, 36, New York, NY, laborer, private (not present)

Owens, Charles, 24, New Orleans, LA, cook, private, Co. E, survived

Owens, James, 28, Savannah, GA, private (not present)

Paine, William, 38, Fredericktown, VA, laborer, private, transferred to 55th Mass. (not present)

Palmer, Ishmael, 25, Springboro, OH, laborer, private, Co. K, survived

*Palmer, Joseph A., 23, Dayton, OH, barber, private, promoted to sergeant, Co. K, survived [p. 17, fig. 10]

Parker, George, 21, Cleveland, OH, painter, private, Co. E, survived

Parker, Henry, 22, Lancaster County, PA, laborer, private, Co. D, survived

Parker, Jeremiah, 21, West Chester, PA, farmer, private, Co. B, survived

Parker, John, 23, Philadelphia, PA, teamster, private, Co. B, survived

Parker, John H., 21, Bridgeville, DE, laborer, private, Co. E, survived

Parker, William, 21, Martinsburg, PA, farmer, private, Co. I, survived

Parkis, Francis, 40, Russell, MA, laborer, private, Co. K (not present)

Parks, Edward, 43, Carlisle, PA, hostler, private, Co. I, survived

Parks, Henry, 39, Woodstock, VT, farmer, private, Co. I (not present)

Parritt, William, 20, Sharon, CT, glassmaker, private, Co. G (not present)

Partridge, David A., 29, Medway, MA, bootmaker (?), 2nd lieutenant, promoted to captain, Cos. E,G,C, survived

Passiby, William (alt.: Passaby, Passidy), 27, Camden County, NJ, farmer, private, Co. D, survived

Patten, Benjamin, 23, Cincinnati, OH, laborer, private, Co. G, survived

Patterson, Alexander, 28, Boston, MA, barber, private, Co. G (not present)

Patterson, Charles T., 26, Boston, MA, barber, private, Co. F (not present)

Patterson, Henry, 20, Oberlin, OH, mason, private, promoted to sergeant, Co. F, survived

Patterson, Robert, 19, Norfolk, VA, Butcher, private, transferred to 55th Mass. (not present)

Payne, Nelson, 23, Adrian, MI, farmer, private, Co. G, survived

Peal, Henry T., 25, Cleveland, OH, shoemaker, private, Co. F, survived

Pease, Giles M., 24, Boston, MA, physician, asst. surgeon, promoted to 1st lieutenant & asst. surgeon (not present)

Peer, John W., 21, Philadelphia, PA, barber, private, Co. B, survived

Pegram, Edward, 25, Cleveland, OH, laborer, private, Co. H, survived

Pell, George M., 30, North Lee, MA, farmer, private, Co. A (not present)

Pennington, William F., 18, Coatesville, PA, farmer, private, Co. C, survived

Perkins, Washington, 35, Boston, MA, laborer, private, Co. A, survived

Pernell, George, 19, New Haven, CT, farmer, private, transferred to 55th Mass. (not present)

Perow, Joseph, 29, Burlington, NJ, butcher, private, Co. A, wounded July 18, 1863, at Ft. Wagner

Perry, C. O., 19, Hartford County, NC, farmer, private, transferred to 55th Mass. (not present)

Perry, Thomas, 39, Adams County, MS, farmer, private (not present)

Perry, William, 20, Elmira, NY, laborer, private, Co. H, survived

Pertiller, Richard, 19, Owego, NY, farmer, private, Co. F, survived

Peters, Amasa A., 21, Bristol, VT, laborer, private, Co. G (not present)

Peters, Daniel P. (alt.: David), 39, Brooklyn, CT, farmer, private, transferred to 55th Mass. (not present)

Peters, George G., 19, Lenox, MA, farmer, private, Co. A, survived

Peters, Joseph F., 26, Laconia, NH, farmer, private, Co. F, survived

Peters, William, 27, Pittsfield, MA, porter, private, Co. E (not present)

Phelps, Emery, 18, New Bedford, MA, shoemaker, private, Co. C, survived

Phelps, William J., 18, St. Albans, VT, laborer, private, Co. C, survived

Philips, Anderson, Denver, CO, laborer, private (not present)

Philops, Jeremiah, 28, Marshall, MI, boot maker, private, Co. H, survived

Phoenix, James, 24, Pottsville, PA, laborer, private, Co. K, survived

Pierce, Harrison, 21, Monson, MA, farmer, private, Co. A, killed July 18, 1863, at Ft. Wagner

Pierce, Solomon, 42, Monson, MA, farmer, private, Co. A (not present)

Pierce, Warren, 19, Monson, MA, farmer, private, Co. A (not present)

Pillow, William, 23, farmer, private, Co. I, missing July 18, 1863, after Ft. Wagner

Pinckney, Alexander, 28, Chatham, Canada, peddler, private, promoted to sergeant, Co. D, survived

Piner, Philip, 22, seaman, private, Co. D (not present)

Pinn, Samuel, 19, Lancaster County, PA, barber, private, promoted to corporal, Co. D, survived

Piper, Charles H., 23, Stockbridge, MA, farmer, private, Co. A (not present)

Platner, Thomas Edward, 17, Hudson, NY, laborer, private, Co. A, survived

Pleasant, William H., 18, Cleveland, OH, farmer, private, promoted to sergeant, Co. H, survived

Plowden, John, 22, Chambersburg, PA, laborer, served as corporal, Co. D, wounded July 18, 1863, at Ft. Wagner

Pope, George, 19, Brookline, MA, clerk (?), captain, promoted to lieutenant colonel, wounded July 18, 1863, at Ft. Wagner

Porter, Charles C., 34, New Haven, CT, farmer, private, Co. D (not present)

Porter, Edward, 44, Washington, MA, farmer, private, transferred to 55th Mass. (not present)

Porter, Marshall, 18, Pownall, VT, farmer, private, Co. G (not present)

Porter, William, 23, New Bedford, MA, waiter, private, Co. A (not present)

Porter, William D., 25, New York, NY, musician (?), private, Co. A, survived

Postley, James, 19, Elmira, NY, laborer, private, Co. F, survived

Potter, Charles, 18, Pittsfield, MA, laborer, private, Co. F, survived

Potter, Charles W., 28, Hinsdale, MA, barber, private, Co. B (not present)

Potter, Franklin, 26, New York, NY, laborer, private, Co. A, wounded July 18, 1863, at Ft. Wagner

Powell, Allen, 25, Front Royal, VT, blacksmith, private, Co. I, wounded July 18, 1863, at Ft. Wagner

Powell, James H., 20, Buffalo, NY, farmer, private, promoted to corporal, Co. F, survived

Powers, Francis, 21, CT, farmer, private (not present)

Prator, Anson (alt.: Praytor), 28, Lucas County, OH, farmer, private, Co. D, survived

Pratt, James Albert, 24, West Roxbury, MA, carpenter (?), served as 2nd lieutenant, Co. G, wounded July 18, 1863, at Ft. Wagner

Preston, Charles Henry, 22, West Chester, PA, farmer, private, Co. B, survived

Price, Cornelius, 25, Underhill, VT, laborer, private, Co. A (not present)

Price, David, 26, Saratoga County, NY, farmer, private, Co. G, survived

Price, George, 30, Montrose, PA, farmer, private, Co. C, missing July 18, 1863, after Ft. Wagner

Price, James, 26, VA, private (not present)

Price, James F., 31, Buffalo, NY, laborer, private, Co. H, survived

Price, John E., 27, Cincinnati, OH, farmer, private, Co. I, wounded July 18, 1863, at Ft. Wagner

Price, John P., 38, Elmira, NY, barber, private, Co. F, survived

Price, John P., 23, Essex County, MA, private (not present)

Price, William

Prime, Daniel, 19, Easton, PA, laborer, private, Co. H, survived

Prince, Abel, 35, St. Albans, VT, farmer, private, Co. K (not present)

Prince, Charles, 21, St. Albans, VT, farmer, private, Co. C (not present)

Prince, Daniel, 21, St. Albans, VT, laborer, private, Co. C (not present)

Prince, Henry, 24, Charlotte, VT, farmer, private, Co. H (not present)

Prince, Isaac, 21, Charlotte, VT, farmer, private, Co. H (not present)

Prince, Isaac, 18, St. Albans, VT, farmer, private, Co. C (not present)

Prince, Jason, 24, Scituate, MA, farmer, private, Co. G (not present)

Princeton, William, 33, Cleveland, OH, farmer, private, Co. E (not present)

Pritchet, Robert, 18, Pontiac, IN, laborer, private, Co. K, survived

Proctor, Joseph, 24, Chambersburg, PA, cook, private, Co. H, survived

Proctor, Joseph J., 25, Detroit, MI, carpenter, private, promoted to corporal, Co. E, missing July 18, 1863, after Ft. Wagner

Prosser, George T., 21, Columbia, PA, laborer, private, Co. D, captured July 18, 1863, at Ft. Wagner

Pruyn, Peter H., 26, Lenox, MA, farmer, private, Co. A, wounded July 18, 1863, at Ft. Wagner

Pryce, James H., 19, Wilmington, NC, laborer, private, Co. H (not present)

Quinn, James C., 23, Rutland, VT, laborer, private, Co. K (not present)

Radzinsky, Louis D., 29, physician (?), asst. surgeon, promoted to 1st lieutenant/asst. surgeon (not present)

Ragens, George, 18, Chambersburg, PA, chimney sweep, private, Co. I, wounded July 18, 1863, at Ft. Wagner

Raimer, Newman, 18, Newport, IN, laborer, private, Co. H, survived

Raymuor, William, 19, Shippensburg, PA, laborer, private, Co. G, survived

Reader, George J., 36, Granby, CT, farmer, private, Co. E (not present)

Reason, Charles K., 23, Syracuse, NY, laborer, private, Co. E, wounded July 18, 1863, at Ft. Wagner

Rector, Napoleon B., 28, Sandusky, OH, porter, private, Co. F, survived

Redmond, William H., 21, Newport, IN, farmer, private, Co. K, survived

Reed, Charles, 21, Barre, MA, farmer, private, Co. D (not present)

Reed, John W., 22, Philadelphia, PA, laborer, private, Co. B (not present)

Reed, Joseph W., 23, Plymouth, NH, farmer, private, Co. D (not present)

Reed, Lewis, 21, Abington, MA, stitcher (?), 2nd lieutenant, promoted to captain, Cos. F,H,I,C,G,K,A (not present)

Reid, David, 35, Boston, MA, bookkeeper (?), 2nd lieutenant, promoted to 1st lieutenant, Cos. C,A,E,G, survived

Remley, George 19, Green County OH, laborer, private, Co. C, survived

Renkins, Alexander W., 21, Buffalo, NY, sailor, private, promoted to corporal, Co. D, wounded July 18, 1863, at Ft. Wagner

Rensellear, Charles M., 21, Easthampton, MA, blacksmith, private, Co. C (not present)

Reynolds, George, 20, Corning, NY, laborer, private, Co. G, survived

Reynolds, Samuel, 16, Littleton, MA, laborer, private, Co. H (not present)

Rice, Joseph J., 22, Camden, NJ, farmer, private, Co. D, survived

Rice, Thomas, 28, Mercersburg, PA, laborer, private, Co. F, survived

Richardson, Andrew, 23, Philadelphia, PA, stevedore, private, Co. B, survived

Richardson, Joseph T., 18, Cleveland, OH, mason, private, Co. E, survived

Rickman, James M., 19, Greenville, OH, laborer, private, Co. K, survived

Rideout, Charles, 22, Mercersburg, PA, farmer, private, Co. I, survived

Rideout, James, 17, Mercersburg, PA, laborer, private, Co. I, survived

Ridgeley, Richard, 26, Detroit, MI, laborer, private, Co. H, survived

Ridgeway, Oliver B., 36, Oberlin, OH, wagoner, private, Co. F, survived

Rigby, William, 21, West Chester, PA, farmer, private, Co. B, captured July 18, 1863, at Ft. Wagner

Riggs, Thomas Peter, 19, Georgetown, Canada, upholsterer, private, Co. D, killed July 18, 1863, at Ft. Wagner

Riley, George, 21, Fleming County, KY, cook, private (not present)

Riley, James, 17, Chicago, IL, farmer, private, Co. H, survived

Ringgold, George N., 20, Pittsfield, MA, barber, private, promoted to corporal, Co. A, survived

Ringold, James W., 18, Philadelphia, PA, farmer, private, Co. B, survived

Ritchie, John, 26, Boston, MA, student (?), 1st lieutenant, promoted to 1st lieutenant/quartermaster, survived

Roberts, Mark, 43, Bristol, VT, laborer, private, Co. I (not present)

Robinson, Charles R., 18, Philadelphia, PA, waiter, private, Co. G, survived

Robinson, Frank, 28, East Liberty, PA, laborer, private, Co. K, survived

Robinson, George, 20, Plymouth, MA, laborer, private, Co. E (not present)

Robinson, John, 19, Halifax, Nova Scotia, Canada, sailor, private, Co. D (not present)

Robinson, Lewis, 21, Columbia, PA, farmer, private, Co. A (not present)

Robinson, Milton, 21, Indianapolis, IN, laborer, private, Co. F, survived

Robinson, Peter, 28, New York, NY, laborer, private, Co. E, survived

Robinson, Richard, 25, Worcester, MA, barber, private, Co. F, survived

Robinson, Samuel, 21, Rochester, NY, groom, private, Co. D (not present)

Robinson, Thomas Peter, 21, Staten Island, NY, farmer (?), private, Co. A, wounded July 1863 (date not specified)

Robinson, William, 23, Detroit, MI, farmer, private, Co. G, survived

Robinson, William, 19, Sandy Hill, NY, boatman, private, Co. G, survived

Robinson, William, 21, bricklayer, private, Co. E (not present)

Robinson, William H., 21, Lynn, MA, laborer, private, Co. E, survived

Rogers, Edward, 26, Burlington, VT, farmer, private, Co. C (not present)

Rogers, Frederick E., 20, Chelsea, MA, clerk (?), served as 2nd lieutenant, Co. A (not present)

Rollings, Robert, 35, Andover, MA, farmer, private, Co. A (not present)

Rolls, Jeremiah, 22, Cincinnati, OH, boatman, private, promoted to 1st sergeant, Co. I, survived

Rome, George, 29, Providence, RI, Fireman, private, transferred to 55th Mass. (not present)

Roper, David R., 22, Indianapolis, IN, farmer, private, Co. F, killed July 18, 1863, at Ft. Wagner

Ross, Benjamin, 21, Boston, MA, laborer, private, Co. K, survived

Ross, Daniel, 19, Adrian, MI, farmer, private, Co. G, survived

Ross, James, 28, Boston, MA, laborer, private, Co. B (not present)

Roundtree, Tyrel (alt.: Tyrell, Tyrrel), 28, New Bedford, MA, farmer, private, Co. H (not present)

Rouse, Elias S., 22, Chatham, Canada, laborer, private, Co. K, wounded July 18, 1863, at Ft. Wagner

Roy, Lindsley, 22, Boston, MA, waterman, private, Co. A (not present)

Rudolph, Francis J., 19, West Chester, PA, farmer, private, Co. K, survived

Ruker, Daniel, 19, Knoxbury County, AL, brush maker, private, transferred to 55th Mass. (not present)

Russ, Jordan, 28, Detroit, MI, blacksmith (?), private, Co. E, wounded July 18, 1863, at Ft. Wagner

*****Russell, Cabot J.,** 18, Boston, MA, student (?), 1st lieutenant, promoted to captain, Co. H, killed July 18, 1863, at Ft. Wagner [pl. 40]

Russell, Henry, 21, Oxford, OH, laborer, private, Co. I, survived

Russell, James R., 35, Carlisle, PA, laborer, private, Co. H, survived

Rutledge, William, 34, Oberlin, OH, woodcutter, private, Co. G, survived

Ryan, Warner, 19, Frederick County, MD, farmer, private, Co. D, survived

Sampson, David H., 19, Boston, MA, teamster, private, transferred to 55th Mass. (not present)

Sanders, Nathan, 19, Holt County, MO, waiter, private (not present)

Saunders, Enoch, 38, Cambridge, MA, laborer, private, Co. A, survived

Saunders, John, 22, Chatham, Canada, laborer, private, Co. D, survived

Sawyer, Isaac, 21, Brattleboro, VT, hostler, private, Co. E, survived

Schenck, Anthony, 26, Buffalo, NY, laborer, private, Co. H (not present)

Schuyler, Arthur, 18, Lawrence, MA, laborer, private, Co. C, survived

Scott, Alfred Freeman, 20, Falmouth, MA, farmer, private, Co. H (not present)

Scott, Charles, 24, Ann Arbor, MI, laborer, private, Co. H, survived

Scott, George, 18, Dorchester, MA, farmer, private, Co. H (not present)

Scott, George, 24, Harrisburg, PA, laborer, private, promoted to corporal, Co. D (not present)

Scott, George H., 18, Rutland, VT, laborer, private, Co. B (not present)

Scott, Thomas, 28, Boston, MA, confectioner, private, Co. H (not present)

Scott, William, 21, Newark, NJ, coachman, private, Co. C, survived

Scott, William, 42, Rutland, VT, laborer, private, Co. I (not present)

Scott, William H., 22, Ypsilanti, MI, waiter, private, Co. K, survived

Seaman, Alfred, 25, Parksburg, PA, laborer, private, Co. G, survived

Seaman, Richard, 19, Brooklyn, NY, laborer, private, Co. D, survived

Sessor, Oscar, 24, Portsmouth, NH, sailor, private, promoted to corporal, Co. D (not present)

Shaffer, John, 22, Newport, IA, laborer, private, promoted to corporal, Co. H, survived

Sharts, James E., 24, North Lee, MA, farmer, private, Co. A, wounded July 18, 1863, at Ft. Wagner

Sharts, William H., 23, North Lee, MA, laborer, private, Co. A, survived

*Shaw, Robert G., 25, New York, NY, businessman, major, promoted to colonel, killed July 18, 1863, at Ft. Wagner [pl. 16]

Shaw, Thomas, 23, Cincinnati, OH, boatman, private, promoted to corporal, Co. K, survived

Sherman, William, 23, Newport, RI, farmer, private, transferred to 55th Mass. (not present)

Shirk, John, 20, Shippensburg, PA, farmer, private, Co. K, survived

Shirley, John L., 23, West Chester, PA, farmer, private, Co. B, survived

Shorter, John, 16, Amboy, MI, farmer, private, Co. G, survived

Shrewsbury, John, 21, Cincinnati, OH, boatman, private, Co. I, wounded July 18, 1863, at Ft. Wagner

Sidney, Dolby, New Haven, CT, farmer, private, Co. D (not present)

Silvers, William, 31, Toronto, Canada, steward, private, transferred to 55th Mass. (not present)

Simmons, John, 24, Kalamazoo, MI, foundryman, private, promoted to corporal, Co. I, survived

Simmons, Robert J., 26, Bermuda, clerk, private, promoted to 1st sergeant, Co. B, wounded and imprisoned July 18, 1863, at Ft. Wagner

Simms, Abram C., 20, Oxford, OH, farmer, private, promoted to corporal, Co. I, survived

Simpkins, William H., 23, West Roxbury, MA, clerk (?), served as captain, Co. K, killed July 18, 1863, at Ft. Wagner

Simpson, Henry, 21, Columbus, OH, barber, private, Co. G, survived

Simpson, Louis L., 22, Hingham, MA, shoemaker, private, Co. G (not present)

Sims, John, 36, Boston, MA, engineer, private, promoted to corporal, Co. G, survived

Sisco, Stephen H. (alt.: Scisco), 22, Mendon, MA, farmer, private, Co. G (not present)

Siscoe, John H., 20, Catskill, NY, farmer, private, promoted to corporal, Co. A, survived

Siscoe, Richard, 19, Catskill, NY, farmer, private, Co. A, survived

Slaughter, Simon, 24, NC, Hostler, private, transferred to 55th Mass. (not present)

Slider, John, 21, Mercersburg, PA, laborer, private, Co. I, survived

Smith, Augustus, 18, Orange County, NY, farmer, private, Co. D, survived

Smith, Baltimore, 41, Cincinnati, OH, carpenter, private, Co. I, missing July 18, 1863, after Ft. Wagner

Smith, Burrill, 18, Boston, MA, clerk, private, promoted to 1st sergeant, Co. A, wounded July 18, 1863, at Ft. Wagner

*Smith, Charles A., 19, Montrose, PA, laborer, private, Co. C, survived [pl. 33]

Smith, Edward H., 18, Lockhaven, PA, cabinetmaker, private, Co. H, survived

Smith, Edward H., 21, West Chester, PA, farmer, private, Co. B, survived

Smith, Enos, 30, Easton, PA, laborer, private, Co. H (not present)

Smith, George, 27, Cincinnati, OH, laborer, private, Co. K, survived

Smith, George, 24, Elmira, NY, laborer, private, Co. F, survived

Smith, George W., 19, Toledo, OH, laborer, private, Co. K, survived

Smith, Grimm Z., 23, Boston, MA, painter, private, Co. I (not present)

Smith, Henry, 18, Chicago, IL, laborer, private, Co. H, survived

Smith, Henry, 22, Niles, MI, farmer, private, Co. I, survived

Smith, Henry

Smith, Isaac, 30, Cincinnati, OH, cook, private, Co. G, survived

Smith, Isaac 19, Mount Pleasant, OH, farmer, private, Co. G, survived

Smith, James, 20, Philadelphia, PA, butcher, private, Co. B, survived

Smith, James H., 22, Harrisburg, PA, laborer, private, Co. I, survived

Smith, James H., 19, Toronto, Canada, sailor, private, promoted to corporal, Co. D, survived

Smith, John, 18, Coatesville, PA, farmer, private, Co. C, survived

Smith, John, 26, Somerset County, MD, laborer, private, Co. A, wounded July 18, 1863, at Ft. Wagner

Smith, Lewis, 19, Philadelphia, PA, laborer, private, promoted to corporal, Co. B, survived

Smith, Louis, 25, Columbus, OH, painter, private, Co. I, survived

Smith, Orren E., 24, Webster, MA, seaman (?), 1st lieutenant, promoted to captain, Co. G, wounded July 18, 1863, at Ft. Wagner

Smith, Peter, 24, Central America, sailor, private, transferred to 55th Mass. (not present)

Smith, Richard R., 22, Unionville, PA, farmer, private, Co. K, survived

Smith, Robert, 23, Cleveland, OH, laborer, private, Co. H, survived

Smith, Robert, 21, Elmira, NY, laborer, private, Co. F, survived

Smith, Robert, 36, Springfield, OH, brickmaker, private, Co. E, survived

Smith, Samuel, 30, Boston, MA, laborer, private, promoted to corporal, Co. A, survived

Smith, Samuel, 20, Pettes County, MO, farmer, private, Co. G, survived

Smith, Thomas F., 24, Montreal, Canada, laborer, private, transferred to 55th Mass. (not present)

Smith, William, 22, Morgan County, VA, laborer, private, promoted to corporal, Co. I, survived

Smith, William, 24, Salem, OH, laborer, private, Co. K, survived

Smith, William A., 18, Utica, NY, laborer, private, transferred to 55th Mass. (not present)

Smith, William P., 24, New Haven, CT, farmer, private, Co. F, wounded July 18, 1863, at Ft. Wagner

Snowden, Charles, 19, Lewiston, PA, barber, private, promoted to sergeant, Co. F, survived

Snowden, John A., 20, Philadelphia, PA, laborer, private, Co. B, missing July 18, 1863, after Ft. Wagner; supposed killed

Snowdon, John, 23, Montgomery County, MD, laborer, private, transferred to 55th Mass. (not present)

Snowden, Philip, 18, Elmira, NY, laborer, private, Co. F, survived

South, Edward, 25, Norristown, DE, waiter, private, transferred to 55th Mass. (not present)

Soward, John, 30, Cleveland, OH, cook, private, Co. G, survived

Spain, William, 22, Havanna, OH, farmer, private, Co. E, survived

Sparrow, Nathaniel, 34, Boston, MA, carpenter, private, promoted to corporal, Co. D, survived

*****Spear, Daniel,** 21, Boston, MA, sailmaker (?), served as 2nd lieutenant, Co. C (not present) [pl. 35]

Spencer, Aaron, 20, North Lee, MA, laborer, private, promoted to corporal, Co. A, survived

Sprague, Nathan, 23, Rochester, NY, gardener, private, Co. D (not present)

Spriggs, Enos, 21, West Chester, PA, farmer, private, Co. B, survived

*****Spriggs, Isaiah,** 19, Chelsea, MA, laborer, private, Co. A, survived [p. 17, fig. 9]

Stackhouse, John, 30, Lynn, MA, laborer, private, Co. F (not present)

Stanley, Romulus, 24, Charlestown, MA, seaman, private, transferred to 55th Mass. (not present)

Stanton, Charles, 21, Glens Falls, NY, boatman, private, Co. G, wounded and captured July 18, 1863, at Ft. Wagner

States, Daniel, 18, Philadelphia, PA, teamster, private, Co. B, wounded and imprisoned July 18, 1863; returned June 7, 1865

Stephens, George, 31, Boston, MA, cabinetmaker, private, Co. B, survived

Stephens, George, 18, Shiloh, NC, laborer, private, transferred to 55th Mass. (not present)

Stevens, Edward L., 21, Brighton, MA, clerk (?), 2nd lieutenant, promoted to 1st lieutenant, Co. H (not present)

Stevens, John, 23, Pontiac, MI, farmer, private, Co. G, missing July 18, 1863, after Ft. Wagner

Stevens, Robert, 27, New Bedford, MA, farmer, private, Co. C, survived

Stevens, William A., 19, Great Barrington, MA, laborer, private, Co. A, survived

Stevenson, Allen W., 21, Cincinnati, OH, tobacconist, private, Co. K, wounded and missing July 18, 1863, at Ft. Wagner

Stevenson, Samuel, 27, Washington, DC, farmer, private, promoted to corporal, Co. K, survived

Stevenson, William, 18, Fayetteville, PA, laborer, private, Co. I, survived

Steward, Charles, 23, sailor, private, Co. F (not present)

*****Steward, Henry F.,** 23, Adrian, MI, farmer, private, promoted to sergeant, Co. E, survived [pl. 22]

Steward, Latinia (alt.: Stuart, Latimer), 39, Chesterfield, VA, barber, private (not present)

Stewart, Charles, 18, Fairhaven, VT, farmer, private, Co. D (not present)

Stewart, Edward, 24, Pittsburgh, PA, fireman, private, promoted to corporal, Co. E, survived

Stewart, George H., 35, Watertown, NY, laborer, private, Co. G, survived

Stewart, Henderson, 26, Fall River, MA, farmer, private, Co. H (not present)

Stewart, Henry, 19, Rutland, VT, laborer, private (not present)

Stewart, Henry F., 19, Horseheads, NY, barber, private, Co. E, survived

Stewart, Hezekiah, 19, Shelby County, OH, laborer, private, Co. D, survived

Stewart, Jefferson B., 18, Brownsville, MI, laborer, private, Co. H, survived

Stilles, Joseph, 25, Middletown, PA, laborer, private, promoted to corporal, Co. F, survived

Stimpson, Royal

Stone, Edward, 26, Toledo, OH, blacksmith, private, Co. K, wounded July 18, 1863, at Ft. Wagner

*****Stone, Lincoln R.,** 29, Salem, MA, physician (?), surgeon, promoted to major and surgeon, survived [pl. 38]

Stoner, Thomas, 18, Medford, MA, laborer, private, Co. I, missing July 18, 1863, after Ft. Wagner

Storms, George F., 23, Rutland, VT, laborer, private, Co. G (not present)

Story, Charles A., 20, Hadley, MA, farmer, private, promoted to sergeant, Co. B (not present)

Story, Samuel P., 18, Russell, MA, laborer (?), private, Co. K (not present)

Story, William A., 26, Hadley, MA, barber, private, Co. B (not present)

Stotts, John H., 26, Lancaster County, PA, laborer, private, promoted to corporal, Co. D, survived

Streets, George Washington, 19, Hollidaysburg, PA, laborer, private, Co. B, wounded July 18, 1863, at Ft. Wagner

Sufphay, Samuel, 17, Philadelphia, PA, drummer, private, served as drummer, Co. B, survived

Sugland, John G., 21, Vernon, VT, farmer, private, Co. K (not present)

Sulsey, Joseph, 21, Mount Holly, NY, dentist, private, promoted to sergeant, Co. E, wounded July 18, 1863, at Ft. Wagner

Sutherland, John (Suderland?), 30, Stockport, NY, farmer, private, Co. A, survived

Swails, Stephen A., 31, Elmira, NY, boatman, private, promoted to 1st sergeant, Cos. F,C, survived

Swan, Charles, 33, Monterey, MA, laborer, private, Co. B (not present)

Swan, Henry, 45, Monterey, MA, laborer, private, Co. B (not present)

Sylvia, Samuel, 22, Gardsborough, Nova Scotia, Canada, sailor, private, Co. F (not present)

Tabb, America C., 37, Boston, MA, trader, private, Co. A, survived

Talbot, Jacob, 18, West Bridgewater, MA, farmer, private, Co. G (not present)

Tanner, John N., 26, Southbridge, MA, mechanic, private, Co. B, survived

Tappin, Elisha (alt.: Toppin), paperhanger, private, transferred to 55th Mass. (not present)

Taylor, Alexander, 27, Amherst, MA, farmer, private, Co. C (not present)

Taylor, Charles T., 22, Rochester, NY, private (not present)

Taylor, Robert L., 20, Boston, MA, sailor, private, promoted to sergeant, Co. A, survived

Taylor, Thomas, 18, Tyringham, MA, farmer, private, Co. A (not present)

Taylor, William T., 18, Tyringham, MA, farmer, private, Co. A (not present)

Taylor, Willis, 21, Kalamazoo, MI, drummer, private, Co. I, survived

Teale, Jefferson, 31, Mercersburg, PA, farmer, private, Co. I, survived

Terry, Johnson L., 22, Reading, PA, barber, private, Co. H (not present)

Terry, Marion, 30, Detroit, MI, farmer, private, Co. E, survived

Terry, Stephen, 24, Middleboro, MA, seaman, private, Co. I (not present)

Thomas, Andrew, 18, Middletown, PA, boatman, private, Co. F, survived

Thomas, George W., 19, Buffalo, NY, sailor, private, Co. F, survived

Thomas, Isaac, 22, Baltimore, MD, laborer, private, Co. C (not present)

Thomas, Jacob H., 26, Great Barrington, MA, farmer, private, Co. A, survived

Thomas, James W., 31, Barbados, West Indies, seaman, private, transferred to 55th Mass. (not present)

Thomas, Jeremiah, 18, London, Canada, waiter, private, promoted to corporal, Co. E, survived

Thomas, John, 22, Philadelphia, PA, laborer, private, Co. B, survived

Thomas, John, 31, Philadelphia, PA, farmer, private, Co. F, survived

Thomas, John H., 37, Toledo, OH, barber, private, Co. E, survived

Thomas, Richard, laborer, private

Thomas, Samuel, 32, Binghampton, NY, engineer, private, Co. F, survived

Thomas, Sheldon (alt.: Sheldon, Thomas), 23, Middletown, PA, laborer, private, Co. F, killed July 18, 1863, at Ft. Wagner

Thomas, William, 28, Boston, MA, hostler, private, Co. D (not present)

Thomas, William H., 22, Baltimore, MD, porter, private, Co. D, survived

Thompson, Abraham, 36, Albany, NY, farmer, private, Co. F (not present)

Thompson, Albert D., 18, Buffalo, NY, porter, sergeant, promoted to 1st sergeant, Co. D, survived

Thompson, Alexander, 25, Albany, NY, laborer, private, Co. E, survived

Thompson, Benjamin, 24, Jackson, MI, blacksmith, private, Co. F, wounded July 18, 1863, at Ft. Wagner

Thompson, Charles P., 21, Great Barrington, MA, laborer, private, Co. A, survived

Thompson, David E., 20, Shippensburg, PA, farmer, private, promoted to corporal, Co. K, survived

Thompson, Freeman, 36, Hinsdale, MA, farmer, private, Co. I (not present)

Thompson, George, 42, Reading, PA, laborer, private, Co. E, wounded July 18, 1863, at Ft. Wagner

Thompson, George A., 23, Montrose, PA, barber, private, Co. E, survived

Thompson, James, 38, Amherst, MA, farmer, private, Co. C, survived

Thompson, James, 30, Monson, MA, laborer, private, Co. F (not present)

Thompson, Jeremiah, 19, Bono, OH, farmer, private, Co. C, survived

Thompson, William, 29, St. Thomas, West Indies, laborer, private, transferred to 55th Mass. (not present)

Thompson, William, 18, Thomas, OH, laborer, private, Co. E, survived

Thorn, James P., laborer, private, transferred to 55th Mass. (not present)

Tilden, Joseph, 24, Boston, MA, merchant (?), enlisted as 1st lieutenant, Co. H (not present)

Till, Benjamin A., 19, Hadley, MA, laborer, private, Co. I (not present)

Till, Samuel C., 18, Hadley, MA, broom tier, private, Co. C (not present)

Tillman, Henry, 24, Greensboro, MD, private, transferred to 55th Mass. (not present)

Tillman, Martin, 22, Pittsburgh, PA, boatman, private, Co. G, survived

Timms, William H.H., 23, Galesburg, IL, barber, private, Co. H, survived

Tiptin, Samuel, 18, Battle Creek, MI, farmer, private, Co. I, wounded July 18, 1863, at Ft. Wagner

Titus, James H., 23, Trenton, NJ, teamster, private, promoted to corporal, Co. G, survived

Titus, John H., 20, Albany, NY, laborer, private, Co. E, survived

Titus, William R., 19, Erie, PA, laborer, private, Co. H (not present)

Tobias, Ezra, 27, Montgomery, MA, laborer (?), private, Co. K (not present)

Tolbert, George W., 22, Cecil County, MD, farmer, private, Co. I, survived

*****Tomlinson, Ezekiel G.,** 22, clerk (?), 2nd lieutenant, promoted to 1st lieutenant (not present) [pl. 35]

Toney, Henry, stonecutter, private, transferred to 55th Mass. (not present)

Torrance, Abram, 43, New Bedford, MA, laborer, corporal, demoted to private, Co. C, missing July 18, 1863, after Ft. Wagner

Townsend, Charles, 24, Detroit, MI, laborer, private, Co. H, survived

*****Townsend, James M.,** 20, Oxford, OH, teamster, private, Co. I, survived [pl. 19]

Townsend, Ralsey R., 35, Springfield, MA, teamster (?), private, Co. A, missing July 18, 1863, after Ft. Wagner

Treadwell, Joshua B., 24, Boston, MA, physician, served as 1st lieutenant & asst. surgeon (not present)

Tripp, Abram, 22, Littleton, MA, farmer, private, Co. G (not present)

Tucker, C. Henry, 18, Battle Creek, MI, farmer, private, promoted to corporal, Co. I, wounded July 18, 1863, at Ft. Wagner

Tucker, Charles E., 25, Boston, MA, clerk (?), 2nd lieutenant, promoted to captain, Cos. I,E,H, wounded July 18, 1863, at Ft. Wagner

Tucker, Henry J., 34, Sheffield, MA, laborer, private, Cos. C,E,H, survived

Tucker, Jeremiah, 19, Boston, MA, laborer, private, Co. A, survived

Tucker, John, 21, Racine, WI, cook, private, Co. F, survived

Turner, Henderson, 22, Martinsburg, PA, farmer, private, Co. I, survived

Turner, John J., 20, Columbia, PA, laborer, private, Co. D, survived

Turner, John W., private (not present)

Turner, Solomon, 22, Lancaster County, PA, farmer, private, Co. D, survived

Turner, Treadwell, 21, New Bedford, MA, laborer, private, Co. C, missing July 18, 1863, after Ft. Wagner

Tyler, John, 23, Columbus, MO, laborer, private (not present)

Tyler, William, 22, Hamilton, Canada, dyer, private (not present)

Tyler, William H., 23, Henry County, KY, dyer, private, Co. G, missing July 18, 1863, after Ft. Wagner

Underwood, William, 25, Mason County, KY, laborer, private, Co. G, missing July 18, 1863, after Ft. Wagner

Valentine, Andrew H., 21, Chambersburg, PA, brickmaker, private, Co. I, survived

Valentine, Samuel, 21, Boston, MA, shoemaker, private, promoted to sergeant, Co. B, survived

Van Allen, Charles, 29, Lenox, MA, farmer, private, Co. A, survived

Van Allen, David H., 33, Great Barrington, MA, laborer, private, promoted to corporal, Co. G (not present)

Van Alstine, William, 19, East Troy, NY, farmer, private, Co. C, survived

Van Alstyne, Charles, 22, Hudson, NY, boatman, private, Co. A, survived

Van Alstyne, Henry, 23, blacksmith, private, Co. D, survived

Van Blake, John, 21, Pittsfield, MA, laborer, private, Co. A, survived

Van Buskirk, Richard Henry (alt.: Busckirk), 16, MA, laborer, private, Co. A (not present)

Van Schaik, Solomon, 28, Troy, NY, cook, private, Co. C, survived

Van Volkenberg, Richard (alt.: Van Valkenberg), 18, Cocksackie, NY, laborer, private, Co. H, survived

Vanalstine, William W., 23, Plainfield, MA, farmer, private, Co. B (not present)

Vanderburgh, Lewis, 30, Burlington, VT, private (not present)

Vanderpool, George, 18, Cocksackie, NY, laborer, private, Co. H, survived

Vanleer, George R., 21, West Chester, PA, farmer, private, Co. B (not present)

Vernonhaus, Alexander, 29, Philadelphia, PA, horseman, private, Co. A, survived

Vinson, Joseph, 43, Barrington, VT, farmer, private, Co. I (not present)

Vogelsang, Peter, 46, Brooklyn, NY, clerk, private, promoted to 1st lieutenant/regimental quartermaster, Cos. H,C, survived

Voorhees, Isaac, 22, Philadelphia, PA, teamster, private, Co. E, survived

Vorce, James W., 21, Cleveland, OH, sailor, private, Co. H (not present)

Vosburgh, John E., 24, Lenox, MA, blacksmith, private, Co. A, survived

Vroman, Samuel, 26, Schoharie, NY, blacksmith, private, Co. D, survived

Wade, Benjamin, 25, Murphreesboro, TN, laborer, private, Co. I, survived

Wakefield, Clinton, 20, Springfield, KY, Washer, private (not present)

Walker, Daniel, 19, VA, farmer, private, transferred to 55th Mass. (not present)

Walker, David, 22, Battle Creek, MI, blacksmith, private, Co. H, survived

Walker, James, 25, Cincinnati, OH, barber, private, Co. G (not present)

Wall, Albert G., 20, Oberlin, OH, laborer, private, Co. G, survived

Wall, John, 20, Oberlin, OH, farmer, private, promoted to sergeant, Co. G, survived

Wallace, Frederick, 20, Cincinnati, OH, barber, private, Co. H (not present)

Wallace, George H., 30, Rutland, VT, farmer, private (not present)

Wallace, Samuel, currier, private, transferred to 55th Mass. (not present)

Walley, William W., 34, fireman, private, Co. I (not present)

Wallis, Alanson, 21, Monson, MA, farmer, private, Co. A, survived

Wallis, James, 23, Monson, MA, farmer, private, Co. A, survived

Walls, Albert, 29, Philadelphia, PA, farmer, private, Co. B, missing July 18, 1863, after Ft. Wagner; supposed killed

Walters, John, 16, Philadelphia, PA, waiter, private, served as musician, Co. D, survived

Walton, James M., 24, Philadelphia, PA, lawyer (?), 1st lieutenant, promoted to major, survived

Ward, Augustus, 19, Jackson, MS, sailor, private, Co. G, survived

Warrick, James, 22, Boston, MA, boatman, private, Co. D (not present)

Washington, Charles, 18, Baltimore, MD, farmer, private, Co. C (not present)

Washington, David, 23, Buffalo, NY, butcher, private, Co. F, survived

Washington, Edward, 26, Philadelphia, PA, laborer, private, promoted to sergeant, Co. B, wounded July 18, 1863, at Ft. Wagner

Washington, Geo. A., 42, Philadelphia, PA, sailor, private, Co. B, survived

Washington, George, 25, Charlottesville, VA, laborer, private, transferred to 55th Mass. (not present)

Washington, George, 29, Syracuse, NY, sailor, private, Co. E, wounded July 18, 1863, at Ft. Wagner

Washington, John, 35, Richmond, VA, shoemaker, private (not present)

Washington, Josiah, 18, Boonsboro, MD, farmer, private, Co. K, survived

Washington, Peter, 21, Middletown, PA, coach driver, private, Co. F, survived

Washington, Stephen, 27, West Chester, PA, laborer, private, Co. B, survived

Washington, William, 18, Washington, DC, farmer, private, Co. G (not present)

Washington, Wm. Henry, 21, West Chester, PA, laborer, private, Co. B, survived

Waterman, George F., 27, Lenox, MA, farmer, private, Co. A, missing July 18, 1863, after Ft. Wagner

Waterman, Henry, 22, South Gardiner, ME, farmer, private, Co. I (not present)

Waterman, Ira, 19, Sheffield, MA, farmer, private, Co. I (not present)

Watson, Anderson, 26, Memphis, TN, boatman, private, Co. I, wounded July 18, 1863, at Ft. Wagner

Watson, Cornelius, 31, Newburgh, NY, preacher (?), private, Co. A, killed July 18, 1863, at Ft. Wagner

Watson, Henry, 18, Chatham Four Corners, NY, laborer, private, promoted to corporal, Co. C, survived

Watson, Hezekiah, 18, Mercersburg, PA, quarryman, private, promoted to corporal, Co. I, wounded July 18, 1863, at Ft. Wagner

Watson, Jacob, 20, Mercersburg, PA, butcher, private, promoted to sergeant, Co. K, survived

Watson, William, 21, Dublin, MD, laborer, private, Co. E, survived

Watson, William H., 27, Elmira, NY, laborer, private, Co. F, survived

Watt, Charles, 19, Cincinnati, OH, shoemaker, private, Co. I, wounded July 18, 1863, at Ft. Wagner

Watts, Isaac J., 18, New Bedford, MA, laborer, private, served as drummer, Co. H, survived

Way, Charles T., 21, Stockbridge, MA, laborer, private, Co. H (not present)

Weathers, Albert, 21, Clay County, MO, laborer, private (not present)

Webber, Sylvester, 21, Ripley, OH, farmer, private, Co. G, survived

Webster, Edward, 24, Harrisburg, PA, laborer, private, Co. E, survived

Webster, Frederick H., 20, Boston, MA, clerk (?), served as 2nd lieutenant, Co. G (not present)

Weeden, Cornelius A., 21, Cambridge, MA, porter, private, promoted to corporal, Co. C, survived

Weeks, John, 19, Chatham, Canada, cook, private, Co. E, missing July 18, 1863, after Ft. Wagner

Weeks, John, 36, Rutland, VT, farmer, private, Co. I (not present)

Weevel, George, 29, Mount Healthy, OH, laborer, private, Co. K, survived

Weever, Samuel, 30, Lenox, MA, farmer, private, Co. D, wounded July 18, 1863, at Ft. Wagner

Weir, James S., 18, Rochester, NY, farmer, private, Co. D (not present)

Welch, Frank M., 21, West Meriden, CT, barber, private, promoted to 1st lieutenant, Co. F, wounded July 18, 1863, at Ft. Wagner

Welcome, Clay, 19, Galesburg, IL, laborer, private, Co. H, survived

Wells, Augustus, 20, Philadelphia, PA, laborer, private, Co. B, survived

Wells, Samuel, 23, Galesburg, IL, laborer, private, promoted to corporal, Co. H, survived

Wells, William, 30, Monterey, MA, laborer, private, Co. E (not present)

Wentworth, Charles B., 45, Woodstock, VT, barber, private, Co. B (not present)

Wentworth, Charles B., 21, Woodstock, VT, barber, private, Co. K (not present)

Wentworth, William H., 23, Woodstock, VT, barber (?), private, Co. I, survived

Wesley, James, 21, private, Co. G

West, Lewis, 22, Lancaster County, PA, waiter, private, Co. D, survived

West, Peter, 39, Chicago, IL, cook, private, Co. H, survived

Wheatland, Simeon J., 38, Salem, MA, porter, private (not present)

Whettebourne, Charles (alt.: Whetburne), 22, Boston, MA, cooper, private, Co. G (not present)

Whipple, George, laborer, private, transferred to 55th Mass.

Whipple, William Henry, 21, Scituate, MA, waiter, private, Co. A, wounded July 18, 1863, at Ft. Wagner

White, Addison, 41, Mechanicsburg, OH, saltmaker, private, Co. E, survived

White, Alexander, 22, Washington, DC, private, transferred to 55th Mass. (not present)

White, George S., farmer, private, transferred to 55th Mass.

White, Harvey, 21, Toledo, OH, laborer, private, Co. K, wounded July 18, 1863, at Ft. Wagner

White, Isaac, 27, Philadelphia, PA, teamster, private, Co. B, survived

White, John, 19, Brantford, CT, shoemaker, private, Co. F (not present)

White, Joseph H.C., 20, Galesburg, IL, laborer, private, Co. H, survived

White, Peter, 35, Buchanan County VA, farmer, private (not present)

Whiten, Charles, 26, Syracuse, NY, laborer, private, Co. E, wounded July 18, 1863, at Ft. Wagner

Whitford, Charles H., 26, Hudson, NY, farmer, private, Co. A, survived

Whiting, Alford, 23, Carlisle, PA, waiter, private, promoted to sergeant, Co. I, wounded and captured July 18, 1863, at Ft. Wagner

Whitney, William L., 21, Cambridge, MA, student (?), 2nd lieutenant, promoted to 1st lieutenant, Cos. G,K (not present)

Wiggins, Albert, farmer, private, transferred to 55th Mass.

Wild, Walter H., 22, Brookline, MA, clerk (?), enlisted as served as 1st lieutenant, Co. K, survived

Wilder, John, 29, Cambridge, MA, served as 2nd lieutenant, survived

Wilkins, James H., 21, New Haven, CT, painter, private, promoted to sergeant, Co. D, survived

Willard, Luther F., 20, New Haven, CT, laborer, private, Co. H (not present)

Willard, Samuel, 24, Boston, MA, tradesman (?), served as captain, Co. B, wounded July 18, 1863, at Ft. Wagner

Willey, Peter, 21, Suffolk, VA, private (not present)

William, John, 18, West Indies, farmer, private (not present)

Williams, Alexander, 33, New York, NY, coachman (?), private, Co. A, survived

Williams, Amos, 25, Tyringham, MA, farmer, private, Co. A, survived

Williams, Benjamin, farmer, private, transferred to 55th Mass.

Williams, Charles, 20, Philadelphia, PA, brickmaker, private, Co. B, captured July 18, 1863, at Ft. Wagner

Williams, Charles A., 21, Mount Healthy, OH, farmer, private, Co. G, wounded July 18, 1863, at Ft. Wagner

Williams, Charles E., 19, Chatham Four Corners, NY, laborer, private, Co. C (not present)

Williams, Curtis, 18, Newbern, NC, servant, private, Co. B (not present)

Williams, Cyrus, 18, Rutland, VT, laborer, private, Co. K (not present)

Williams, Daniel, 21, Boston, MA, farmer, private, Co. C (not present)

Williams, Edward, 18, New York, NY, laborer, private, Co. K, wounded July 18, 1863, at Ft. Wagner

Williams, Edward, 28, Oberlin, OH, laborer, private, Co. F, killed July 18, 1863, at Ft. Wagner

Williams, Edward H., 34, Great Barrington, MA, laborer, private, Co. I (not present)

Williams, Eugene T., 20, Oxford, MA, shoemaker, private, Co. F (not present)

Williams, Ezekiel, 20, Harrisburg, PA, laborer, private, Co. I, missing July 18, 1863, after Ft. Wagner

Williams, George, 25, Chicago, IL, barber, private, Co. H, survived

Williams, George, porter, private, transferred to 55th Mass.

Williams, George W., private, Co. I

Williams, Henry, 18, Chester County, PA, farmer, private, Co. I, missing July 18, 1863, after Ft. Wagner

Williams, Isaac, 22, Windsor, VT, farmer, private, Co. H (not present)

Williams, Jacob, 35, White Plains, NY, farmer, private, Co. F, survived

Williams, James, 19, Glens Falls, NY, boatman, private, Co. G, survived

Williams, James O., 35, Carlisle, PA, laborer, private, Co. H (not present)

Williams, John, 19, Boston, MA, sailor, private, Co. B, survived

Williams, John, 20, Chicago, IL, laborer, private, Co. H, survived

Williams, John, 23, Isle of Brando, Canary Islands, cook, private (not present)

Williams, John Q., 21, Stockbridge, MA, farmer, private, Co. B (not present)

Williams, John W., 24, Brattleboro, VT, laborer, private, Co. G (not present)

Williams, Joseph, 21, Detroit, MI, farmer, private, Co. E, survived

Williams, Neff, 21, Paris, TN, laborer, private, Co. K, survived

Williams, Norman B., 29, Woodstock, VT, private, Co. K (not present)

Williams, Olmstead, 36, Detroit, MI, laborer, private, promoted to corporal, Co. H (not present)

Williams, Preston, 23, Galesburg, IL, laborer (?), private, Co. H, wounded July 18, 1863, at Ft. Wagner

Williams, Richard E., 21, Detroit, MI, bricklayer, private, Co. I, survived

Williams, Valorous W., 43, Stockbridge, MA, laborer, private, Co. B (not present)

Williams, Warton A., 24, New Bedford, MA, teamster, corporal, promoted to sergeant, Co. C, survived

Williamson, John, 19, Hamilton, OH, laborer, private, Co. I, missing July 18, 1863, after Ft. Wagner

Willis, Charles J., 24, Syracuse, NY, machinist (?), private, Co. E, survived

Willis, Franklin, 33, Chatham, Canada, farmer, private, Co. D, killed July 18, 1863, at Ft. Wagner

Willis, Jeremiah, 21, Philadelphia, PA, farmer, private, Co. B, survived

Wilmore, Elias, 19, Jamaica, NY, hostler, private, Co. D, survived

Wilson, A., 2nd lieutenant

Wilson, Bonaparte, 20, GA, private (not present)

Wilson, Eli, 28, Springfield, MA, farmer, private, promoted to corporal, Co. A, survived

Wilson, George, 32, Hudson, NY, laborer, private, Co. A, wounded July 18, 1863, at Ft. Wagner

Wilson, George, 20, Toledo, OH, laborer, private, Co. K, survived

Wilson, George A., 23, private, Co. I (not present)

Wilson, Henry, 19, Pittsfield, MA, laborer, private, Co. I (not present)

Wilson, Isaiah, 21, Oberlin, OH, laborer, private, Co. F, survived

Wilson, James H., 19, Owego, NY, laborer, private, Co. F, survived

*****Wilson, John H.,** 23, Cincinnati, OH, boatman, private, promoted to sergeant major, Co. G, survived [pl. 26]

Wilson, John H., 22, Richmond, IN, blacksmith, private, Co. K, wounded and missing July 18, 1863, at Ft. Wagner

Wilson, Joseph, 27, Newport, IN, blacksmith, private, Co. K, survived

Wilson, Joseph D., 25, Chicago, IL, farmer, private, promoted to sergeant, Co. H (not present)

Wilson, Joseph T., 27, New Bedford, MA, seaman, private, Co. C (not present)

Wilson, Robert E., 35, Cambridge, MA, barber (?), private, Co. K, survived

Wilson, Samuel R., 21, West Chester, PA, farmer, private, Co. B, missing July 18, 1863, after Ft. Wagner; supposed to have died in prison

Wilson, Thomas C., seaman, private, transferred to 55th Mass.

Wilson, Uriah, 22, Pontiac, MI, blacksmith, private, promoted to corporal, Co. K, survived

Wilson, Webster, 24, laborer, private, Co. D, survived

Wilson, William, 29, Indianapolis, IN, laborer (?), private, promoted to corporal, Co. A, survived

Wilson, William H., 22, West Chester, PA, farmer, private, Co. A, survived

Winnie, Samuel, 27, Fulton County, NY, hostler, private, promoted to sergeant, Co. G, wounded July 18, 1863, at Ft. Wagner

Winslow, Henry T., 18, South Scituate, MA, shoemaker, private, Co. H (not present)

Winslow, John W., 24, Louisville, IN, laborer, private, Co. K, survived

Winslow, Richard S., 33, South Scituate, MA, shoemaker, private, Co. H (not present)

Winston, Joseph, 21, Philadelphia, PA, farmer, private, Co. B, survived

Wise, William, 21, Auburn, NY, cook, private, Co. G, survived

Wood, Charles, 19, Detroit, MI, chair maker, private, promoted to corporal, Co. E, survived

Wood, Henry, 18, Albany, NY, waiter, private, Co. H, survived

Wooden, George, 21, Laurel, DE, laborer, private, Co. D (not present)

Woods, Robert, 23, Philadelphia, PA, farmer, private, Co. B, survived

Woods, Stewart W., 27, Carlisle, PA, laborer, private, Co. I, captured July 18, 1863, at Ft. Wagner

Woods, Thomas, 38, New York, NY, teamster, private, promoted to corporal, Co. A, survived

Woodson, Samuel, 23, Knox County, KY, Cook, private (not present)

Worthington, Henry, 18, Defiance, OH, farmer, private, Co. H (not present)

Wright, John, 31, East Chester, MA, farmer, private, Co. K (not present)

Wright, John, 39, New Bedford, MA, laborer, private, Co. C, survived

Wright, John, 19, Philadelphia, PA, laborer, private, served as musician, Co. B, survived

Wright, William, 22, Carlisle, PA, laborer, private, Co. H, survived

Wulff, Erick, 26, Boston, MA, soldier (?), 2nd lieutenant, promoted to 1st lieutenant, Co. F, survived

Wyncoop, John R., 23, Philadelphia, PA, waiter, private, Co. D (not present)

Yates, John W., 19, Reading, PA, hostler, private, Co. E, survived

Young, Hamilton, 29, Montrose, PA, farmer, private, promoted to corporal, Co. C, survived

Young, John W., 23, Columbia, PA, laborer, private, Co. D, survived

Young, Nathan L., 21, New Bedford, MA, barber, private, Co. C, wounded July 18, 1863, at Ft. Wagner

Young, William, 39, Spencer, MA, yeoman, private, Co. F (not present)

Younger, Simpson, private, Co. G (not present)

Younger, Thomas, 19, Chatham, Canada, butcher, private, Co. G, survived

TRANSCRIPTS OF LETTERS IN THE EXHIBITION

Plate 15

From Governor John A. Andrew of Massachusetts
Boston, Jan. 30th, 1863
Francis G. Shaw, Esq., Staten Island, N.Y.

Dear Sir:
As you may have seen by the newspapers, I am about to raise a Colored Regiment in Massachusetts. This I cannot but regard as perhaps the most important corps to be organized during the whole war, in view of what must be the composition of our new levies, and therefore I am very anxious to organize it judiciously in order that it may be a model for all future Colored Regiments. I am desirous to have for its officers—particularly for its field officers—young men of military experience, of firm Anti Slavery principles, ambitions, superior to a vulgar contempt for color, and having faith in the capacity of colored men for military service. Such officers must be necessarily gentlemen of the highest tone and honor, and I shall look for them in those circles of Educated Anti Slavery Society, which next to the colored race itself, has the greatest interest in the success of this experiment.

Reviewing the young men of the character I have described, now in the Massachusetts service, it occurs to me to offer the Colonelcy of such a Regiment to your son, Captain Shaw of the 2nd Mass. Infantry, and the Lt-Colonelcy to Capt. Hallowell of the 20th Mass. Infantry, the son of Mr. Morris L. Hallowell of Philadelphia. With my deep conviction of the importance of this undertaking, in view of the fact that it will be the first Colored Regiment to be raised in the Free States, and that its success or its failure, will go far to elevate or to depress the estimation in which the character of the Colored Americans will be held throughout the World, the command of such a Regiment seems to me to be a high object of ambition for any officer. How much your son may have reflected upon such, a subject I do not know, nor have I any information of his disposition for such a task except what I have derived from his general character and reputation, nor should I wish him to undertake it, unless he could enter upon it with a full sense of its importance, with an earnest determination for its success, and with the assent and sympathy and support of the opinion of his immediate family. I therefore beg to enclose to you the letter in which I make him the offer of this commission, and I will be obliged to you, if you will forward it to him accompanying it with any expression to him of your own views, and if you will also write to me upon the subject.

My mind is drawn towards Captain Shaw by many considerations. I am sure that he would attract the support, sympathy and active co-operation of many besides his immediate family and relatives. The more ardent, faithful, true Republicans and friends of Liberty would recognize in him, a scion of a tree whose fruit and leaves have alike contributed to the strength and healing of our generation. So, also is it with Captain Hallowell. His father is a quaker gentleman of Philadelphia, two of whose sons are officers in our regiments, and another is a Merchant in Boston. Their house in Philadelphia is a hospital almost, for Mass. officers, and the family are full of good works; Mr. H. being my constant advisor in the interest of our soldiers, when sick or in distress in that city. I need not add that young Captain H. is a gallant and fine fellow, true as steel to the cause of Human Nature, as well as to the flag of the Country.

I wish to engage the field officers and then get their aid in selecting those of the line. I have offers from "Oliver T. Beard, of Brooklyn, N.Y. Late Lt.-Col.

48th N. Y. V.," who says he can already furnish 600 men, and from others, wishing to furnish men from New York and from Conn., but I do not wish to start the regiment under a stranger to Massachusetts. Still I have written to Col. H. E. Howe to learn about Col. Beard, since he may be useful in some contingency hereafter. If in any way, by suggestion or otherwise, you can aid the purpose which is the burden of this letter, I shall receive your cooperation with the heartiest gratitude.

[The previous sections were most likely transcribed by a member of the Governor's staff, whereas the following lines and signature were penned by John A. Andrew.]

I don't want the office to go begging; and if this offer is refused I would prefer its being kept reasonably private. Hoping to hear from you immediately on yr receiving this note, I am, with high regard,

Your obdt servant and friend,
John A. Andrew.

Plate 43

Anonymous letter to Shaw family announcing Shaw's death
Beaufort S°C°, July 31st 1863

I regret to inform you that Col Shaw is killed. The 54th Mass., of which he was Col, fought so bravely that Gen. Gilmore put them in a white Brigade. When the attack was to be made on Fort Wagner, the Gen selected his best troops, and among the rest, the 54th. The black soldiers marched side by side with their white comrades in arms to the assault. (Tell it with pride to the world.) The parapct is 30 feet high. Col. Shaw was the first man to mount that high parapet. He waved is sword and shouted "come on boys," and then he fell dead. He died well. Neither Greece nor Rome can excell his heroism.

Plate 45

From Corporal James Henry Gooding
Morris Island [SC]. Sept 28th 1863

Your Excelency Abraham Lincoln:
Your Excelency will pardon the presumtion of an humble individual like myself, in addressing you. but the earnest Solicitation of my Comrades in Arms, besides the genuine interest felt by myself in the matter is my excuse, for placing before the Executive head of the Nation our Common Grievance: On the 6th of the last Month, the Paymaster of the department, informed us, that if we would decide to recieve the sum of $10 (ten dollars) per month, he would come and pay us that sum, but, that, on the sitting of Congress, the Regt would, in his opinion, be *allowed* the other 3 (three.) He did not give us any guarantee that this would be, as he hoped, certainly *he* had no authority for making any such guarantee, and we can not supose him acting in any way interested. Now the main question is. Are we *Soldiers*, or are we LABOURERS. We are fully armed, and equipped, have done all the various Duties, pertaining to a Soldiers life, have conducted ourselves, to the complete satisfaction of General Officers, who, were if any, prejudiced *against* us, but who now accord us all the encouragement, and honour due us: have shared the perils, and Labour, of Reducing the first stronghold, that flaunted a traitor Flag: and more, Mr. President. Today, the Anglo Saxon Mother, Wife, or Sister, are not alone, in tears for departed Sons, Husbands, and Brothers. The patient Trusting Decendants of Africs Clime, have dyed the ground with blood, in defense of the Union, and Democracy. Men too your Excellecny, who know in a measure, the cruelties of the iron heel of oppression, which in years gone by, the very Power, their blood is now being spilled to maintain, ever ground them to the dust. But When the war trumpet sounded o'er the land, when men knew not the Friend from the Traitor, the Black man laid his life at the Altar of the Nation,—and he was refused. When the arms of the Union, were beaten, in the first year of the War,

And the Executive called more food. for its ravaging maw, again, the black man begged, the privilege of Aiding his Country in her need, to be again refused, And now, he is in the War: and how has he conducted himself? Let their dusky forms, rise up, out the mires of James Island, and give the answer. Let the rich mould around Wagners parapets be upturned, and there will be found an Eloquent answer. Obedient and patient, and Solid as a wall are they. all we lack, is a paler hue, and a better acquaintance with the Alphabet. Now Your Excellency, We have done a Soldiers Duty. Why cant we have a Soldiers pay? You caution the Rebel Chieftan, that the United States, knows, no distinction, in her Soldiers: She insists on having all her Soldiers, of whatever, creed or Color, to be treated, according to the usages of War. Now if the United States exacts uniformity of treatment of her Soldiers, from the Insurgents, would it not be well, and consistent, to set the example herself, by paying all her *Soldiers* alike: We of this Regt. were not enlisted under any "contraband" act. But we do not wish to be understood, as rating our Service, of more Value to the Government, that the service of the exslave, Their Service is undoubtedly worth much to the Nation, but Congress made express, provision touching their case, as slaves freed by military necessity, and assuming the Government, to be their temporary Guardian: — Not so with us — Freemen by birth, and consequently, having the advantage of *thinking*, and acting for ourselves, so far as the Laws would allow us. We do not consider ourselves fit subjects for the Contraband act. We appeal to You, Sir: as the Executive of the Nation, to have us Justly Dealt with. The Regt, do pray, that they be assured their service will be fairly appreciated, by paying them as American SOLDIERS, not as menial hirelings. Black men You may well know, are poor, three dollars per month, for a year, will suply their needy Wives, and little ones, with fuel. If you, as chief Magistrate of the Nation, will assure us, of our whole pay. We are content, our Patriotism, our enthusiasm will have a new impetus, to exert our energy more and more to aid Our Country. Not that our hearts ever flagged, in Devotion, spite the evident apathy displayed in our behalf, but We feel as though, our Country spurned us, now we are sworn to serve her.

    Please give this a moments attention

ALS   James Henry Gooding

NOTES

Foreword: Augustus Saint-Gaudens' Devotional Memorial

RICHARD J. POWELL

1   Thomas Wentworth Higginson, "The Shaw Memorial and the Sculptor St. Gaudens," *Century Illustrated Magazine* 54 (June 1897): 176–200.
2   Higginson 1897, 184. For an art historical exegesis of the sculptural relief, see Deborah Stott, "Style and Theory in Italian Renaissance Reliefs," *Bunting Institute Colloquium*, April 12, 1983, http://bit.ly/10hNorB (accessed October 6, 2012).
3   Saint-Gaudens' contemporary and fellow sculptor Lorado Taft also declared the Shaw Memorial a "masterpiece" and without any precedents. See Lorado Taft, *The History of American Sculpture* (New York, 1903), 302. For an examination of Benin bronzes (especially their modes of figural conceptualization), see Barbara Plankensteiner, ed., *Benin: Kings and Rituals: Court Arts from Nigeria* (Museum für Völkerkunde, Vienna, 2007).
4   Higginson 1897, 184.
5   Freeman Henry Morris Murray, *Emancipation and the Freed in American Sculpture: A Study in Interpretation* (Washington, DC, 1916), 168–169.

Seeing What Ought to Be: Photography and the 54th Massachusetts Regiment

SARAH GREENOUGH

Epigraph   Frederick Douglass, "Pictures and Progress," [1864 or 1865], Frederick Douglass Papers, Library of Congress, as quoted in John Stauffer, *The Black Hearts of Men: Radical Abolitionists and the Transformation of Race* (Cambridge, MA: Harvard University Press, 2002), 54. This is a later version of a talk Douglass gave in Boston in 1861, which Stauffer dates to 1864. Maurice O. Wallace and Shawn Michelle Smith, eds., *Pictures and Progress: Early Photography and the Making of African American Identity* (Durham, NC: Duke University Library, 2012), date it as probably 1865.
1   Military regulations at the time did not allow African Americans to be officers.
2   Following a recruiting rally organized by then-Lieutenant J.W.M. Appleton (see pl. 18) at which Edward L. Pierce and Wendell Phillips encouraged free blacks to join the regiment, African Americans fanned out across the Northeast and Canada seeking enlistments for the 54th. The journalist and lawyer Thomas Morris Chester enlisted men in Pennsylvania; the noted black nationalist Martin Delany sought recruits in Canada and Boston; the orator Frederick Douglass worked in Boston and in Rochester, New York; the minister Henry Highland Garnet encouraged men to enlist in New York; the businessman and politician Lewis Hayden concentrated on men in his adopted home of Boston; the attorney, educator, and politician John Mercer Langston recruited in Ohio; the abolitionist and women's rights activist Robert Purvis worked in Philadelphia; the orator Charles Lenox Remond focused on his hometown of Salem, Massachusetts; the attorney John S. Rock urged men to join while working as the justice of the peace for Boston and Suffolk County; and the women's rights activist Sojourner Truth worked in Michigan. Several had children or grandchildren who joined the 54th, such as Martin Delany (Touissant L'Ouverture Delany); Frederick Douglass (Charles and Lewis Douglass); and Sojourner Truth (James Caldwell). See also Edwin S. Redkey, "Brave Black Volunteers: A Profile of the Fifty-fourth Massachusetts Regiment," in Martin H. Blatt, Thomas J. Brown, and Donald Yacovone, eds., *Hope and Glory: Essays on the Legacy of the Fifty-fourth Massachusetts Regiment* (Amherst: University of Massachusetts in association with the Massachusetts Historical Society, Boston, 2001), 20–22.
3   "How a Negro Regiment Looks," *Springfield Republican*, as quoted in *Memorial: RGS* (Cambridge, MA: University Press, 1864), 18.
4   Luis F. Emilio, *A Brave Black Regiment: The History of the Fifty-fourth Regiment of Massachusetts Volunteer Infantry, 1863–1865*, intro. by Gregory J. W. Urwin (1894, 2nd enlarged ed.; repr., New York: DaCapo Press, 1995), 32 (hereafter cited as Emilio 1995).
5   Emilio 1995, 32.
6   "The Fifty-fourth Massachusetts," *New York Daily Tribune*, as quoted in *Memorial: RGS*, 1864, 24. Many years later, Captain Garth W. James provided another perspective on their departure, noting, "prejudice of the rankest sort ... assailed us. No historian of that day will ever forget the alternating cheers and groans, the alternate huzza and reproach which attempted to deafen each other on our march down State street." See Garth W. James, "The Assault on Fort Wagner," *War Papers: Read before the Commandery of the State of Wisconsin, Military Order of the Loyal Legion of the United States* (Milwaukee: Burdick, Armitage, and Allen, 1891), 13.
7   Emilio 1995, 34.
8   Emilio 1995, 44.
9   Emilio 1995, 61.
10   Emilio 1995, 77, 78, 80.
11   William H. Carney in the *Cleveland Gazette*, as quoted in Ronald S. Coddington, *African American Faces of the Civil War: An Album*, foreword by J. Matthew

Gallman (Baltimore: Johns Hopkins University Press, 2012), 59. Coddington (p. 281), notes that Sergeant John W. Wall, who had been chosen as the color-bearer while at Camp Meigs, was reduced to the rank of private in November 1863 for "unsoldierly and cowardly conduct."

12 *Memorial: RGS*, 1864, 57.

13 William H. Carney in *The Topeka Plaindealer* [Kansas], June 4, 1904, as quoted in Coddington 2012, 60.

14 "Letter from a Private in the Fifty-fourth Regiment," *New Bedford Mercury*, August 16, 1863, reprinted in *Memorial: RGS*, 1864, 96–97.

15 It is difficult to compile accurate casualty figures for the Civil War, as battle reports and official histories contain different counts of the number of killed, wounded, and missing soldiers. See Redkey in Blatt et al. 2001, 279–280. Emilio 1995, 392, lists 281 soldiers who were killed, died of wounds or in captivity, were wounded or missing, or were captured and exchanged; Redkey's count totals 284.

16 William B. Taliaferro, as quoted by Brian C. Pohanka, "Fort Wagner and the 54th Massachusetts Volunteer Infantry," *American's Civil War Magazine*; see http://bit.ly/j8FGNN.

17 *The Anti-Slavery Standard*, as quoted in *Memorial: RGS*, 1864, 115, and "The Massachusetts 54th," *New York Post*, as quoted in *Memorial: RGS*, 1864, 106.

18 See Nancy Anderson, "For All Time to Come: Memorializing Robert Gould Shaw and the 54th Massachusetts Regiment," in this publication.

19 After the battle, Carney was sent to a military hospital in Beaufort and returned to the 54th about five months later. He was discharged with a medical disability in June 1864. See Coddington 2012, 60–61.

20 See Adam Goodheart, *1861: The Civil War Awakening* (New York: Alfred A. Knopf, 2011), 180.

21 Emilio 1995.

22 Robert T. Teamoh, *Sketch of the Life and Death of Col. Robert Gould Shaw* (Boston, 1904); Peter Burchard, *One Gallant Rush: Robert Gould Shaw and His Brave Black Regiment* (New York: St. Martin's Press, 1965).

23 Russell Duncan, *Where Death and Glory Meet: Colonel Robert Gould Shaw and the 54th Massachusetts Infantry* (Athens: University of Georgia Press, 1999); and Blatt et al. 2001.

24 Dudley Taylor Cornish, *The Sable Arm: Negro Troops in the Union Army, 1861–1865* (1956; repr., Lawrence: University Press of Kansas, 1987); James M. McPherson, *The Negro's Civil War: How American Negroes Felt and Acted during the War for the Union* (1953; repr., Boston: Little, Brown, 1969); Benjamin Quarles, *The Negro in the Civil War* (Boston: Little, Brown, 1953). See also Hondon Hargrove, *Black Union Soldiers in the Civil War* (Jefferson, NC: McFarland, 1988); Joseph T. Glatthaar, *Forged in Battle: The Civil War Alliance of Black Soldiers and White Officers* (Baton Rouge: Louisiana State University Press, 2000); Edwin S. Redkey, *A Grand Army of Black Men: Letters from African-American Soldiers in the Union Army, 1861–1865* (Cambridge: Cambridge University Press, 1992); William Gladstone, *Men of Color* (Gettysburg, PA: Thomas Publications, 1993); Noah Andre Trudeau, *Like Men of War: Black Troops in the Civil War, 1862–1865* (Boston: Little, Brown, 1998); John David Smith, *Black Soldiers in Blue: African American Troops in the Civil War Era* (Chapel Hill: The University of North Carolina Press, 2002); David Blight, *Race and Reunion: The Civil War in American Memory* (Cambridge, MA: Belknap Press of Harvard University, 2001); and Keith P. Wilson, *Campfires of Freedom: The Camp Life of Black Soldiers during the Civil War* (Kent, OH: Kent State University Press, 2002).

25 Russell Duncan, ed., *The Blue-Eyed Child of Fortune: The Civil War Letters of Colonel Robert Gould Shaw* (Athens: University of Georgia Press, 1992); James Henry Gooding, *On the Altar of Freedom: A Black Soldier's Civil War Letters from the Front*, ed. Virginia M. Adams, foreword by James M. McPherson (Amherst: University of Massachusetts Press, 1991); *Freedom: A Documentary History of Emancipation, 1861–1867* (Cambridge: Cambridge University Press, 1982).

26 See, for example, Kathleen Collins, "Shadow and Substance: Sojourner Truth," *History of Photography* 7 (July–September 1983), 183–205; Deborah Willis, ed., *Picturing Us: African American Identity in Photography* (New York: New Press, 1994); Nell Irvin Painter, *Sojourner Truth: A Life, A Symbol* (New York: W. W. Norton, 1996); Brian Wallis, "Black Bodies, White Science: The Slave Daguerreotypes of Louis Agassiz," *The Journal of Blacks in Higher Education*, no. 12 (Summer, 1996), 102–106; Colin L. Westerbeck, "Frederick Douglass Chooses His Moment," *Art Institute of Chicago Museum Studies* 24, no. 2 (1999), 144–161, 260–262; Shawn Michelle Smith, *Photography on the Color Line: W.E.B. Du Bois, Race, and Visual Culture* (Durham, NC: Duke University Press, 2004); Richard J. Powell, *Cutting a Figure: Fashioning Black Portraiture* (Chicago: University of Chicago Press, 2008); Molly Rogers, *Delia's Tears: Race, Science, and Photography in Nineteenth-Century America* (New Haven, CT: Yale University Press, 2010); and Wallace and Smith 2012. Deborah Willis and Barbara Krauthamer reproduce several photographs of Civil War soldiers, including two members of the 54th, as well as a number of others associated with that regiment in *Envisioning Emancipation: Black Americans and the End of Slavery* (Philadelphia: Temple University Press, 2013).

27 In Coddington 2012, the author reproduces several photographs of 54th soldiers and provides valuable new biographical information about them.

28 Ira Berlin, Joseph P. Reidy, Leslie S. Rowland, eds., *Freedom's Soldiers: The Black Military Experience in the Civil War* (Cambridge: Cambridge University Press, 1998), xvi.

29 See Laura Wexler, "A More Perfect Likeness," in Wallace and Smith 2012, 18–40, for her extensive analysis of this talk.

30 Frederick Douglass, "Pictures and Progress: An Address Delivered in Boston, Massachusetts, on 3 December 1861," in John W. Blassingame, ed., *The Frederick Douglass Papers, Series One: Speeches, Debates, and Interviews*, vol. 3: 1855–63 (New Haven, CT: Yale University Press, 1985), 453; see also introduction to Wallace and Smith 2012, 5–6.

31 Douglass in Blassingame 1985, 453–454; see also introduction and Wexler in Wallace and Smith 2012, 5–6, 21.

32 Douglass in Blassingame 1985, 461, and Frederick Douglass, "Pictures and Progress" [1864 or 1865], Frederick Douglass Papers, Library of Congress, as quoted in introduction to Wallace and Smith 2012, 6–7.

33 Douglass in Blassingame 1985, 454.

34 Douglass in Blassingame 1985, 455; see also Wexler in Wallace and Smith 2012, 21.

35 See Powell 2008, 66–67.

36 Elizabeth Cady Stanton, as quoted in Frederick S. Voss, *Majestic in His Wrath: A Pictorial Life of Frederick Douglass*, introduction by Robert K. Sutton, foreword by Waldo E. Martin Jr. (Washington, DC: Smithsonian Institution Press for the National Portrait Gallery and the National Park Service, 1995), v.

37 Douglass [1864 or 1865], as quoted in the introduction to Wallace and Smith 2012, 7.

38 Introduction to Wallace and Smith 2012, 7.

39 John Rock's middle name has often been cited as "Swett," but a marriage announcement published in the *National Standard and Salem County Advertiser*, August 25, 1852, n.s., vol. 1, no. 52, and *The Salem Sunbeam and Democratic Journal*, August 27, 1852, vol. 9, no. 424, gives the name as "Stewart." Courtesy Harlan Buzby, Salem County Historical Society, Salem, NJ.

40 See Ray Allen Billington, ed., *The Journal of Charlotte Forten: A Free Negro in the Slave Era* (New York: The Dryden Press, 1953), 20–29; 191–197.

41 See Robert Ewell Greene, *Swamp Angels: A Biographical Sketch of the 54th Massachusetts Regiment* (BoMark/Greene Publisher, 1990), 112–113.

42 See William C. Darrah, *Cartes-de-Visite in Nineteenth-Century Photography* (Gettysburg, PA: William C. Darrah, 1981), 19.

43 In the months immediately after the 1861 Battle of Fort Sumter, E. & H. T. Anthony in New York, a photography studio and supply company, was said to have sold 1,000 cartes de visite a day of George S. Cook's portrait of Major Robert Anderson, the Union officer who valiantly but unsuccessfully attempted to defend Fort Sumter. See Beaumont Newhall, *The History of Photography: From 1839 to the Present* (1937; repr., New York: The Museum of Modern Art, 1964), 50. For Holmes, see Darrah 1981, 24.

44 See Collins 1983, 183–205; and Painter 1996, 185–199.

45 A Rochester newspaper, as quoted by Carleton Mabee with Susan Mabee Newhouse, *Sojourner Truth: Slave, Prophet, Legend* (New York: New York University Press, 1993), 187; see also Powell 2008, 46–48.

46 See Willis and Krauthamer 2013, 30.

47 See Emilio 1995, 373.

48 Walt Whitman, "The Real War Will Never Get in the Books," from *Specimen Days* in *Leaves of Grass and Selected Prose*, ed. with introduction by John Kouwenhoven (New York: The Modern Library, 1950), 634–635.

49 The letters of the Demus and Christy families are housed in the National Archives and Record Service, U.S. National Archives and Records Administration, Washington, DC (hereafter cited as NARA). Many have been transcribed and published online, "The Valley of the Shadow: Demus and Christy Family": http://bit.ly/ZsstAN.

50 Whitman in Kouwenhoven 1950, 635.

51 Edward Ayers, William G. Thomas III, and Anne Sarah Rubin, "Black and on the Border," Digital Commons@ University of Nebraska—Lincoln: http://bit.ly/X1OVbH.

52 Ayers, Thomas, and Rubin, online publication.

53 See Donald Yacovone, "The Fifty-fourth, the Pay Crisis, and the 'Lincoln Despotism,'" in Blatt et al. 2001, 35–51.

54 Whitman in Kouwenhoven 1950, 302.

55 Emilio, 1995, 23. This carte de visite has been identified as having been made in Readville because of the similarity of the curtain and floor covering to the background seen in a photograph in the Alfred Stedman Hartwell Collection at the State Library of Massachusetts, which is identified on the verso as "Joe / Head Quarters Camp Meigs / Readville Mass / Oct 1862," as well as those seen in several photographs reproduced in Michael K. Sorenson, "The Mystery Photographer," *Military Images* 25 (March/April 2004), np. See also Erina Duganne, "Black Civil War Portraiture in Context," http://bit.ly/135y9Sf.

56 As quoted in Coddington 2012, 69, 71.

57 Other African American soldiers from Company I, as well as from other companies, appear to have had their portraits made in this same studio: see, for example, "Robert J. Jones, Pvt. Co. I" and "Moses Jackson, Sergt., Co. E," in Emilio 1995, 32A, 208A.

58 See Duganne, "Black Civil War Portraiture in Context."

59 Coddington 2012, 65. A "minnie" (*minié*) was a cylindrical bullet with a hollow base that expanded when it fired and proved lethal over long distances. Invented in 1849, it was used by both Union and Confederate soldiers.

60 Lewis Douglass to Helen Amelia Loguen, July 20, 1863, Carter G. Woodson Papers, Manuscript Division, 117.00.00, Library of Congress.

61 Coddington 2012, 81.

62 Frederick Douglass, "Should the Negro Enlist in the Union Army?" talk given at National Hall, Philadelphia, July 6, 1863, "Addresses of the Hon. W. D. Kelley, Miss Anna E. Dickinson, and Mr. Frederick Douglass," p. 7, Frederick Douglass Papers, Library of Congress. See http://1.usa.gov/Wb61FY.

63 See Harvey S. Teal, *Partners with the Sun: South Carolina Photographers, 1840–1940* (Columbia: University of South Carolina Press, 2000), 107–110, and 112; see also Bob Zeller, *The Blue and Gray in Black and White: A History of Civil War Photography* (Westport, CT: Praeger, 2005), 120.

64 Teal 2000, 107.

65 Coddington 2012, 53.

66 Coddington 2012, 221; and Emilio 1995, 339.

67 An inscription on the back of a duplicate print of this image in the collection of the Museum of African American History, Boston, notes that it was made on Morris Island on June 3, 1864.

68 Coddington 2012, 55, 229.

69 Gooseberry, Johnson, and Palmer are standing in front of the same backdrop as Bush, whose carte de visite is stamped on the back "H. C. Foster, Morris Island, S.C." Although Spriggs stands in front of a different backdrop, the back of his carte de visite is also stamped "H. C. Foster, Morris Island, S.C."
70 Emilio 1995, frontispiece. The only known vintage photograph (fig. 2) is in the Journal of Major John W.M. Appleton, 54th Massachusetts Infantry, West Virginia University Libraries, West Virginia and Regional History Collection. Appleton could also have had a hand in its creation.
71 See Emilio 1995, 131, 146.
72 See Emilio 1995, xvi.
73 Carl Cruz, as quoted in Eleanor Wachs, ed., "'It wasn't in her lifetime but it was handed down': Four Black Oral Histories of Massachusetts," Office of the Massachusetts Secretary of State, Boston, 1989, 16–17.
74 Emilio 1995, 54 and 131; see also Coddington 2012, 54, 82–83, 89. On the back of pl. 32, Major John W.M. Appleton wrote: "Nicknamed 'Slickey' at the time, Capt. Homan's servant. He was said to have been moon struck at times thereby dangerous. Said to have made several assaults on Capt. Homans and at other times was fond and kind. He shot and killed Corpl Wilson, Co. A." See John W.M. Appleton Papers, West Virginia University Libraries, West Virginia and Regional History Collection.
75 Coddington 2012, 67, 70–71, 229.
76 First awarded in October 1863 and also called the Fort Sumter Medal, the Gillmore Medal was given to all Union soldiers who served under Major General Quincy A. Gillmore, who commanded Union troops attempting to seize Fort Sumter in 1863.
77 William H. Carney to Assistant Secretary of War G. D. Meiklejohn, May 26, 1900, Documents Relating to the Military and Naval Service of Blacks Awarded the Congressional Medal of Honor From the Civil War to the Spanish American War (M929), roll 1, NARA. My thanks to Joe McPhillips for this reference.
78 Although other African Americans had received the Congressional Medal of Honor by 1900, Carney's award came almost thirty-seven years after his actions of July 18, 1863, which were the earliest deemed worthy of the honor. General Gillmore had issued a Medal of Honor to Carney in November 1863, but by some oversight the case was never brought to the attention of the War Department; see Report of Chief of Record and Pension Office on application for award of Medal of Honor to William Harvey Carney, sergeant, Company C, 54th Massachusetts Volunteers (Colored), in pension record for William H. Carney, Records and Pension Office, NARA.
79 James E. Reed was a New Bedford photographer, active from the 1880s through 1914, who had photographed Frederick Douglass. See *New Bedford through the Lens: A Walk through History*, available online, http://bit.ly/11W0NFV; and International Center of Photography: http://bit.ly/XlMwOg.
80 Walt Whitman as quoted by Horace Traubel in Alan Trachtenberg, *Reading American Photographs: Images as History, Mathew Brady to Walker Evans* (New York: Hill and Wang, 1989), 60.
81 Walt Whitman, "Out from Behind This Mask: (To Confront a Portrait)," in Kouwenhoven 1950, 302.

For All Time to Come: Memorializing Robert Gould Shaw and the 54th Massachussets Regiment

NANCY K. ANDERSON

Epigraph Abraham Lincoln, "Speech to the 166th Ohio Regiment, Washington, D.C., August 22, 1864," *Speeches and Writings, 1859–1865* (New York: Library of America, 1989), 624: "It is not merely for today, but for all time to come that we should perpetuate for our children's children this great and free government, which we have enjoyed all our lives."
1 Marine Lieutenant Timothy Fallon and his family visited the National Gallery of Art on January 11, 2011. Conservator Shelley Sturman and curator Nancy Anderson accompanied the family to the gallery where the Shaw Memorial (on long-term loan from the National Park Service and the Saint-Gaudens National Historic Site) is on view. Permission for Lieutenant Fallon to touch the sculpture was granted by the superintendent of the Saint-Gaudens site.
2 Timothy Fallon shared his recollections with the author in an e-mail dated August 16, 2012. All statements by Lieutenant Fallon in subsequent paragraphs are drawn from this e-mail.
3 James Barnes, "The Shaw Memorial," *Harper's Weekly* 41 (May 29, 1897): 546.
4 "Topics of the Time: The Hero," *Century Magazine* 54 (June 1897): 312.
5 Both quotations are taken from Lewis Douglass' letter, dated July 20, 1863, which appeared in the August 1863

issue of *Douglass' Monthly* under the heading "From Charleston. The 54th Massachusetts at Fort Wagner—Letter from Sergeant Lewis," 852–853.

6 Letter written by Brigadier General Rufus Saxton, under the heading "Tribute to the Late Col. Shaw," July 27, 1863, also in *Douglass' Monthly* (August 1863), 853.

7 On September 4, 1863, *The Liberator* quoted *Beaufort Free South*: "A collection was taken on Sunday in the Baptist church of Beaufort, in aid of the fund for the proposed monument to the late Robert G. Shaw. Sixty dollars were contributed. The colored people seem to take a great interest in this effort to honor Col. Shaw's memory, and we learn that a large sum has already been promised by different colored regiments. There are now six regiments of colored men in this department, and a little energy is all that is required to raise a monument honorable alike to the noble dead and to the donors."

On November 5, 1864, under the heading "The Shaw Monument," *Anglo-African* printed an exchange of letters between Colonel E. N. Hallowell and Brigadier General Rufus Saxton, reporting, by company, the contributions from the members of the 54th Massachusetts Regiment for a "monument in memory of Col. Robert G. Shaw and those who died with him." Saxton wrote: "The glorious work which our armies in the field, and patriots at home are now doing, means that the day is not far distant when a granite shaft shall stand unmolested on South Carolina soil to mark the spot where brave men died, not, as recent developments have shown, alone as soldiers, but as *martyrs* in the cause of freedom." See also Marilyn Richardson, "Taken from Life: Edward M. Bannister, Edmonia Lewis, and the Memorialization of the Fifty-fourth Massachusetts Regiment," in Martin H. Blatt, Thomas J. Brown, and Donald Yacovone, eds., *Hope and Glory: Essays on the Legacy of the Fifty-fourth Massachusetts Regiment* (Amherst: University of Massachusetts in association with the Massachusetts Historical Society, Boston, 2001), 94–115. Richardson quotes Benjamin Quarles, *The Negro in the Civil War* (1953; repr., Boston: Little, Brown, 1969), as an additional source regarding memorial funds.

8 In 1865 funds originally raised for a monument to Shaw and the 54th Massachusetts Regiment, supplemented with funds from the New England Freedmen's Society and a number of Northern philanthropists, were used to establish the Shaw Memorial School for free black children in Charleston.

9 See Richardson in Blatt et al. 2001, 95; and Charles Sumner, "Monument to Colonel Shaw," *The Liberator*, December 22, 1865. Discussion of a monument was also prompted by the report that Shaw had been buried with his troops in a mass grave. Subsequently, articles and poems regarding a monument were published: see "A Monument to Colonel Shaw," *New York Tribune*, October 8, 1863.

10 Sumner in *The Liberator* (1865) recounts early efforts to erect a monument to Shaw. See also Richardson in Blatt et al. 2001, 95; and Gregory C. Schwarz et al., *The Shaw Memorial: A Celebration of an American Masterpiece*, Saint-Gaudens National Historic Site (Fort Washington, PA: Eastern National, 1997; rev. ed. 2002), 19–20.

11 The twenty-one members of the committee are listed by Edward Atkinson in part 1 of the three-part article on the Shaw Memorial published in *Century Magazine* 54 (June 1897): 176.

12 The marble version of the bust of Shaw in the collection of the Museum of African American History in Boston is inscribed "Rome 1867" and may have been commissioned by the Shaw family.

13 The origin of the Sanitary Commission is detailed in Charles J. Stillé, *History of the United States Sanitary Commission* (New York: Hurd and Houghton, 1868); chap. 14 (pp. 402–422) addresses issues related to the siege at Fort Wagner.

14 In the fall of 1863, the Sanitary Commission based in Chicago organized the Northwestern Soldiers' Fair, which raised nearly $100,000. Large fairs often included an "art department" with paintings and other objects donated by artists to be sold or raffled for the benefit of the troops.

15 For Christiana Carteaux Bannister (1819/1820?–1902), see Jane Lancaster, "'I would have made out very poorly had it not been for her': The Life and Work of Christiana Bannister, Hair Doctress and Philanthropist," *Rhode Island History* 59 (November 2001): 102–121.

16 "An Appeal to the Public," *The Liberator*, May 20, 1864. The issue of unequal pay for African American soldiers ($13 for white soldiers, $10 for African American soldiers—with $3 deducted for uniform/supplies from the already reduced pay) had been a contentious issue since the formation of the 54th Massachusetts Regiment. Governor Andrew believed he had assurances of equal pay when he called for an African American regiment, but the federal government issued reduced pay. Members of the 54th refused all pay until the issue was resolved shortly before the Colored Ladies' Sanitary Fair opened in October 1864.

17 "The Colored Ladies' Sanitary Commission of Boston," *Anglo-African*, May 28, 1864.

18 For Edward Bannister, see Juanita Marie Holland, *The Life and Work of Edward Mitchell Bannister, 1828–1901* (New York: Kenkeleba House, 1992); Juanita Marie Holland, "To Be Free, Gifted and Black: African American Artist, Edward Mitchell Bannister," *International Review of African American Art* 12, no. 1 (1995): 4–25; Juanita Marie Holland, "Co-Workers in the Kingdom of Culture: Edward Bannister and the Boston Community of African-American Artists, 1848–1901," PhD diss., Columbia University, 1998; and Lynda Roscoe Hartigan, *Sharing Traditions: Five Black Artists in Nineteenth-Century America*, Smithsonian American Art Museum (Washington, DC: Smithsonian Institution Press, 1985), 69–84.

19 "Emancipation Day," *The Liberator*, December 26, 1862.

20 In a letter to the editor of *The National Anti-Slavery Standard*, reprinted in *The Liberator*, November 18, 1864, Lydia Marie Child described the installation of Bannister's portrait of Shaw at the Colored Ladies' Sanitary Fair.

21 "The Colored Ladies' Sanitary Fair," *Boston Evening Transcript*, October 19, 1864. The initial announcements for the fair included reference to the soldiers' "having received no pay." The issue was settled in the summer of 1864 (equal pay for all), thus later solicitations for the Colored Ladies' Sanitary Fair do not refer to the pay dispute.

22 "Col. Shaw," *Boston Evening Transcript*, November 4, 1864: "A few shares in the portrait of Col. Shaw … which was for sale at the Colored Ladies' Sanitary Fair now on exhibition at Childs & Jenks's, Tremont Street, may be had. The book may be found at 31 Winter Street, Madame C. Bannister's. The drawing will take place as soon as the list is full."

23 In response to a request from Colonel M. S. Littlefield of the 54th Massachusetts Regiment, William Carney provided biographical information in a letter dated October 18, 1863, later published in *The Liberator*, November 6, 1863. Additional information regarding Carney's life after the war may be found in Eleanor Wachs, ed., "'It wasn't in her lifetime but it was handed down': Four Black Oral Histories of Massachusetts," Office of the Massachusetts Secretary of State, Boston, 1989.

24 The story of Sergeant Carney's heroism is reported in correspondence from Morris Island, dated August 1, 1863, for the *New York Tribune* and reprinted by the *Chicago Tribune*, August 5, 1863, under the heading "From Charleston."

25 A letter to the editor of the *Anglo-African* signed "G.W.P." and published November 5, 1864, described the small statue of Carney by Edmonia Lewis. In an article titled "Edmonia Lewis," published in *The Broken Fetter* [Detroit], March 3, 1865, Lydia Marie Child wrote, "She also made a clever little statuette of the colored Sergeant, who, when wounded, exerted himself to hold up the Stars and Stripes, exclaiming, 'The dear old Flag hasn't touched the ground, boys!'"

26 For Edmonia Lewis, see Richardson in Blatt et al. 2001, 94–115; Kirsten Pai Buick, *Child of Fire: Mary Edmonia Lewis and the Problem of Art History's Black and Indian Subject* (Durham, NC: Duke University Press, 2010); Harry Henderson and Albert Henderson, *The Indomitable Spirit of Edmonia Lewis: A Narrative Biography* (Milford, CT: Esquiline Hill Press, 2012); PDF e-book.

27 Bannister and Lewis had studios near each other in Boston's Studio Building (Bannister in no. 85, Lewis in no. 89). Lewis' commitment to abolitionist activism became evident early in her career when she began selling portrait medallions of John Brown, the martyred abolitionist (see *The Liberator*, January 29, 1864).

28 Some confusion exists regarding the exhibition history of the original version of Lewis' bust of Shaw. Richardson in Blatt et al. 2001, 105, and Henderson and Henderson 2012 ("The Colored Soldiers' Fair") write that the bust was exhibited at the Colored Ladies' Sanitary Fair and both cite a letter from John Greenleaf Whittier, but no contemporary published references reporting the bust on view at the fair have come to light. Bannister's painting of Shaw was described repeatedly in contemporary accounts. A bust of Shaw, presumably, would have attracted similar attention. It seems more likely that Lewis' bust of Shaw remained in her studio, where Lydia Marie Child described seeing it (*The Liberator*, January 20, 1865), as did members of the Shaw family before it was placed on view in a commercial gallery (*Boston Evening Transcript*, November 14, 1864).

29 *Boston Evening Transcript*, November 11, 1864. The National Sailors' Fair, held in Boston in November 1864, was a large and successful benefit that the *Transcript* reported (November 14, 1864) raised more than $10,000 per day.

30 *Boston Evening Transcript*, November 11, 1864.

31 *Boston Evening Transcript*, November 11, 1864. Augustus Marshall, photographer, maintained a studio near those of Bannister and Lewis in the Studio Building in Boston.

32 *Boston Evening Transcript*, November 14, 1864.

33 "Lady-Artists in Rome [Rome, March 1866]," *The Art-Journal* [London], June 1, 1866, 177: "A bust of Colonel Shaw, who commanded the first coloured regiment ever formed, is a meritorious work, and has been ordered by the family of the brave colonel who died fighting for his country."

34 Although references to one hundred plaster copies of the bust having been produced and sold for $15 each have been repeated in the literature, no example has come to light.

35 William Lloyd Garrison published his weekly abolitionist newspaper, *The Liberator*, from Boston beginning in January 1831. The final issue was dated December 29, 1865.

36 "The 54th Massachusetts," *The Liberator*, August 7, 1863.

37 See Sumner 1865 (note 9 above) for an account of the revival of the project.

38 See note 11 above.

39 Atkinson 1897, 176.

40 Atkinson, who served as treasurer for the committee, documented the growth of the fund (see Atkinson 1897, 176).

41 Governor Andrew died October 30, 1867; Senator Sumner died March 11, 1874.

42 Atkinson 1897, 176. In the interim, the Soldiers and Sailors Monument designed by Martin Milmore had been erected and dedicated (1877) on Boston Common. The monument included four bas-relief panels, one of which depicted Shaw and the 54th Regiment passing by the State House.

43 *The Reminiscences of Augustus Saint-Gaudens*, edited and amplified by Homer Saint-Gaudens, vol. 1 (New York: The Century Co., 1913), 332. William A. Coffin, "The Shaw Memorial and the Sculptor St. Gaudens II: The Sculptor St. Gaudens," in *Century Magazine* (June 1897), 179, 181, wrote: "The original idea of the equestrian figure with the troops in the background has always been adhered to; but the horseman and the monument thought it should take the form of an equestrian statue on a high pedestal: but the family of Colonel Shaw felt that this would give too much importance to the single figure, the idea of the memorial that it should typify patriotic devotion, and embody a modern spirit with heroic attributes."

44 Atkinson 1897, 176.

45 Sumner in *The Liberator*, 1865 (see note 9 above).

46 Saint-Gaudens 1913, 1: 332.

47 "The Shaw Monument," *Anglo-African*, November 5, 1864 (see note 7 above).
48 Saint-Gaudens 1913, 1: 332.
49 Saint-Gaudens 1913, 1: 333.
50 See Edward Atkinson, William A. Coffin, and Thomas Wentworth Higginson, "The Shaw Memorial and the Sculptor St. Gaudens," *Century Magazine*, 54 (June 1897), 176–200; Schwarz et al. 2002; Lois Goldreich Marcus, "The *Shaw Memorial* by Augustus Saint-Gaudens: A History Painting in Bronze," *Winterthur Portfolio* 14, no. 1 (Spring 1979), 1–23.
51 Saint-Gaudens 1913, 1: 335.
52 Saint-Gaudens 1913, 1: 333–338.
53 Saint-Gaudens 1913, 1: 343.
54 James Barnes, in *Harper's Weekly*, May 29, 1897, identified the figure as "Humanity ... the embodiment of Sympathy." Others have described her as Fame, the Angel of Death, the Angel of Victory.
55 Saint-Gaudens 1913, 1: 343–345.
56 John W.M. Appleton, "That Night at Fort Wagner, by One Who Was There," *Putnam's Magazine* 4 (July 1869).
57 Deborah Willis and Barbara Krauthamer, *Envisioning Emancipation: Black Americans and the End of Slavery* (Philadelphia: Temple University Press, 2013), 129.
58 "Address of Booker T. Washington," in Schwarz et al. 2002, 119–121.
59 William James, "Robert Gould Shaw," *Essays in Religion and Morality* (Cambridge, MA: Harvard University Press, 1982), 66–68.
60 James 1982, 73.
61 Coffin 1897, 179.
62 Schwarz et al. 2002, 47.
63 Kirk Savage, *Standing Soldiers, Kneeling Slaves: Race, War, and Monument in Nineteenth-Century America* (Princeton, NJ: Princeton University Press, 1997), 75. David Blight has also written thoughtfully about the Shaw Memorial. See his *Race and Reunion: The Civil War in American Memory* (Cambridge, MA: Harvard University Press, 2001), 338–345.
64 Savage 1997, 124.
65 Coffin 1897, 181.

Before the Eyes of Thousands: The 54th Massachusetts Regiment and the Shaw Memorial in Twentieth-Century Art

LINDSAY HARRIS

Epigraph Romare Bearden, "The Negro Artist and Modern Art," *Opportunity* (December 1934), reprinted in David Levering Lewis, ed., *The Portable Harlem Reader* (New York: Viking, 1994), 103.

I am grateful to Sarah Greenough and Nancy Anderson for the opportunity to contribute to this catalogue, and to Victoria Sams and Clarisse Fava-Piz for their helpful comments on earlier drafts of this essay.

1 Robert Gould Shaw, quoted in Peter Burchard, *One Gallant Rush: Robert Gould Shaw and His Brave Black Regiment* (New York: Saint Martin's Press, 1965), 128.
2 Burchard 1965, 136.
3 Denise Von Glahn, "The Musical Monument of Charles Ives," in Martin H. Blatt, Thomas J. Brown, and Donald Yacovone, eds., *Hope and Glory: Essays on the Legacy of the Fifty-fourth Massachusetts Regiment* (Amherst: University of Massachusetts Press in association with the Massachusetts Historical Society, Boston, 2001), 191–201; and Sidney Kaplan, "The Black Soldier of the Civil War in Literature and Art," *The Chancellor's Lecture Series* (Amherst: University of Massachusetts, 1981), 26.
4 William James, quoted in Russell Duncan, ed., *Blue-Eyed Child of Fortune: The Civil War Letters of Colonel Robert Gould Shaw* (Athens: University of Georgia Press, 1992), 56.
5 David Blight, "The Shaw Memorial in the Landscape of Civil War Memory," in Blatt et al. 2001, 80; Ben W. Heineman Jr., "The Sculptor Who Brought Dead Civil War Heroes to Life," *The Atlantic* (online) (May 25, 2012); and Kaplan 1981, 3.
6 Scholarship on the Shaw Memorial is extensive. In addition to the aforementioned sources, see Kirk Savage, *Standing Soldiers, Kneeling Slaves: Race, War, and Monument in Nineteenth-Century America* (Princeton, NJ: Princeton University Press, 1997), 193–208; Albert Boime, *The Art of Exclusion: Representing Blacks in the Nineteenth Century* (Washington, DC: Smithsonian Institution Press, 1990), 199–219; Sidney Kaplan, "The Sculptural World of Augustus Saint-Gaudens," *The Massachusetts Review* 30, no. 1 (Spring 1989): 17–74; Stephen J. Whitfield, "'Sacred in History and in Art': The Shaw Memorial," *New England Quarterly* 60, no. 1 (March 1987): 3–27; Lois Goldreich Marcus, "The *Shaw Memorial* by Augustus Saint-Gaudens: A History Painting in Bronze," *Winterthur Portfolio* 14, no. 1 (Spring 1979): 1–23.
7 Chapter 6, "Common Soldiers," in Savage 1997, 162–209.
8 Savage 1997, 188.
9 Smith began soliciting funds among the African American community in Boston to erect a monument to Shaw and the 54th as early as 1865. It was not until the early 1880s, however, that Saint-Gaudens was brought into the project. On the commission

of the Shaw Memorial, see Savage 1997, 194–197; and Nancy Anderson's essay in the present publication.

10 Booker T. Washington, quoted in Whitfield 1987, 14, and in Lincoln Kirstein, "The Memorial to Robert Gould Shaw and His Soldiers by Augustus Saint-Gaudens," *Lay This Laurel* (New York: Eakins Press Foundation, 1973), n.p.

11 Washington, quoted in Whitfield 1987, 14.

12 *Cleveland Gazette* (June 28, 1895), quoted in Henry Louis Gates Jr., "The Trope of a New Negro and the Reconstruction of the Image of the Black," *Representations* 24, Special Issue: *America Reconstructed, 1840–1940* (Autumn, 1988), 129.

13 David McCullough, *The Greater Journey: Americans in Paris* (New York: Simon & Schuster, 2011), 449.

14 Thomas Junius Calloway, quoted in Robert W. Rydell, "Gateway to the 'American Century': The American Representation at the Paris Universal Exposition of 1900," in *Paris 1900: The "American School" at the Universal Exposition*, ed. Diane P. Fischer (New Brunswick, NJ: Rutgers University Press, 1999), 141.

15 On Calloway's organization of the American Negro Exhibit, see Shawn Michelle Smith, *Photography on the Color Line: W.E.B. Du Bois, Race, and Visual Culture* (Durham, NC: Duke University Press, 2004), 12–24.

16 Calloway, quoted in Rydell 1999, 141.

17 Calloway, "The American Negro Exhibit and the Paris Exposition," quoted in Smith 2004, 21, 171 n. 67.

18 Letter from Assistant Secretary of War to William H. Carney, May 9, 1900, ARC Identifier 594893, File Unit: William Harvey Carney, Sgt. C. 54. Mass. Vol., Record and Pension Office 574146, National Archives and Records Administration.

19 Calloway, quoted in Smith 2004, 171 n. 67; and in Rydell 1999, 141. In addition to the shows discussed here, African American photographer Harry Shepherd presented photographs of the Tuskegee Institute at the 1900 exposition. See Deborah Willis-Thomas, *Black Photographers, 1840–1940: An Illustrated Bio-Bibliography* (New York: Garland Publishing, 1985), 11.

20 Douglass, quoted in Juanita Marie Holland, "The Color of Art: African American Artistic Identities in the Twentieth Century," in *Narratives of African American Art and Identity: The David C. Driskell Collection* (San Francisco: Pomegranate Communications, 1998), 26.

21 Frederick Rudolph, "Samuel Chapman Armstrong: Founder of the Hampton Institute," in *Carrie Mae Weems: The Hampton Project* (New York: Aperture Foundation, 2000), 61.

22 Armstrong, quoted in Frances Benjamin Johnston and Lincoln Kirstein, *The Hampton Album* (New York: The Museum of Modern Art, 1966), 6.

23 Armstrong, quoted in Johnston 1966, 6; and in Rudolph 2000, 60.

24 Johnston 1966, 9.

25 For a detailed account of these albums, see Shawn Michelle Smith, "'Looking at One's Self through the Eyes of Others': W.E.B. Du Bois' Photographs for the Paris Exposition of 1900," in Maurice O. Wallace and Shawn Michelle Smith, eds., *Pictures and Progress: Early Photography and the Making of African American Identity* (Durham, NC: Duke University Press, 2012), 274–298. See also Smith 2004, 1–42.

26 Gates 1988, 129; Kevin K. Gaines, *Uplifting the Race: Black Leadership, Politics, and Culture in the Twentieth Century* (Chapel Hill: University of North Carolina Press, 1997). See also Smith 2004.

27 Smith 2004, 4–5.

28 Langston Hughes, "The Negro Artist and the Racial Mountain," *The Nation* (June 23, 1926), reprinted in David Levring Lewis, ed., *The Portable Harlem Renaissance Reader* (New York: Viking, 1994), 95.

29 Rayford W. Logan, *The Betrayal of the Negro, from Rutherford B. Hayes to Woodrow Wilson* (New York: Collier Books, 1965), 335.

30 On the importance of a two- or three-room cottage as an indicator of social and economic advancement, see Booker T. Washington, "The Awakening of the Negro," *Atlantic Monthly* (September 1896), 322–328.

31 Washington 1896. On the "uplift" of African Americans, see Gaines 1996.

32 Gates 1988, 132.

33 "About Copley Prints," *The Copley Prints* (Boston: Curtis & Cameron, 1902), 7–9.

34 Gaines 1996, 26.

35 Mary Frances Berry, *Black Resistance, White Law: A History of Constitutional Racism in America* (New York: Appleton-Century-Crofts, 1971), 139–154.

36 Arnold Rampersad, "Introduction," in Alain Locke, ed., *The New Negro: Voices of the Harlem Renaissance* (New York: Maxwell Macmillan International, 1992), xiv.

37 Lewis Hine, quoted in Alan Trachtenberg, *America & Lewis Hine: Photographs 1904–1940* (New York: Aperture, 1977), 12.

38 In 1919–1920 Hine developed new studio publicity that read "Lewis Wickes Hine: Interpretive Photography." See *America & Lewis Hine* 1977, 21. See also Kate Sampsell-Willmann, *Lewis Hine as Social Critic* (Jackson: University of Mississippi Press, 2009), 129–174.

39 On the history of *Survey* magazine, see Rampersad's introduction to Locke 1992 [1925], ix–xi.

40 Rudolph Fisher, "The South Lingers On," *Survey Graphic* (March 1925), 644–647. Hine's photograph appears on the first page of the article.

41 Rampersad 1992, ix–xxiii.

42 James Weldon Johnson, cited in Aberjhani and Sandra L. West, *Encyclopedia of the Harlem Renaissance* (New York: Facts on File, Inc., 2004), xviii.

43 On the political and cultural development of the civil rights movement after the First World War, see Lauren Rebecca Sklaroff, *Black Culture and the New Deal: The Quest for Civil Rights in the Roosevelt Era* (Chapel Hill: University of North Carolina, 2009); Glenda Gilmore, *Defying Dixie: The Radical Roots of Civil Rights 1919–1950* (New York: W.W. Norton, 2008); Jacquelyn Dowd Hall, "The Long Civil Rights Movement and the Political Uses of the Past," *Journal of American History* 91, no. 4 (March 2005), 1234–1262.

44 For an overview of artists' interest in African American heritage during the Harlem Renaissance, see Samella Lewis, "New Americanism and Ethnic Identity," *African*

American Art and Artists, rev. and exp. ed. (Berkeley: University of California Press, 2003), 59–114; Lowery Stokes-Sims, *Challenge of the Modern: African American Artists 1925–1945*, vol. 1 (New York: The Studio Museum in Harlem, 2003); *Harlem Renaissance Art of Black America* (New York: The Studio Museum in Harlem, 1987).

45 On this series, see Ellen Harkins Wheat, *Jacob Lawrence: The Frederick Douglass and Harriet Tubman Series of 1938–40*, Hampton University Museum, Hampton, VA (Seattle: University of Washington Press, 1991).

46 Frederick Douglass, "Douglass' Monthly" (March 1863), quoted in Kaplan 1981, 2.

47 "Press Release Competition for the Mural Decoration of the Recorder of Deeds Building, Washington, D.C.," (April 7, 1943), 2. Carlos and Rhoda LeBlanc Lopez papers, 1932-1973, microfilm reel 2105, Archives of American Art, Smithsonian Institution. On the history of the Recorder of Deeds Building, its decoration, and its patronage, see Sara A. Butler, "Ground Breaking in New Deal Washington, DC: Art, Patronage, and Race at the Recorder of Deeds Building," *Winterthur Portfolio* 45, no. 4 (Winter 2011): 277–320.

48 Carlos and Rhoda LeBlanc Lopez papers, AAA.

49 Whitfield 1987, 7–8; see also Nancy Anderson's essay in this publication.

50 Carlos and Rhoda LeBlanc Lopez papers, AAA.

51 President Harry S. Truman issued an Executive Order on July 26, 1848, establishing equality of treatment and opportunity in the Armed Services. Executive Order 9981, Harry S. Truman Library and Museum.

52 David W. Blight, *American Oracle: The Civil War in the Civil Rights Era* (Cambridge, MA: Harvard University Press, 2011).

53 *Illinois Negro Historymakers* (Chicago: Illinois Emancipation Centennial Commission, 1964), 23.

54 *Illinois Negro Historymakers*, organized by the Illinois Emancipation Centennial Commission, was shown at *A Century of Negro Progress Exposition*, held at McCormick Place in Chicago in the fall of 1963. *Illinois Negro Historymakers*, 1964, 37. I am grateful to Kathryn M. Harris at the Abraham Lincoln Presidential Library & Museum for providing me with information about this exhibition.

55 Sidney Kaplan, "Notes on the Exhibition: The Portrayal of the Negro in American Painting," in Allan D. Austin, ed., *Sidney Kaplan: American Studies in Black and White. Selected Essays 1949–1989* (Amherst: University of Massachusetts, 1991), 211–226.

56 Richard Benson, "Working with Lee," in Peter Galassi, ed., *Friedlander* (New York: The Museum of Modern Art, 2005), 438.

57 Walker Evans, *American Photographs* (New York: The Museum of Modern Art, 1938); Robert Frank, *The Americans* (New York: Grove Press, Inc., 1959).

58 Leslie George Katz, "Afterword," in Lee Friedlander, *The American Monument* (New York: Eakins Press, 1976), n.p.

59 Kirstein 1973, n.p.

60 Heinrich Wölfflin, quoted in Tobia Bezzola, "From Sculpture in Photography to Photography as Plastic Art," in Roxana Marcoci, ed., *The Original Copy: Photography of Sculpture, 1839 to Today* (New York: The Museum of Modern Art, 2010), 29. Heinrich Wölfflin, "Wie man Skulpturen aufnehmen soll," parts 1 and 2, *Zeitschrift für bildende Kunst*, no. 7 (1896), 224–228.

61 On Saint-Gaudens' interest in photography and use of varied photographic processes, see John H. Dryfhout and Sandy and Stephen Dorros, *Photographs and Historical Processes* (Cornish, NH: Saint-Gaudens National Historic Site, 1995).

62 Kirstein 1973, n.p.

63 Cherise Smith, "Fragmented Documents: Works by Lorna Simpson, Carrie Mae Weems, and Willie Robert Middlebrook at the Art Institute of Chicago," *Art Institute of Chicago Museum Studies* 24, no. 2 (1999), 254.

64 Weems, quoted in Smith 1999, 252.

65 Weems, quoted in "Carrie Mae Weems: The Hampton Project, January 13, 2004–April 29, 2007," Williams College Museum of Art website, http://wcma.williams.edu/exhibit/hampton-project/.

66 *Gettysburg: A Journey in Time* (Philadelphia: Esther M. Klein Art Gallery, University City Science Center, 1997).

67 William Earle Williams, quoted in "William Earle Williams, Unsung Heroes: African American Soldiers in the Civil War, January 16 – March 16, 2007," Light Work Gallery website, http://www.lightwork.org/exhibitions/past/williams.html.

Commemorating Black Soldiers: The African American Civil War Memorial in Washington, DC

RENÉE ATER

Epigraph Ex-slave Elijah Marrs quoted in Joseph T. Glatthaar, *Forged in Battle: The Civil War Alliance of Black Soldiers and White Officers* (Baton Rouge: Louisiana State University Press, 2000), 79; and Christian G. Samito, *Becoming American under Fire: Irish Americans, African Americans, and the Politics of Citizenship during the Civil War Era* (Ithaca, NY: Cornell University Press, 2009), 47.

1 See Alois Riegl, "Modern Cult of Monuments: Its Character and Its Origins," trans. Kurt W. Forster and Diane Ghirardo, *Oppositions* 25 (Fall 1982): 20–51 (published in German as "Der Moderne Denkmalkultus: sein Wesen und seine Entstehung," 1903); Freeman Henry Morris Murray, *Emancipation and the Freed in American Sculpture: A Study in Interpretation*, Black Folk in Art Series (Washington, DC, private publication, 1916), xvii–xxiv; Marianne Doezema, "The Public Monument in Tradition and Transition," in *The Public Monument and Its Audience* (Cleveland: Cleveland Museum of Art, 1977), 9–21; John Bodnar, *Remaking America: Public Memory, Commemoration, and Patriotism in the Twentieth Century* (Princeton, NJ: Princeton University Press, 1992), 3–20; Sanford Levinson, *Written in Stone: Public Monuments in Changing Societies* (Durham, NC: Duke University Press, 1998); James E. Young, "Memory/Monument," in *Critical*

Terms for Art History (2nd ed.), ed. Robert S. Nelson and Richard Shiff (Chicago: University of Chicago Press, 2003), 234–247; Marita Sturken and James E. Young, "Monuments," in *Encyclopedia of Aesthetics*, ed. Michael Kelly, Oxford Art Online, http://bit.ly/159PUOE; and Erika Doss, *Memorial Mania: Public Feeling in America* (Chicago: University of Chicago Press, 2010), 1–60.

2 For a discussion of "sites of memory," see Pierre Nora, "Between Memory and History: *Les Lieux de Mémoire*," *Representations* 26 (Spring 1989): 7–24; and Jay Winter, "Sites of Memory," in *Memory: Histories, Theories, Debates*, ed. Susannah Radstone and Bill Schwarz (New York: Fordham University Press, 2010), 312–324.

3 Frederick Douglass, "Men of Color, To Arms!" Broadside (Rochester, March 2, 1863), Library of Congress, Washington, DC, Rare Books and Special Collections Division.

4 "Bill Summary and Status, 102nd Congress (1991–1992), H.J. Res. 320," THOMAS, Library of Congress, http://1.usa.gov/159Q88p and "Memorial Planned for Civil War's Black Soldiers," *New York Times*, August 11, 1991.

5 *African-Americans Civil War*, 102nd Cong., October 14, 1992, Public Law 102–412, H.J. Res. 320.

6 "Memorial Planned for Civil War's Black Soldiers," *New York Times*, August 11, 1991; Mark E. McCormick, "Louisville Sculptor Has Designs on Washington," *Courier-Journal* [Louisville], August 20, 1993; and Kathryn Allamong Jacob, *Testament to Union: Civil War Monuments in Washington, DC* (Baltimore: Johns Hopkins University Press, 1998), 146.

7 James E. Goode, "Four Salutes to the Nation: The Equestrian Statues of General Andrew Jackson," *White House History* 17 (2010): 13.

8 Marita Sturken, "The Wall, the Screen, and the Image: The Vietnam Veterans Memorial," *Representations* 35 (Summer 1991): 126.

9 Edward D. Dunson Jr., discussion with Renée Ater, October 24, 2012.

10 Camp Barker was at 1200 S Street NW, Wisewell Barracks and Hospital at 7th and P Streets NW, and Campbell Hospital at 6th Street and Florida Avenue NW. See Jane Freundel Levey and Paul K. Williams, *Midcity at the Crossroads: Shaw Heritage Trail* (Washington, DC, 2006); and Kathryn S. Smith and Paul K. Williams, *City within a City: Greater U Street Heritage Trail* (Washington, DC, 2001). For a brief overview of contraband camps, see Eric Wills, "The Forgotten: The Contraband of America and the Road to Freedom," *Preservation* (May/June 2011), http://bit.ly/ftRapg.

11 Pamela G. Holt (executive director, DC Commission on the Arts and Humanities) to the artist, October 1992; Pamela G. Holt to Ed Hamilton, December 7, 1992; and Alec Simpson (assistant director, DC Commission on the Arts and Humanities) to Ed Hamilton, March 9, 1993. All letters cited in this essay are in the Papers of Ed Hamilton, Louisville, KY.

12 Matt Radford (coordinator, Art in Public Spaces, DC Commission on the Arts and Humanities) to Ed Hamilton, May 17, 1993; Radford to Hamilton, June 8, 1993; and Radford to Hamilton, July 16, 1993.

13 Radford to Hamilton, August 6, 1993.

14 Holt to Hamilton, December 22, 1994.

15 Ed Hamilton, *The Birth of an Artist: A Journey of Discovery* (Louisville, KY: Chicago Spectrum Press, 2006), 28–29.

16 Hamilton 2006, 49–66.

17 Hamilton 2006, 96–98; and Ed Hamilton, interview with Renée Ater, August 21, 2012.

18 Hamilton interview, 2012.

19 "Addresses of the Hon. W.D. Kelley, Miss Anna E. Dickinson, and Mr. Frederick Douglass at a Mass Meeting, Held at National Hall, Philadelphia, July 6, 1863, for the Promotion of Colored Enlistments," p. 7, The Frederick Douglass Papers at the Library of Congress, Manuscript Division, Library of Congress.

20 Glatthaar 1990, 79.

21 Keith P. Wilson, *Campfires of Freedom: The Camp Life of Black Soldiers during the Civil War* (Kent, OH: Kent State University Press, 2002), 157–158.

22 Hamilton interview, 2012.

23 Hamilton interview, 2012.

24 James M. McPherson, *The Negro's Civil War: How American Blacks Felt and Acted during the War for the Union* (1965; repr., New York: Vintage Books, 2003), 197–207; and Jacqueline Jones, *Labor of Love, Labor of Sorrow: Black Women, Work, and the Family from Slavery to the Present* (New York: Basic Books, 1985), 44–78.

25 Hamilton 2006, 102; and Hamilton interview, 2012.

26 See Kirk Savage, *Standing Soldiers, Kneeling Slaves: Race, War, and Monument in Nineteenth-Century America* (Princeton, NJ: Princeton University Press, 1997), 89–128.

27 See Deborah Chotner and Shelley Sturman, *Augustus Saint-Gaudens' Memorial to Robert Gould Shaw and the Massachusetts Fifty-fourth Regiment* (National Gallery of Art, Washington, 1997); Savage 1997, 192–208; David W. Blight, "The Shaw Memorial in the Landscape of Civil War Memory"; and Kathryn Greenthal, "Augustus Saint-Gaudens and the Shaw Memorial," in Martin H. Blatt, Thomas J. Brown, and Donald Yacovone, eds., *Hope and Glory: Essays on the Legacy of the Fifty-fourth Massachusetts Regiment* (Amherst: University of Massachussets in association with the Massachussets Historical Society, 2001), 79–93, 116–129.

28 See Katie Mullis Kresser, "Power and Glory: Brahmin Identity and the Shaw Memorial," *American Art* 20, no. 3 (Fall 2006): 32–57.

29 Stuart McConnell, *Glorious Contentment: The Grand Army of the Republic, 1865–1900* (Chapel Hill: University of North Carolina Press, 1992), 1–17. A separate and modest Grand Review of United States Colored Troops took place on November 14, 1865, in which the all-black regiments from Pennsylvania and Massachusetts marched through the streets of Harrisburg, Pennsylvania.

30 Glatthaar 1990, 231–264; Steven Hahn, *A Nation under Our Feet: Black Political Struggles in the Rural South from Slavery to the Great Migration* (Cambridge, MA: Belknap Press of Harvard University Press, 2003), 165–215; and Kate Masur, *An Example for All the Land: Emancipation and the Struggle over Equality*

in Washington, D.C. (Chapel Hill: University of North Carolina Press, 2010).

31 David W. Blight, *Race and Reunion: The Civil War in American Memory* (Cambridge, MA: Harvard University Press, 2001), 381–397; and Cecilia Elizabeth O'Leary, *To Die For: The Paradox of American Patriotism* (Princeton, NJ: Princeton University Press, 1999), 194–205.

32 Frank Smith Jr. quoted in Richard W. Stevenson, "Civil War Regiment Receives Capital Tribute," *New York Times*, July 12, 1998.

33 Peter Burke, "History as Social Memory," in *Memory: History, Culture and the Mind*, ed. Thomas Butler (Oxford: B. Blackwell, 1989), 108.

34 Kirk Savage, *Monument Wars: Washington, D.C., the National Mall, and the Transformation of the Memorial Landscape* (Berkeley: University of California Press, 2009), 10.

35 Winter 2010, 313. See also Edward Casey, *Remembering: A Phenomenological Study*, 2nd ed. (Bloomington: Indiana University Press, 2000), 216–257.

36 Bill Broadway, "Honoring a Past of Blacks in Uniform: Bikers Celebrate Heroic Heritage in Face of Racism," *Washington Post*, May 26, 2003. In 2009 President Barack Obama began an annual tradition of sending a wreath to the African American Civil War Memorial on Memorial Day. See Sheryl Gay Stoulberg, "'They Answered a Call,' Obama Says of Veterans: A Traditional Tribute, and a New One," *New York Times*, May 26, 2009.

Sources for quotations in the plate sections

p. 22
Frederick Douglass, from *Men of Color. To Arms!* Rochester, March 2, 1863.

pp. 36 and 66
Lewis Douglass in a letter to his fiancée Amelia Lougen, Morris Island, SC, July 20, 1863. Carter G. Woodson Papers, Manuscript Division, Library of Congress, Washington, DC. Amelia Lougen's full name was Helen Amelia Lougen, but she is addressed as "Amelia."

p. 128
Lincoln Kirstein, *Lay This Laurel* (New York: Eakins Press, 1973).

Roster of the 54th Massachusetts Regiment

1 The following primary sources—themselves derived from oral communications and handwritten copies—were consulted in the creation of the roster: "Records of the 54th Massachusetts Infantry Regiment (Colored), 1863–1865," Regimental and Company Books of Civil War Volunteer Union Organizations (M1659), U.S. National Archives and Records Administration, Washington, DC [hereafter NARA]; and Luis F. Emilio, *A Brave Black Regiment: History of the Fifty-fourth Regiment of Massachusetts Volunteer Infantry, 1863–1865* (Boston: The Boston Book Co., 1891; repr. of 2nd enlarged ed. [1894], with intro. by Gregory J. W. Urwin, New York: DaCapo Press, 1995).

Additional resources included: "Compiled Service Records for the United States Colored Troops (USCT), 1890–1912" (M1898), NARA; "Register of U.S. Colored Troop Deaths during the Civil War, 1861–1865," NARA; Civil War Soldiers and Sailors system database, National Park Service; and genealogical records at the African American Civil War Memorial and Museum. Finally, individual pension records were consulted at NARA, when available.

2 Although Henry Augustus Monroe gave his age as sixteen when he enlisted, he was in fact only thirteen. See Ronald S. Coddington, *African American Faces of the Civil War: An Album*, foreword by J. Matthew Gallman (Baltimore: The Johns Hopkins University Press, 2012), 229.

3 Where alternate spellings of names exist, the information found in the regimental record books (NARA M1659) precedes that listed in the appendix of Luis Emilio's book.

4 As the mechanisms for keeping military and pension records were themselves fairly new at the time, standardized and accurate information about these soldiers is not always available.

SELECTED BIBLIOGRAPHY

ARCHIVES

Demus and Christy Family Papers, U.S. National Archives and Records Administration, Washington, DC [hereafter NARA].

Frederick Douglass Papers, Rare Books and Special Collections, Library of Congress, Washington, DC.

Ed Hamilton Papers, Collection of the artist, Louisville, KY.

Carter G. Woodson Papers, Manuscript Division, Library of Congress, Washington, DC.

"Compiled Service Records of the 54th Massachusetts Infantry Regiment (Colored), 1863–1865," NARA.

"Regimental and Company Books of the 54th Massachusetts Infantry Regiment (Colored), 1863–1865," Regimental and Company Books of Civil War Volunteer Union Organizations, NARA.

"Register of U.S. Colored Troop Deaths during the Civil War, 1861–1865," NARA.

U.S. Military Pension Records, NARA.

BOOKS, ARTICLES, AND EXHIBITION CATALOGUES

Appleton, John M. W. "That Night at Fort Wagner, by One Who Was There." *Putnam's Magazine* 4, no. 19 (July 1869): 8–15.

Atkinson, Edward, W. A. Coffin, and Thomas Higginson. "The Shaw Memorial and the Sculptor St. Gaudens." *Century* 54 (June 1897): 176–200.

Barnes, James. "The Shaw Memorial." *Harper's Weekly*, no. 41 (May 29, 1897): 546.

Benson, Robert, and Lincoln Kirstein. *Lay This Laurel*. New York: Eakins Press, 1973.

Berlin, Ira, Joseph P. Reidy, and Leslie Rowland. *Freedom's Soldiers: The Black Military Experience in the Civil War*. Cambridge: Cambridge University Press, 1998.

Billington, Ray Allen, ed. *The Journal of Charlotte Forten: A Free Negro in the Slave Era*. New York: Dryden Press, 1953.

Birrer, Christopher. "The Fifty-fourth Massachusetts: A Revolutionary Symbol of the Black Struggle for Equality." *Journal of America's Military Past* (Spring/Summer 2005): 5–35.

Blassingame, John W., ed. *The Frederick Douglass Papers, Series One: Speeches, Debates, and Interviews*. Vol. 3. 1855–63. New Haven, CT: Yale University Press, 1985.

Blatt, Martin H., Thomas J. Brown, and Donald Yacavone, eds. *Hope and Glory: Essays on the Legacy of the Fifty-fourth Massachusetts Regiment*. Amherst: University of Massachusetts in association with the Massachusetts Historical Society, Boston, 2001.

Blight, David W. *American Oracle: The Civil War in the Civil Rights Era*. Cambridge, MA: Harvard University Press, 2011.

———. *Race and Reunion: The Civil War in American Memory*. Cambridge, MA: Belknap Press of Harvard University Press, 2001.

———. "The Meaning of the Fight: Frederick Douglass and the Memory of the Fifty-fourth Massachusetts." *The Massachusetts Review* 36, no. 1 (Spring 1995): 141–153.

Bodnar, John E. *Remaking America: Public Memory, Commemoration, and Patriotism in the Twentieth Century*. Princeton, NJ: Princeton University Press, 1992.

Boime, Albert. *The Art of Exclusion: Representing Blacks in the Nineteenth Century*. Washington, DC: Smithsonian Institution Press, 1990.

Buick, Kristen Pai. *Child of the Fire: Mary Edmonia Lewis and the Problem of Art History's Black and Indian Subject*. Durham, NC: Duke University Press, 2010.

Burchard, Peter. *One Gallant Rush: Robert Gould Shaw and His Brave Black Regiment*. New York: St. Martin's Press, 1965.

———. *"We'll Stand by the Union": Robert Gould Shaw and the Black 54th Massachusetts Regiment*. Makers of America. New York: Facts on File, 1993.

Burke, Peter. "History as Social Memory." In *Memory: History, Culture and the Mind*. Edited by Thomas Butler, 97–113. Oxford: B. Blackwell, 1989.

Caffin, Charles H. *American Masters of Sculpture; Being Brief Appreciations of Some American Sculptors and of Some Phases of Sculpture in America*. New York: Doubleday, Page & Co., 1913.

Carney, William H. "I Was There." Edited by Brian C. Pohanka. *Civil War* (June 1990): 8, 57.

Coddington, Ronald S. *African American Faces of the Civil War: An Album*. Foreword by J. Matthew Gallman. Baltimore: The Johns Hopkins University Press, 2012.

Collins, Kathleen. "Shadow and Substance: Sojourner Truth." *History of Photography* 7 (September 1983): 183–205.

Cornish, Dudley Taylor. *The Sable Arm: Negro Troops in the Union Army, 1861–1865*. Modern War Studies. 1956; Lawrence: University Press of Kansas, 1987.

Cox, Kenyon. "Augustus Saint-Gaudens." *Century* 35 (November 1887): 30.

Craven, Wayne. *Sculpture in America.* New York: Crowell, 1968.

Curtis & Cameron. *The Copley Prints: Reproductions of Notable Paintings Publicly and Privately Owned in America....* Boston: Curtis & Cameron, 1902.

Darrah, William C. *Cartes-de-Visite in Nineteenth-Century Photography.* Gettysburg, PA: William C. Darrah, 1981.

Doezema, Marianne, and June Hargrove. *The Public Monument and Its Audience.* Cleveland: Cleveland Museum of Art, 1977.

Doss, Erika Lee. *Memorial Mania: Public Feeling in America.* Chicago: University of Chicago Press, 2010.

Douglass, Frederick. *The Life and Writings of Frederick Douglass: 1910 – 1994.* New York: International Publishers, 1950.

Dryfhout, John H. *The Works of Augustus Saint-Gaudens.* Hanover, NH: University Press of New England, 1982.

Duganne, Erina. "Black Civil War Portraiture in Context." http://bit.ly/135y9Sf

Duncan, Russell, ed. *Blue-Eyed Child of Fortune: The Civil War Letters of Colonel Robert Gould Shaw.* Athens: University of Georgia Press, 1992.

———. *Where Death and Glory Meet: Colonel Robert Gould Shaw and the 54th Massachusetts Infantry.* Athens: University of Georgia Press, 1999.

Emilio, Luis F. *A Brave Black Regiment: History of the Fifty-fourth Regiment of Massachusetts Volunteer Infantry, 1863 – 1865.* Boston: The Boston Book Co., 1891. Reprint of 2nd enlarged edition (1894), with new introduction by Gregory J. W. Urwin. New York: DaCapo Press, 1995.

———. *The Assault on Fort Wagner, July 18, 1863: The Memorable Charge of the Fifty-fourth Regiment of Massachusetts Volunteers, Written for "The Springfield Republican."* Boston: Rand Avery, 1887.

Freedom, a Documentary History of Emancipation, 1861 – 1867. Cambridge: Cambridge University Press, 1982.

Gaines, Kevin Kelly. *Uplifting the Race: Black Leadership, Politics, and Culture in the Twentieth Century.* Chapel Hill: University of North Carolina Press, 1996.

Gates, Henry Louis, Jr.. "The Trope of a New Negro and the Reconstruction of the Image of the Black." *Representations* 24, Special Issue: *America Reconstructed, 1840 – 1940* (Autumn 1988): 129.

Gips, Terry, et al. *Narratives of African American Art and Identity: The David C. Driskell Collection, University of Maryland.* San Francisco: Pomegranate Communications, 1998.

Gladstone, William A. *Men of Color.* Gettysburg, PA: Thomas Publications, 1993.

Glatthaar, Joseph T. *Forged in Battle: The Civil War Alliance of Black Soldiers and White Officers.* Baton Rouge: Louisiana State University Press, 2000.

Goode, James E. "Four Salutes to the Nation: The Equestrian Statues of General Andrew Jackson." *White House History* 17 (2010): 4 – 19.

Gooding, James Henry. *On the Altar of Freedom: A Black Soldier's Civil War Letters from the Front.* Edited by Virginia M. Adams. Amherst: University of Massachusetts Press, 1991.

Greenthal, Kathryn. *Augustus Saint-Gaudens: Master Sculptor.* The Metropolitan Museum of Art. Boston: G.K. Hall & Co., 1985.

Hahn, Steven. *A Nation under Our Feet: Black Political Struggles in the Rural South, from Slavery to the Great Migration.* Cambridge, MA: Belknap Press of Harvard University Press, 2003.

Hamilton, Ed. *The Birth of an Artist: A Journey of Discovery.* Louisville, KY: Chicago Spectrum Press, 2006.

Hargrove, Hondon B. *Black Union Soldiers in the Civil War.* Jefferson, NC: McFarland & Co, 1988.

Hartigan, Lynda Roscoe. *Sharing Traditions: Five Black Artists in Nineteenth-Century America.* Smithsonian American Art Museum. Washington, DC: Smithsonian Institution Press, 1985.

Heller, Charles E. *Portrait of an Abolitionist: A Biography of George Luther Stearns, 1809 – 1867.* Westport, CT: Greenwood Press, 1996.

Henderson, Harry, and Albert Henderson. *The Indomitable Spirit of Edmonia Lewis: A Narrative Biography.* Milford, CT: Esquiline Hill Press, 2012. PDF e-book.

Henig, Gerald S. "Glory at Battery Wagner: William H. Carney Became the First Black Soldier to Earn the Medal of Honor." *Civil War Times* (June 2009): 36 – 39.

Holland, Juanita Marie. *The Life and Work of Edward Mitchell Bannister, 1828 – 1901.* Whitney Museum of American Art at Champion. New York: Kenkeleba House, 1992.

Holzer, Harold, and Mark E. Neely Jr. "Days of 'Glory': How America First Saw the 54th Mass." *Civil War* (June 1990): 46 – 49, 61.

Jacob, Kathryn Allamong. *Testament to Union: Civil War Monuments in Washington, D.C.* Photographs by Edwin Harlan Remsberg. Baltimore: Johns Hopkins University Press, 1998.

James, William. *Essays in Religion and Morality.* Cambridge, MA: Harvard University Press, 1982.

Johnston, Frances Benjamin, and Lincoln Kirstein. *The Hampton Album: 44 Photographs from an Album of Hampton Institute.* New York: The Museum of Modern Art, 1966.

Kaplan, Sidney. *American Studies in Black and White: Selected Essays, 1949 – 1989.* Amherst: University of Massachusetts Press, 1991.

———. "The Black Soldier of the Civil War in Literature and Art." *The Chancellor's Lecture Series,* 26 – 27. Amherst: University of Massachusetts, 1981.

———. "The Sculptural World of Augustus Saint-Gaudens." *The Massachusetts Review* 30, no. 1 (Spring 1989): 17 – 64.

Karcher, Carolyn L. *The First Woman in the Republic: A Cultural Biography of Lydia Maria Child.* Durham, NC: Duke University Press, 1994.

———, ed. *A Lydia Maria Child Reader.* New Americanists. Durham, NC: Duke University Press, 1997.

Lancaster, Jane. "'I would have made out very poorly had it not been for her': The Life and Work of Christiana Bannister, Hair Doctress and Philanthropist." *Rhode Island History* 59 (November 2001).

Levinson, Sanford. *Written in Stone: Public Monuments in Changing Societies.* Durham, NC: Duke University Press, 1998.

Lincoln, Abraham. *Speeches and Writings. 1859–1865.* New York: Library of America, 2009.

Locke, Alain. *The New Negro: Voices of the Harlem Renaissance.* Introduction by Arnold Rampersad. New York: Maxwell Macmillan International, 1992.

Logan, Rayford W. *The Betrayal of the Negro, from Rutherford B. Hayes to Woodrow Wilson.* New York: Collier Books, 1965.

Lowell, James Russell. "Memoria Positum: R.G.S." *Atlantic Monthly* 13 (January 1864): 88–90.

Mabee, Carleton, with Susan Mabee Newhouse. *Sojourner Truth: Slave, Prophet, Legend.* New York: New York University Press, 1993.

Marcus, Lois Goldreich. "The *Shaw Memorial* by Augustus Saint-Gaudens: A History Painting in Bronze." *Winterthur Portfolio* 14, no. 1 (Spring 1979): 1–23.

Masur, Kate. *An Example for All the Land: Emancipation and the Struggle over Equality in Washington, D.C.* Chapel Hill: University of North Carolina Press, 2010.

McPherson, James M. *The Negro's Civil War: How American Blacks Felt and Acted During the War for the Union.* 1965; New York: Vintage Books, 2003.

"Memorial Planned for Civil War's Black Soldiers." *New York Times*, August 12, 1991.

Memorial R.G.S. [Robert Gould Shaw]. Cambridge, MA: University Press, 1864.

Murray, Freeman Henry Morris. *Emancipation and the Freed in American Sculpture: A Study in Interpretation.* Black Folk in Art Series. Washington, DC: private publication, 1916.

New Bedford through the Lens: A Walk through History. A Photography Exhibition Presented by the New Bedford Art Museum. 2011. http://bit.ly/11W0NFV

Nora, Pierre. "Between Memory and History: Les Lieux De Memoire." *Representations* 26 (Spring 1989): 7–24.

O'Connor, Thomas H. *Civil War Boston: Home Front and Battlefield.* Boston: Northeastern University Press, 1997.

O'Leary, Cecilia Elizabeth. *To Die For: The Paradox of American Patriotism.* Princeton, NJ: Princeton University Press, 1999.

Painter, Nell Irvin. *Sojourner Truth: A Life, A Symbol.* New York: W.W. Norton, 1996.

Patterson, Vivian Johnston, Carrie Mae Weems, and Frances Benjamin Johnston. *Carrie Mae Weems: The Hampton Project.* Williams College Museum of Art, Williamstown. New York: Aperture, 2000.

Pearson, Henry Greenleaf. *The Life of John A. Andrew, Governor of Massachusetts, 1861–1865.* Boston, New York: Houghton, Mifflin and Co., 1904.

Powell, Richard J. *Cutting a Figure: Fashioning Black Portraiture.* Chicago: University of Chicago Press, 2008.

Quarles, Benjamin. *The Negro in the Civil War.* 1953; Boston: Little, Brown, 1969.

Redkey, Edwin S. *A Grand Army of Black Men: Letters from African-American Soldiers in the Union Army, 1861–1865.* Cambridge Studies in American Literature and Culture. Cambridge: Cambridge University Press, 1992.

Van Rensselaer, Mariana. "Saint-Gaudens' Lincoln." *Century* 35 (November 1887): 37, 39.

Richardson, Marilyn. "Edmonia Lewis at McGrawville: The Early Education of a Nineteenth-Century Black Woman Artist." *Nineteenth-Century Contexts* 22 (September 1, 2000): 239–256.

Riegl, Alois. "Modern Cult of Monuments: Its Character and Its Origins." Translated by Kurt W. Forster and Diane Ghirardo. *Oppositions* 25 (Fall, 1903, Reprint, 1982): 20–51.

Riley, Stephen T. "A Monument to Colonel Robert Gould Shaw." *Proceedings of the Massachusetts Historical Society* 75 (1963): 36.

Rydell, Robert W. "Gateway to the 'American Century': The American Representation at the Paris Universal Exposition of 1900." In *Paris 1900: The "American School" at the Universal Exposition.* Edited by Diane P. Fischer. New Brunswick, NJ: Rutgers University Press, 1999.

Saint-Gaudens, Augustus. *The Reminiscences of Augustus Saint-Gaudens*, Vols. 1–2. Edited and amplified by Homer Saint-Gaudens. John Davis Batchelder Collection (Library of Congress). New York: The Century Co., 1913.

Samito, Christian G. *Becoming American under Fire: Irish Americans, African Americans, and the Politics of Citizenship During the Civil War Era.* Ithaca, NY: Cornell University Press, 2009.

Sampsell-Willmann, Kate. *Lewis Hine as Social Critic.* Jackson: University Press of Mississippi, 2009.

Savage, Kirk. *Monument Wars: Washington, D.C., the National Mall, and the Transformation of the Memorial Landscape.* Berkeley: University of California Press, 2009.

———. *Standing Soldiers, Kneeling Slaves: Race, War, and Monument in Nineteenth-Century America.* Princeton, NJ: Princeton University Press, 1997.

Scharnhorst, Gary. "From Soldier to Saint: Robert Gould Shaw and the Rhetoric of Racial Justice." *Civil War History* (December 1988): 308–322.

BIBLIOGRAPHY

Schwarz, Gregory C., et al. *The Shaw Memorial: a Celebration of an American Masterpiece*. Saint-Gaudens National Historic Site (Fort Washington, PA: Eastern National, 1997; rev. ed. 2002.

Shaw, Gwendolyn DuBois. *Portraits of a People: Picturing African Americans in the Nineteenth Century*. Addison Gallery of American Art. Seattle: University of Washington Press, 2006.

Smith, Cherise. "Fragmented Documents: Works by Lorna Simpson, Carrie Mae Weems, and Willie Robert Middlebrook at the Art Institute of Chicago." *Art Institute of Chicago Museum Studies* 24, no. 2 (1999).

Smith, John David. *Black Soldiers in Blue: African American Troops in the Civil War Era*. Chapel Hill: University of North Carolina Press, 2002.

Smith, Marion Whitney. *Colonel Robert Gould Shaw*. New York: Carlton Press, 1990.

Smith, Shawn Michelle. *Photography on the Color Line: W.E.B. Du Bois, Race, and Visual Culture*. Durham, NC: Duke University Press, 2004.

Stevenson, Richard W. "Civil War Regiment Receives Capital Tribute." *New York Times*, July 12, 1998.

Stillé, Charles J. *History of the United States Sanitary Commission*. New York: Hurd and Houghton, 1868.

Teal, Harvey S. *Partners with the Sun: South Carolina Photographers, 1840–1940*. Columbia: University of South Carolina Press, 2000.

Teamoh, Robert T. *Sketch of the Life and Death of Col. Robert Gould Shaw*. Boston, MA, 1904.

Trachtenberg, Alan. *America & Lewis Hine: Photographs 1904–1940*. New York: Aperture, Inc., 1977.

———. *Reading American Photographs: Images as History, Mathew Brady to Walker Evans*. 1st ed. New York, NY: Hill and Wang, 1989.

Trudeau, Noah Andre. *Like Men of War: Black Troops in the Civil War, 1862–1865*. Boston: Little, Brown, 1998.

Urwin, Gregory. "I Want You to Prove Yourselves Men." *Civil War Times Illustrated* (December 1989): 42–44, 46–51.

Voss, Frederick. *Majestic in His Wrath: A Pictorial Life of Frederick Douglass*. Introduction by Robert K. Sutton. Foreword by Waldo E. Martin Jr. Washington, DC: Smithsonian Institution Press for the National Portrait Gallery and the National Park Service, 1995.

Wachs, Eleanor, ed. "'It wasn't in her lifetime but it was handed down': Four Black Oral Histories of Massachusetts." Boston: Office of the Massachusetts Secretary of State, 1989.

Wallace, Maurice O., and Shawn Michelle Smith, eds. *Pictures and Progress: Early Photography and the Making of African American Identity*. Durham, NC: Duke University Press Books, 2012.

Washington, Booker T. "The Awakening of the Negro." *Atlantic Monthly* (September 1896).

———. *The Monument to Robert Gould Shaw, Its Inception, Completion and Unveiling, 1865–1897*. Boston, New York: Houghton, Mifflin and Co., 1897.

Wheat, Ellen Harkins, and Jacob Lawrence. *Jacob Lawrence: The Frederick Douglass and Harriet Tubman Series of 1938–40*. Hampton University Museum, Hampton, VA. Seattle: University of Washington Press, 1991.

Whitfield, Stephen J. "'Sacred in History and in Art': The Shaw Memorial by Augustus Saint-Gaudens." *New England Quarterly* 60, no. 1 (March 1987): 3–27.

Whitman, Walt. *Leaves of Grass and Selected Prose*. Edited with an introduction by John Kouwenhoven. New York: The Modern Library, 1950.

Williams, George Washington. *A History of the Negro Troops in the War of the Rebellion, 1861–1865*. New York: Harper & Bros., 1888.

Williams, William Earle, and Gerry Badger. *William Earle Williams, Unsung Heroes: African American Soldiers in the Civil War, January 16 - March 16, 2007*. Syracuse, N.Y.: Light Work, Robert B. Menschel Media Center, 2007.

Willis, Deborah. *Reflections in Black: a History of Black Photographers, 1840 to the Present*. New York: W.W. Norton, 2000.

———, ed. *Picturing Us: African American Identity in Photography*. New York: New Press, 1994.

Willis, Deborah, and Barbara Krauthamer. *Envisioning Emancipation: Black Americans and the End of Slavery*. Philadelphia: Temple University Press, 2013.

Willis-Thomas, Deborah. *Black Photographers, 1840–1940: An Illustrated Bio-Bibliography*. New York: Garland Publishing, 1985.

Wilkinson, Burke. *Uncommon Clay: The Life and Works of Augustus Saint Gaudens*. New York: Harcourt Brace Jovanovich, 1985.

Wilson, Keith P. *Campfires of Freedom: The Camp Life of Black Soldiers during the Civil War*. Kent, OH: Kent State University Press, 2002.

Winter, Jay. "Sites of Memory." In *Memory: Histories, Theories, Debates*. Edited by Susannah Radstone and Bill Schwarz, 312–324. New York, 2010.

Wise, Stephen R. *Gate of Hell: Campaign for Charleston Harbor, 1863*. Columbia: University of South Carolina Press, 1994.

Yacovone, Donald. *A Voice of Thunder: The Civil War Letters of George E. Stephens*. Blacks in the New World. Urbana: University of Illinois Press, 1997.

Zeller, Bob. *The Blue and Gray in Black and White: A History of Civil War Photography*. Westport, CT: Praeger, 2005.

ACKNOWLEDGMENTS

In September 2011, Susan and Peter MacGill gave the National Gallery of Art twenty-four photographs by Richard Benson of Augustus Saint-Gaudens' Shaw Memorial, and thus began the fascinating journey that has resulted in this publication and exhibition. Benson made the photographs in 1973 for a book, *Lay This Laurel*, that he and Lincoln Kirstein produced, which was intended to focus renewed attention on the Shaw Memorial in Boston. It included stirring poems by Emily Dickinson and Walt Whitman, among others, as well as an essay by Kirstein himself that addressed not only Shaw and the 54th Massachusetts Regiment but also the profound impact that the Civil War had and continues to have on American life, landscape, and psyche. With their careful examination of single lines of soldiers, Benson's photographs point to the power of the Shaw Memorial and also the anonymity of the men Saint-Gaudens depicted, for besides Shaw, whose likeness was based on a photograph, none were modeled on actual members of the 54th. Inspired by this realization and by the desire to celebrate the 54th in 2013 — the 150th anniversary of the Battle of Fort Wagner, their most famous encounter — our two departments of photographs and American paintings joined forces to collaborate on this exhibition and publication. Our objective was to shine attention on the 54th, showing important documents and works of art that commemorate them and the Battle of Fort Wagner and that address the issues they encountered as one of this country's first African American regiments. In addition, we sought to reveal the ways in which their actions and the Shaw Memorial have been and continue to be a touchstone for twentieth- and twenty-first-century artists.

We owe an enormous debt of gratitude to the United States Department of the Interior, the National Park Service, and the Saint-Gaudens National Historic Site for placing the patinated plaster version of the Shaw Memorial, as well as several plaster heads Saint-Gaudens made of the soldiers, on long-term loan at the National Gallery. We also offer deepest thanks to Susan and Peter MacGill for their donation of Benson's photographs. In addition, we are extremely grateful to Richard Benson, Carrie Mae Weems, and William Earle Williams for their contributions to the exhibition and the generous assistance they have given us throughout this project. During this anniversary year, when there are so many exhibitions related to the Civil War, we also want to thank all the lenders for so graciously parting with their treasures and enabling us to share them with our audience in this very special context.

An exhibition and publication like this one, which includes such diverse materials and comes together quickly, could not be accomplished without great dedication, support, and generosity. As soon as the idea for the show was proposed, Earl A. Powell III, director, and Franklin Kelly, deputy director, recognized its importance and gave it their unwavering support, as did D. Dodge Thompson, head of exhibition programs, Mark Leithauser, chief of design, and Judy Metro, editor in chief. With this encouragement, we assembled a superb team that has aided us every step of the way. Lindsay Harris, research associate in the department of photographs, was among our first, most eager, and loyal recruits. The project has benefited from her insights and her gifted research as well as her excellent essay in the catalogue. Several more recruits joined from the department of American paintings: Zoë Samels and Nicole Stribling, present and former curatorial assistants, lent invaluable organizational assistance and also, along with former intern Megan Sweeney, compiled the roster of the 54th Massachusetts with painstaking care and precision. In the publishing office, our team expanded to include Tam Curry Bryfogle, who edited the catalogue with an unflappable attention to detail, combined with tact and discernment, and Wendy Schleicher, whose design, like a successful regiment, elegantly knit together disparate elements to give a voice and a vision to our project. All of us were greatly assisted by deputy publisher Chris Vogel and permissions coordinator for exhibition objects Sara Sanders-Buell.

No one can work on the Civil War, even only a small aspect of it such as the 54th Massachusetts Regiment, and not acknowledge the pioneering research done by earlier historians and curators to preserve and make sense both of the conflict itself and the documents and works of art it produced. Our bibliography includes the key archives and publications that were of importance for our work, but many scholars and curators gave generously of their time and expertise. We are especially grateful to our colleagues at the Massachusetts Historical Society, Anne E. Bentley, Betsy Boyle, Peter Drummey, and Dennis Fiori, not only for their numerous loans to the exhibition but also for their insights and enthusiastic support. We also give a special thanks to our new colleagues on the National Mall, Jacquelyn D. Serwer as well as Rhea Combs, Michèle Gates Moresi, Drew Talley, and Ruthann R. Uithol of the National Museum of African American History and Culture, Washington, DC, and Nora Lockshin, paper conservator, Smithsonian Center for Archives Conservation, Washington, DC. In addition, we would like to thank: Hari Jones, African American Civil War Museum, Washington, DC; Lauren Hewes, American Antiquarian Society, Worcester, MA; Matthew Witkovsky and Douglas Severson, Art Institute of Chicago; Ann-Marie Harris, Berkshire Athenaeum, Pittsfield, MA; Will Garrison, Berkshire Historical Society, Pittsfield, MA; Catharina Slautterback, Boston Athenaeum; Karen Shafts and Jane Winton, Boston Public Library; Dana Byrd and Richard Lindemann, Bowdoin College, Brunswick, ME; Ronald S. Coddington; Carl J. Cruz; Charleen M. Ward, Department of General Services, Washington, DC; Richard J. Powell, Duke University, Durham, NC; Chris Foard; Kamal McClarin, Frederick Douglass National Historic Site, Washington, DC; Greg French; Alison Nordstrom and Wataru Okada, George Eastman House, Rochester, NY; Greg Goodell, Gettysburg National Military Park Museum; Sandra Trenholm, The Gilder Lehrman Institute of American History, New York; Jon Goodman; Robert Matthias, Grand Army Memorial Building and Museum, Lynn, MA; Thomas Harris; Bruce Bumbarger, and Diana Peterson, Haverford College, Haverford, PA; Samuel W. Black, Senator John Heinz History Center, Pittsburgh; Albert Henderson; Leslie Morris, Houghton Library, Harvard University, Cambridge, MA; Nancy Sherbert, Kansas Historical Society, Topeka; Jane Lancaster; David Wilson, Leominster Historical Society, Leominster, MA; Sarah Weatherwax, The Library Company, Philadelphia; Carol Johnson, Library of Congress, Washington, DC; Allison Andrews, Medford Historical Society, Medford, MA; Peter W. Kunhardt Jr., The Meserve-Kunhardt Foundation, Pleasantville, NY; Joellen ElBashir, Moorland-Spingarn Research Center, Howard University, Washington, DC; Sarah Meister and Drew Sawyer, The Museum of Modern Art, New York; Dennis Edelin, Jane Fitzgerald, and James Zeender, National Archives and Records Administration, Washington, DC; Perry Wheelock, National Park Service, United States Department of the Interior, Washington, DC; Anne and Frank Goodyear, and Ann Shumard, National Portrait Gallery, Washington, DC; Keith Davis, Nelson-Atkins Museum, Kansas City, MO; Paul Cyr, New Bedford Free Public Library, New Bedford, MA; Ken Grossi and Anne Salsich, Oberlin College, Oberlin, OH; Lisa Wood, Ohio Historical Society, Columbus; Randall Pollard; Judy Norrell; Michael O'Connor; Adam Craig and Jennifer Dlugosz, Pamplin Historical Park and the National Museum of the Civil War Soldier, Petersburg, VA; Wendy Grossman, The Phillips Collection, Washington, DC; Callie Hawkins and Erin Carlson Mast, President Lincoln's Cottage at the Soldiers' Home, Washington, DC; Todd Baldwin and Mark Harris, Princeton University Art Museum, Princeton, NJ; Marilyn Richardson; Cindy Herron, Paul Sack Collection, San Francisco; Henry Duffy, Rick Kendall, and Gregory C. Schwarz, Saint-Gaudens National Historic Site, Cornish, NH; J. Harlan Buzby, Salem Historical Society, Salem, NJ; Sandra Phillips, San Francisco Museum of Modern Art; Mary Yearwood, Schomburg Center for Research in Black Culture, New York; Elisabeth Sann and Jack Shainman, Jack Shainman Gallery, New York; James Miller, Sheffield Historical Society, Sheffield, MA; Will Stapp; Deborah Willis, Tisch School of the Arts at New York University; Sarah Beetham, University of Delaware, Newark; Renée Ater, University of Maryland, College Park, MD; Kirk Savage, University of Pittsburgh; Gregory J. W. Urwin; Frances Pollard, Virginia Historical Society, Richmond; John Cuthbert, West Virginia and Regional History Collection, Morgantown, WV; Diane Hart, Christina Olsen, and Rachel Tassone, Williams College Museum of Art, Williamstown, MA; Nancy Kuhl, Beinecke Rare Book and Manuscript Library and Jock Reynolds, Yale University Art Gallery, New Haven, CT; Bob Zeller. We would also like to acknowledge and thank Lieutenant Timothy Fallon, U.S. Marine Corps, for enabling us to see the Shaw Memorial in a new light.

With its compelling form and powerful message, the Shaw Memorial has engendered a loyal following since it was first installed at the National Gallery in 1997. Nicolai Cikovsky Jr., former senior curator and head of the department of American and British paintings, oversaw the initial Shaw Memorial project and exhibition at the Gallery, with guidance from a team of conservators including Mervin Richard, Shelley Sturman, and Michael Palmer of the National Gallery of Art; Brigid Sullivan and Carol Warner of the National Park Service; and Richard Newman of the Museum of Fine Arts, Boston. Gallery curator Deborah Chotner wrote an illustrated brochure that has been recently updated and continues to be distributed free of charge. As we embarked on this present project, we were deeply grateful to have the expertise and advice of many members of this original team. In addition, we wish to thank Bethann Heinbaugh, loans and exhibitions conservation; Connie McCabe and Sarah Wagner, photograph conservation; Christopher Maines and Matthew Clarke, scientists; Julia Burke, textile conservation; and Jenny Ritchie, Hugh Phibbs, and Stephen Muscarella, matting and framing for their care in overseeing the display of these works of art. Registrar Melissa Stegeman ensured that the art was safely transported; Wendy Battaglino coordinated all of the details of the exhibition loans and paperwork; while Nancy Breuer, deputy secretary and deputy general counsel, efficiently handled all of the contractual issues. Special mention should be given to Gordon Anson, Donna Kirk, Andrea D'Amato, Barbara Keyes, and Jeff Wilson, who have designed and executed a graceful and elegant installation. We also acknowledge the support of Alan Newman, chief of imaging and visual services, Lorene Emerson, head of photographic services, Barbara Wood, permissions coordinator for comparative illustrations, Tricia Zigmund for her photographs of Ed Hamilton's *Spirit of Freedom*, and Lee Ewing for his superb new photography of the Shaw Memorial. And we are grateful to special police officers Robert Edwards and Michael Strong for sharing with us their knowledge of military protocol.

Our thanks also go to Faya Causey, Allison Peil, and Ben Masri-Cohen, who have arranged an excellent series of lectures and talks in conjunction with the exhibition; to Melanie Harper-Spears for her educational programs and to Gallery docent Joe McPhillips for sharing with us his research on the 54th; Margaret Parsons, Joanna Raczynska, and Stephen Ackert for the accompanying film and music programs; Lynn Matheny for attentively reviewing the educational materials for both the exhibition and the website. In addition, we are especially grateful to Elizabeth Cropper and Therese O'Malley of the Center for the Advanced Study of Visual Art for organizing a scholarly symposium in conjunction with the exhibition. Christine Myers, Cristina Del Sesto, Cathryn Scoville, and Patty Donovan in the development office all deserve special thanks, as do Deborah Ziska, Sara Beth Walsh, and Sarah Holley in the press office. Finally, in the department of photographs, we wish to thank both Ksenya Gurshstein for her assistance with the roster and Maryanna Ramirez for her efficient, cheerful help with a myriad of details, which made our work on this project far more productive and pleasant.

SARAH GREENOUGH
NANCY K. ANDERSON

INDEX

Note Page numbers in italic type indicate illustrations. Subjects reproduced as plates in the catalogue are listed both under their own name and under the artist's name, if known.

A

African American Civil War Memorial, Washington, DC, 113–126, *114*, 195n36
African American Civil War Memorial Freedom Foundation, 115, 116, 125
African American Civil War Museum, Washington, DC, 126
Alexander, Archer, 123
Allen, Edward L., *Lewis Hayden* (pl. 12), 9–10, *32*
ambrotypes, 14–16
The American Monument (Friedlander, Benson, and Katz), 107–108
American Negro Exhibit (Paris, 1900), 19, 98–100
Anderson, Robert, 187n43
Andrew, John A., 3, *24* (pl. 2), 35, 84, 86, 89, 189n16
Anglo-African (newspaper), 86
Anonymous Letter to Shaw Family Announcing Shaw's Death (pl. 43), *63*
Antietam, battle of, 5
anti-lynching crusade, 91
Appleton, John M. W., 91, 185n2, 188n70, 188n74
Armstrong, Samuel Chapman, 99, 110
Army of Georgia, 124
Army of Tennessee, 124
Army of the Potomac, 124
Arnum, Charles H., *46* (pl. 25)
Askew, Thomas E., 100
photographs by, *101*
Atkinson, Edward, 89, 90
Atlanta University, 100
"The Attack on Fort Wagner—The Stormers Advancing Under Fire," *Harper's Weekly*, 105, *105*
Attucks, Crispus, 3

B

Ball, Thomas, *Freedmen's Memorial to Abraham Lincoln (Emancipation Group)*, 113, 122–123, *123*
Bannister, Christiana Carteaux, 84–86, *85*
Bannister, Edward Mitchell, 85–88, *85*
Barnard, George N., 111
Ruins in Charleston, South Carolina (pl. 54), *iv–v* (detail), *72–73*
Ruins of the Pinckney Mansion, Charleston, South Carolina (pl. 55), *74–75*
Ruins of the Railroad Depot, Charleston, South Carolina (pl. 56), *76–77*
Barton, Clara, 9, *68* (pl. 47)
Bearden, Romare, 94
Beaufort, South Carolina, 5, 10
Becker, Theodore J., 14, 15
Bell, Charles Milton, *Charlotte L. Forten, Teacher* (pl. 49), *69*
Benson, Richard, 107–110
Lay This Laurel, 108–110
Robert Gould Shaw Memorial (pl. 72), 108, *142*
Robert Gould Shaw Memorial (pl. 73), 108, 109, *143*
Robert Gould Shaw Memorial (pl. 74), 108, *144*
Robert Gould Shaw Memorial (pl. 75), *vi* (detail), 108, *145*
Benton, Samuel, 18, *52* (pl. 32), 188n74
Berlin, Ira, 8
Bethune, Mary McLeod, 123
Bion, Paul, 90
Black & Case, *Helen Louise Gilson, Nurse* (pl. 50), *69*
Black Codes, 91
Blatt, Martin H., *Hope and Glory*, 7
Bogardus, Abraham, *Major Martin Robison Delany* (pl. 13), 9–10, *33*
Boston Evening Transcript (newspaper), 86, 87, 88
Boys Choir of Harlem, 119
Brady, Matthew, 111
Governor John A. Andrew (pl. 2), *24*
Bright, Jeptha Bernard "Barney," 118
Louisville Clock, 118
River Horse, 118
Broadbent, Samuel, *Charles Lenox Remond* (pl. 6), 9–10, *28*
Broderick, Matthew, 7
Brown, Abraham F., 16, 18, *44*, *45* (pls. 23, 24)
Brown, John, 3, 8, 104, 190n27
Brown, Thomas J., *Hope and Glory*, 7
Burchard, Peter, *One Gallant Rush*, 7
Bureau of Colored Troops Records, National Archives, 126
Burnite, David C., *Thomas Morris Chester* (pl. 9), 9–10, *30*
Burns, Anthony, 3
Burroughs, Margaret, 107
Bush, James W., 17, *49* (pl. 28)

C

Caldwell, James, 11, 185n2
Calloway, Thomas Junius, 98–99
Camp Barker, 117
Campbell Hospital, 117
Captain Luis F. Emilio (pl. 36), 18, *55*
Captain Norwood P. Hallowell (pl. 39), 18, *58*
Carney, William H., 6–7, *6*, 17–18, *18*, 19, 86, 88, 98, 106, 119, *137*, *139* (pls. 67, 69), 148, 149, 186n19, 188n78
cartes de visite, 10–11, 14–15, 187n43
Case & Getchell, *Sergeant Major Lewis H. Douglass* (pl. 21), 14, *42*
Casualty List of the 54th Massachusetts Infantry Regiment from the Assault on Fort Wagner, SC (pl. 42), *62*
Century Magazine, 82, 90
Charleston, South Carolina, 5, 83, 95, 106
Chester, Thomas Morris, *30* (pl. 9), 185n2
Child, Lydia Marie, 87
Christiana Carteaux Bannister, *85*
Christy, Jacob E., 12, 13
Christy, Joseph, 13
Christy, Samuel A., 12, 13
Christy, William, 12, 13
civil rights movement, 107
Civil War Soldiers and Sailors System database, 126
Civil War Times (magazine), 119
Claflin, Charles R. B., *Clara Barton, Nurse* (pl. 47), *68*
Cleveland Gazette (newspaper), 97
Coffin, William A., 90, 92
Colored Citizens of Boston, 86
Colored Ladies of Massachusetts, 84–86

Colored Ladies' Sanitary Fair, Boston, 84–88
Colored Soldiers Monument (Kentucky African American Civil War Veterans Monument), Frankfort, Kentucky, 119, *119*
Congressional Medal of Honor, 19, 86, 119, *138*, 148, 188n78
Congressional Medal of Honor, Awarded to Sergeant William H. Carney, Co. C, 54th Mass. Inf., for Gallantry at Fort Wagner, S.C., July 18, 1863 (pl. 68), *138*
Cook, George S., 187n43
Cooley, Samuel A., 15
Cornish, Dudley Taylor, *The Sable Arm*, 7, 125
Council of the District of Columbia, 115
Currier & Ives
  The Gallant Charge of the 54th Massachusetts (Colored) Regiment: on the Rebel Works at Fort Wagner, Morris Island, Near Charleston, July 18th, 1863, and Death of Colonel Robt. G. Shaw (pl. 41), *60–61*, 96, 106
Curtis & Cameron Publishers, 102
  Shaw Memorial (pl. 70), *140*

D

Daguerre, Louis-Jacques-Mandé, 8
daguerreotypes, 8, 10, 11
Darby, John G., *Harriet Arminta Tubman, Spy* (pl. 52), 10, *70*
Darien, Georgia, 5
Davis, William C., *The Fighting Men of the Civil War*, 119
DC Commission on the Arts and Humanities, 115, 117
Delany, Martin Robison, 9, *33* (pl. 13), 185n2
Delany, Touissant L'Ouverture, 185n2
Demus, David, 12, 13
Demus, George, 13
Demus, Mary Jane, 12, 13
Devrouax, Paul S., 115, 116
Disdéri, André-Adolphe-Eugène, 10

Dixon, Eddie, 117
Douglas, Aaron, 104
Douglass, Amelia (née Lougen), 14–15, 36, 66, *67*
Douglass, Anna, 83
Douglass, Charles, 5, 185n2
Douglass, Frederick, 2, 3, 5, 8–9, *9*, 14, 15, 22, *27* (pl. 5), 83, 99, 104–105, 115, 119–120, 185n2
Douglass, Lewis, 5, 14–15, 16, 19, 36, *42* (pl. 21), 66, *67* (pl. 46), 83, 185n2
Douglass' Monthly (journal), 83
Dr. M. M. Marsh (pl. 48), *68*
Du Bois, W.E.B., 19
  Negro Life in Georgia, U.S.A., 99–100, *101*
  Types of American Negroes, Georgia, U.S.A., 99–100, *101*
Dunbar, Paul Laurence, 95
Duncan, Russell, *Where Death and Glory Meet*, 7
Dunson, Edward D., Jr., 115, 116

E

E. & H. T. Anthony, 187n43
8th United States Colored Infantry, 120
Emancipation Proclamation, 3, 7, 8, 23, 86, 88, 104, 119, 123
Emancipation Proclamation (pl. 1), *23*
Emerson, Ralph Waldo, 95
Emilio, Luis, 7, 18, *54, 55* (pls. 35, 36), 109
Enlistment Roll of Company A, 54th Massachusetts Infantry Regiment (pl. 17), *38*
Evans, Walker, 107
Exhibit of the American Negro. *See* American Negro Exhibit (Paris, 1900)
Exposition Universelle (Paris, 1900), 19, 92, 97–100, *97*, 110, 192n19

F

Fallon, Maureen, 81
Fallon, Timothy, 81–82
Fauset, Jessie Redmon, 100

55th Massachusetts Regiment, 85
54th Massachusetts Regiment, xv–xvi, 3, 5–19, 81–92, *91*, 95–96, 100, 102–111, 117, 119, 120, 185n2, 190n42
  casualties, 62, 109, 186n15
  Company A, *38*
  Company C, 98
  Company G, 16
  Company H, 11
  Company I, 13, 14, 15
  enrollment list, *38*
  payment for soldiers of, 13, 85, 189n16, 190n21
1st Regiment, United States Cavalry, 116
Fisher, Abraham, *Private Theodore J. Becker*, 14, 15
Fisher, Rudolph, 103
Flag of the 54th Massachusetts Volunteer Regiment, 7
Fleetwood, Christian, 19
Forten, Charlotte L., 9, *69* (pl. 49)
Fort Sumter, battle of, 187n43, 188n76
Fort Wagner, battle of, 5–6, 10, 12, 14, *60–61, 63, 64*, 88, 95, 105, *105*, 109, 148, 186n15
Foster, H. C., 15, 17
  Private Alexander H. Johnson, Musician (pl. 31) [attributed to], 16–17, *51*
  Private Isaiah Spriggs, Company A, 54th Massachusetts Regiment [attributed to], 17, *17*
  Private John Gooseberry, Musician (pl. 30) [attributed to], 16–17, *50*
  Sergeant and Mrs. William H. W. Gray, 10, *11*
  Sergeant James W. Bush (pl. 28), 17, *49*
  Sergeant Joseph A. Palmer, Company K, 54th Massachusetts Regiment, 17, *17*
4th Regiment of the U.S. Colored Volunteer Infantry, 19
Frank, Robert, 107
Frederick Douglass, 9
Friedlander, Lee
  The American Monument, 107–108

"Robert Gould Shaw and the First Black Volunteer Regiment, Boston, Massachusetts," 107, *108*
Fuller, James, 148

G

Garnet, Henry Highland, *30* (pl. 8), 185n2
Garrison, William Lloyd, 3, 88
General Andrew Jackson equestrian monument, 116
Gettysburg, battle of, 124–125
Gillmore, Quincy A., 5, 188n76, 188n78
Gillmore Medal of Honor, 19, 188n76
Gilson, Helen Louise, 9, *69* (pl. 50)
Gladstone, William A., *Men of Color*, 119
Glatthaar, Joseph T., 120
Glory (film), 7, 81, 95, 119, 125
Gomar, Richard, *53* (pl. 34)
Gooding, James Henry, 7
  letter to Lincoln, 13, 65
Gooseberry, John, 16–17, 18, *50* (pl. 30)
Grand Prix, Exposition Universelle (Paris, 1900), 92, 97
Grand Review of the Armies, 124
Grand Review of United States Colored Troops, 194n29
Gray, Martha, 10, *11*
Gray, William H. W., 10, *11*
Great Migration, 102–103
Grimes, Leonard Andrew, 86

H

Hallett, Charles, 18, *56* (pl. 37)
Hallowell, Norwood P., *58* (pl. 39)
Hamilton, Ed, 117–118
  Amistad Memorial, New Haven, Connecticut, 117
  Booker T. Washington Memorial, Hampton, Virginia, 117, 118
  Joe Louis Memorial, Detroit, Michigan, 117

205

Spirit of Freedom, 114, 115, 117–120, *118*, *118* (detail), *121*, *121* (details), *122*–*125*, *122* (detail)
The Hampton Album (exhibition catalogue), 99
Hampton Institute, 99, 110
Harlem Renaissance, 103, 110
Harper's Weekly (magazine), 82
Harrison, Benjamin, 19
Hatch, Henry F., *William H. Carney*, *18*, 19
Hayden, Lewis, 8, 9, *32* (pl. 12), 185n2
Higginson, Thomas Wentworth, xv, xvi
Hine, Lewis
  Black Family by Fireplace, from the Series "Southern Negroes" (pl. 71), 100, 102, 109, *141*
  "Southern Negroes" series, 100, 102–103
Holmes, Oliver Wendell, 10
Horner, James, 119
Hughes, Langston, 100
Hurd, Gustine L., *Edward Mitchell Bannister*, *85*

I
Ives, Charles, 95

J
Jackson, Andrew, 116
James, Garth Wilkinson, 92, 185n6
James, William, 92
James Island, battle of, 5, 11
J. E. Farwell and Co., *To Colored Men. 54th Regiment! Massachusetts Volunteers, of African Descent!* (pl. 18), *39*
Jefferson, Thomas, 116
Jim Crow laws, 100
Johnson, Alexander Howard, 16–17, *51* (pl. 31)
Johnson, Andrew, 91, 124
Johnson, William Henry, 104
Johnston, Frances Benjamin, 99, 110
  "A Hampton Graduate at Home," 99, *99*
  "The Old Folks at Home," 99, *99*

K
Kaplan, Sidney, 107
Katz, Leslie George, 107–108
Kellogg, Paul, 103
Kirstein, Lincoln, 108–109, 128
Krauthamer, Barbara, 91
Ku Klux Klan, 91, 100

L
Langston, John Mercer, *31* (pl. 11), 185n2
Lawrence, Amos A., 3
Lawrence, Jacob, 104, 110
  The Frederick Douglass Series, panel no. 26, 104, *104*
Lay This Laurel (Benson, Katz, and Kirstein), 108–110
Lee, Robert E., 88
Legion of Honor, 92
Letter from Corporal James Henry Gooding to President Abraham Lincoln (pl. 45), 13, *65*
Letter from Governor John A. Andrew to Francis G. Shaw (pl. 15), *35*
Lewis, Edmonia, 7, 85–88, *85*, 190n27
  Colonel Robert Shaw, 87–88, *87*, 190n28
Lewis and Amelia Douglass (pl. 46), 14, *67*
The Liberator (newspaper), 84–85, 88
Lin, Maya, Vietnam Veterans Memorial, 116
Lincoln, Abraham, 3, 13, 80, 84, 88, 93, 104, 123, *123*
Lindsley, H. B., *Harriet Tubman*, 10
Locke, Alain, 100
  The New Negro, 103
Logan, John A., 115–116
Lopez, Carlos, 106
  The 54th Massachusetts Regiment, under the Leadership of Colonel Shaw in the Attack on Fort Wagner, Morris Island, South Carolina, 105–107, *106*
Lougen, Amelia. *See* Douglass, Amelia (née Lougen)
Lowell, James Russell, 95
lynchings, 88, 91

M
Major General George Henry Thomas equestrian monument, 115–116
Major General James Birdseye McPherson equestrian monument, 116
Major General John A. Logan equestrian monument, 115–116
Major Lincoln R. Stone, Surgeon (pl. 38), 5, 18, *57*
Map of Washington, DC, *114*
Marcus, Lois Goldreich, 90
Marrs, Elijah, 112
Marsh, M. M., *68* (pl. 48)
Marshall, Augustus, Edmonia Lewis' *Colonel Robert Shaw*, 87, *87*
McConnell, Stuart, 124
McPherson, James Birdseye, 116
McPherson, James M., *The Negro's Civil War*, 7
Meadows, Jerome, 117
Medal of Honor. *See* Congressional Medal of Honor
Medal of Honor Men exhibit (Paris, 1900), 98, *98*
Meiklejohn, G. D., 19
Miller, Samuel J., *Frederick Douglass* (pl. 5), *27*
Milmore, Martin, Soldiers and Sailors Monument, Boston, 190n42
Monroe, Henry Augustus, 16–17, 19, *49* (pl. 29)
Montgomery, James, 5
Moore, David Miles, 16–17, *16*
Morris Island, South Carolina, 4, 5, 13, 15, 16, 83, 95
Murray, Freeman Henry Morris, xvi
Museum of Modern Art, New York, 99

N
Napoleon III, Emperor, 10
National Archives and Records Administration, 115, 126
National Council of Negro Women, 123
National Park Service, 90, 115, 126
National Planning Commission, 115
Netson, William J., *48* (pl. 27)
New Negro, 97, 99, 102–103
New York Civil Rights Law, 97
New York Daily Tribune (newspaper), 5
New York draft riots, 88, 91
9th U.S. Colored Troops, 99
Nixon, Richard, 107
Norton, Eleanor Holmes, 115

O
Obama, Barack, 195n36
O'Sullivan, Timothy, 111

P
Pach Brothers, *George Luther Stearns* (pl. 3), *25*
Palmer, Joseph A., 17
Paris Exposition. *See* Exposition Universelle (Paris, 1900)
Peck, Ferdinand W., 97, 98
Phillips, Wendell, 3, 6–7, *26* (pl. 4), 185n2
Pierce, Edward L., 185n2
Pippin, Horace, 104
Plessy v. Ferguson (1896), 97
The Portrayal of the Negro in American Painting (exhibition), 107
Private Abraham F. Brown (pl. 23), 16, *44*
Private Abraham F. Brown (pl. 24), 16, *45*
Private Charles A. Smith (pl. 33), *53*
Private Charles H. Arnum (pl. 25), *46*
Private David Miles Moore, Company C, 54th Massachusetts Regiment, 16–17, *16*
Private Henry A. Monroe, Musician (pl. 29), 16–17, *49*
Private James Matthew Townsend (pl. 19), 13–14, *40*
Private Richard Gomar (pl. 34), *53*
Private Samuel J. Benton (pl. 32), *52*, 188n74
Private William J. Netson, Musician (pl. 27), *48*
Purvis, Robert, 8, 9, *29* (pl. 7), 185n2

INDEX

Q
Quarles, Benjamin, *The Negro in the Civil War*, 7, 125

R
Recorder of Deeds mural, 105–107, *106*
Reed, James E., 19
  William H. Carney (pl. 69), 19, *137*
Reid, James Earl, 117
Reidy, Joseph P., 8
Remond, Charles Lenox, 8, 9, 28 (pl. 6), 86, 185n2
Richards, Frederick DeBourg, *Dr. John S. Rock* (pl. 10), 9–10, *31*
Richardson, Henry Hobson, 89
Ringwalt & Brown, *View of Transparency, in front of Headquarters of Supervisory Committee for Recruiting Colored Regiments, Chestnut Street, Philadelphia, in Commemoration of Emancipation in Maryland, November 1, 1864* (pl. 66), 18, *136*
Robert Purvis (pl. 7), 9–10, *29*
Rocher, H., *Edmonia Lewis*, 85
Rock, John S., 8, 9, *31* (pl. 10), 185n2
Rodin, Auguste, 92, 97, 124
Roosevelt, Franklin D., 105, *106*
Rowland, Leslie S., 8
Rude, François, xv
Russell, Cabot J., *59* (pl. 40)

S
Saint-Gaudens, Augusta, 91
Saint-Gaudens, Augustus, 89–92, 102
  allegorical figure, Shaw Memorial, Boston, 90, *90*, 191n54
  Early Study of the Allegorical Figure for the Shaw Memorial (pl. 57), *129*
  Preliminary Sketch for Shaw Memorial (pl. 58), *129*
  Shaw Memorial (pl. 65), xv–xvii, *xvii*, 7, 81–82, *90* (detail), 124, *134–135*
  Shaw Memorial, Boston, 82–83, *82*, 88–93, *91*, 95–96, 100, 102–103, 106–111, 113, 122, 123–124
  Shaw Memorial, Exposition Universelle (Paris, 1900), 97
  Study Head of a Black Soldier (pl. 59), 90, *130*
  Study Head of a Black Soldier (pl. 60), 90, *130*
  Study Head of a Black Soldier (pl. 61), 90, *131*
  Study Head of a Black Soldier (pl. 62), 90, *132*
  Study Head of a Black Soldier (pl. 63), 90, *132*
  Study Head of a Black Soldier (pl. 64), 90, *133*
Saint-Gaudens, Homer, 90
Savage, Kirk, 92–93, 125
Saxton, Rufus, 83, *83*, 189n7
Schwarz, Gregory C., 90
Second Lieutenant Charles O. Hallett (pl. 37), 18, *56*
Second Lieutenant Ezekiel G. Tomlinson, Captain Luis F. Emilio, and Second Lieutenant Daniel Spear (pl. 35), 18, *54*
2nd Massachusetts Regiment, 5
Sergeant Henry F. Steward (pl. 22), x, 15, *43*
Sergeant Major John H. Wilson (pl. 26), 16, *47*
Sergeant William H. Carney (pl. 7), 6–7, *6*, 17–18
Shaw, Francis G., 35
Shaw, Robert Gould, xv, 3, 5–7, 10, 17, 18, *37* (pl. 25), 83, 86–90, *87*, 92–93, 95, 106, 109, 117, *154*, 190n42
Shepherd, Harry, 192n19
  John Mercer Langston (pl. 11), 9–10, *31*
Sims, John, 3
Smith, Charles A., *53* (pl. 33)
Smith, Cherise, 109
Smith, Frank, Jr., 115, 125
Smith, Joshua B., 83–84, *84*, 88–89, 96
Smith, Shawn Michelle, 9

Sneden, Robert Knox
  Charleston Harbor, S.C., Bombardment of Fort Sumter, ii
  Genl. Q. A. Gillmore's Line of Earthworks in Front of Fort Wagner, Morris Island, SC, July 1863, 4
Sojourner Truth (pl. 14), 10–11, *34*
Sojourner Truth, Advocate (pl. 53), 11, *71*
Sons and Daughters of the United States Colored Troops, 125
Southworth & Hawes, *Wendell Phillips* (pl. 4), *26*
Spear, Daniel, *54* (pl. 35)
Spriggs, Isaiah, 17
Standard Bearer (newspaper), 19
Stead, James U., *Henry Highland Garnet* (pl. 8), 9–10, *30*
Stearns, George Luther, 3, *25* (pl. 3)
Steward, Henry F., x, 15, 18, *43* (pl. 22)
Stone, Lincoln Ripley, 5, 18, *57* (pl. 38)
Story, William Wetmore, 84
Sturken, Marita, 116
Sumner, Charles, 84, *84*, 89, 96
Survey (magazine), 103
Survey Graphic (magazine), 103
Susie King Taylor, Nurse (pl. 51), 10, *70*

T
Taylor, Susie King, 10, *70* (pl. 51)
Teamoh, Robert T., *Sketch of the Life and Death of Col. Robert Gould Shaw*, 7
Thomas, George Henry, 115–116
Thompkins, William J., 105–106
tintypes, 16
Tomlinson, Ezekiel G., *54* (pl. 35)
Townsend, James Matthew, 13–14, 19, *40* (pl. 19)
Truth, Sojourner, 8, 10–11, *34* (pl. 14), *71* (pl. 53), 185n2
Tubman, Harriet, 10, *10*, *70* (pl. 52)
Turner, Nathaniel, 104

Tuskegee Institute, 192n19
23rd Massachusetts Volunteer Infantry, 18

U
Underground Railroad, 86
Unidentified Private, Company I, 54th Massachusetts Regiment (pl. 20), 14, *41*
Union Progressive Association, 86
United States Colored Troops, 113, 116, 119, 120, 124–126, 194n29
United States Sanitary Commission, 84
Universal Exposition. See Exposition Universelle (Paris, 1900)
U.S. Congress, 115
U.S. Constitution, 91

V
Van Der Zee, James, 104
Vesey, Denmark, 104
Vietnam War, 107, 116
Vizetelly, Frank, *Assault on Battery Wagner, Morris Island, Near Charleston, on the Night of the 18th July – the Rush of the Garrison to the Parapet* (pl. 44), *64*

W
Wall, John W., 186n11
Wallace, Maurice O., 9
Wall of Honor, African American Civil War Memorial, 115, 116, *116* (detail), 126
Washington, Booker T., 91–93, 96, 98, 102
Washington, Denzel, 7
Washington Metropolitan Area Transit Authority, 115
Weems, Carrie Mae, 109–110
  Detail from the Shaw Monument, from "The Hampton Project" (pl. 77), *147*
  The Hampton Project, 110
  From Here I Saw What Happened and I Cried, 109–110

Restless after the Longest Winter You Marched & Marched & Marched, from "From Here I Saw What Happened and I Cried" (pl. 76), 109–110, *146*
Wells, Ida B., 91
West Point Monument (Norfolk African American Civil War Memorial), Norfolk, Virginia, 119, *119*
Whipple, John Adams
    Captain Cabot J. Russell (pl. 40), 18, *59*
    Colonel Robert Gould Shaw (pl. 16), 18, *37*, 154
Whitman, Walt, 11, 13, 19
William H. Carney (pl. 67), 19, *137*
William H. Carney (pl. 69), *139*
Williams, Fannie Barrier, 100
Williams, William Earle, 110–111
    Folly Beach, South Carolina, 1999 (pl. 79), *150*
    Folly Beach Looking towards Morris Island, 1999 (pl. 80), 111, *151*
    Sergeant Carney Monument, Norfolk, Virginia, 2004 (pl. 78), 148, *149*
    Unsung Heroes, 110–111
Willis, Deborah, 91
Wilson, John H., 16, *47* (pl. 26)
Winter, Jay, 125
Winterthur Portfolio (journal), 90
Wisewell Barracks and Hospital, 117
Wölfflin, Heinrich, 109

Y

Yacovone, Donald, *Hope and Glory*, 7

Z

Zwick, Edward, *Glory*, 7, 81, 95, 119, 125

PHOTOGRAPHY CREDITS

FRONT COVER AND SECTION DETAILS OF THE SHAW MEMORIAL

Image courtesy of the Board of Trustees, National Gallery of Art, Washington. Photographer: Lee Ewing

PLATES

pl. 5: © The Art Institute of Chicago; pls. 8, 14: National Portrait Gallery, Smithsonian Institution/Art Resource, NY; pls. 9, 49: Photographs and Prints Division, Schomburg Center for Research in Black Culture, The New York Public Library, Astor, Lenox and Tilden Foundations; pl. 12: Courtesy of the Ohio Historical Society; pls. 15, 17, 18, 22–25, 27–31, 33, 34, and p. x: Courtesy of the Massachusetts Historical Society; pls. 16, 41, and p. 154: Boston Athenaeum; pl. 20: Courtesy of The Gilder Lehrman Institute of American History; pl. 21: photographer: Tricia Zigmund (National Gallery of Art); pls. 26, 32: West Virginia and Regional History Collection, West Virginia University Libraries; pls. 35, 66: Courtesy of the Library of Congress; pls. 36–39: Courtesy of Pamplin Historical Park and The National Museum of the Civil War Soldier; pl. 40: © American Antiquarian Society; pls. 47, 48, 50, 51: Image courtesy of the Board of Trustees, National Gallery of Art, Washington; photographer: Tricia Zigmund; pls. 57–65: Image courtesy of the Board of Trustees, National Gallery of Art, Washington; photographer: Lee Ewing; pl. 70: photographer: Jeffrey Nintzel; pl. 71: Courtesy of George Eastman House, International Museum of Photography and Film; pls. 72–75 and p. vi: © Richard Benson. Courtesy Pace/MacGill Gallery, New York. Image courtesy of the Board of Trustees, National Gallery of Art, Washington; photographer: Erica Abbey; pl. 76: Courtesy of the artist and Jack Shainman Gallery, New York; pl. 77: © Carrie Mae Weems

COMPARATIVE ILLUSTRATIONS

Greenough

fig. 1 (in addition to p. ii): Virginia Historical Society; fig. 3: Courtesy Commonwealth of Massachusetts Art Commission; figs. 4, 5: Courtesy of the Library of Congress; figs. 6, 11: photographer: Thomas Lingner/The Able Lens

Anderson

fig. 1: Courtesy Carol M. Highsmith; figs. 2, 4: Courtesy of the Library of Congress; figs. 3, 8: Courtesy of the Massachusetts Historical Society; fig. 6: National Portrait Gallery, Smithsonian Institution/Art Resource, NY; fig. 7: Boston Athenaeum; fig. 10: Courtesy Commonwealth of Massachusetts, Massachusetts Art Commission

Harris

fig. 2, 5–8, 11: Courtesy of the Library of Congress; figs. 3, 4: © The Museum of Modern Art/Licensed by SCALA/Art Resource, NY; fig. 9: © The Jacob and Gwendolyn Lawrence Foundation, Seattle / Artists Rights Society (ARS), New York; fig. 10: reprinted with the permission of Applewood Books, Publishers of America's Living Past, Carlisle, MA 01741; fig. 12: Smithsonian American Art Museum, © Lee Friedlander

Ater

figs. 1, 3–5, 8–11: photographer: Tricia Zigmund (National Gallery of Art); fig. 6: © L. Todd Spencer/The Virginian-Pilot; fig. 7: © Timothy Ross Talbott; fig. 12: Renée Ater